HUMAN AGENCY AND LANGUAGE

PHILOSOPHICAL PAPERS

I

HUMAN AGENCY AND LANGUAGE

PHILOSOPHICAL PAPERS

I

CHARLES TAYLOR

Professor of Philosophy and Political Science
McGill University, Montreal

CAMBRIDGE
UNIVERSITY PRESS

PUBLISHED BY THE PRESS SYNDICATE OF THE UNIVERSITY OF CAMBRIDGE
The Pitt Building, Trumpington Street, Cambridge, United Kingdom

CAMBRIDGE UNIVERSITY PRESS
The Edinburgh Building, Cambridge CB2 2RU, UK   http: //www.cup.cam.ac.uk
40 West 20th Street, New York, NY 10011-4211, USA   http: //www.cup.org
10 Stamford Road, Oakleigh, Melbourne 3166, Australia

First published 1985
Reprinted 1986, 1988, 1990, 1992, 1993, 1995, 1999

Typeset in Sabon

A catalogue record for this book is available from the British Library

Library of Congress Catalogue card number: 84-16966

ISBN 0-521-31750-9 paperback

Transferred to digital printing 2005

CONTENTS

ACKNOWLEDGEMENTS

1. 'What is human agency?', from T. Mischel (ed.), *The Self* (Oxford, Blackwell, 1977), pp. 103–35.
2. 'Self-interpreting animals', September 1977, unpublished.
3. 'Hegel's philosophy of mind', from G. Fløistad (ed.), *Contemporary Philosophy: A New Survey* (The Hague, Martinus Nijhoff, 1983), vol. 4, pp. 133–55.

An earlier version of this paper was read at the conference on Hegel and the Philosophy of Action, sponsored by the Hegel Society of Great Britain, Merton College, Oxford, September 1981.

4. 'The concept of a person', from *Social Theory as Practice*, The B. N. Ganguli Memorial Lectures 1981 (Delhi, Oxford University Press, 1983), pp. 48–67.
5. 'Peaceful coexistence in psychology', from *Social Research*, 40:1 (Spring 1973), pp. 55–82.

This paper was delivered as a lecture to a meeting of Section 24 of the American Psychological Association, Hawaii, 4 September 1972.

6. 'What is involved in a genetic psychology?', from T. Mischel (ed.), *Cognitive Development and Epistemology* (New York and London, Academic Press, 1971), pp. 393–416.
7. 'How is mechanism conceivable?', from Marjorie Grene (ed.), *Interpretations of Life and Mind: Essays around the Problem of Reduction* (London, Routledge and Kegan Paul, 1971), pp. 38–64.

An earlier version of this paper, delivered at the Loyota University Centennial Celebration, October 1970, has been published in A. Karazmar and J. C. Eccles, *Brain and Human Behavior* (New York, Springer-Verlag, 1970).

8. 'Cognitive psychology'; a slightly different version appeared as 'The significance of significance: the case of cognitive psychology', in S. Mitchell and M. Rosen (eds.), *The Need for Interpretation* (London, Athlone Press, 1983), pp. 141–69.
9. 'Language and human nature'; this paper was delivered as the Alan B.

Plaunt Memorial Lecture, University of Carleton, Ottowa, April 1978. A shortened version was published under the title 'Theories of meaning' in *Man and World*, 13 : 3–4 (1980), pp. 281–302.

10. 'Theories of meaning', Dawes Hicks lecture on philosophy, presented to the British Academy, London, 1980, and published in *Proceedings of the British Academy*, 66 (1980), pp. 283–327 (Oxford University Press).

INTRODUCTION

Despite the appearance of variety in the papers published in this collection, they are the work of a monomaniac; or perhaps better, what Isaiah Berlin has called a hedgehog. If not a single idea, then at least a single rather tightly related agenda underlines all of them. If one had to find a name for where this agenda falls in the geography of philosophical domains, the term 'philosophical anthropology' would perhaps be best, although this term seems to make English-speaking philosophers uneasy.

I started on it with a polemical concern. I wanted to argue against the understanding of human life and action implicit in an influential family of theories in the sciences of man. The common feature of this family is the ambition to model the study of man on the natural sciences. Theories of this kind seem to me to be terribly implausible. They lead to very bad science: either they end up in wordy elaborations of the obvious, or they fail altogether to address the interesting questions, or their practitioners end up squandering their talents and ingenuity in the attempt to show that they can after all recapture the insights of ordinary life in their manifestly reductive explanatory languages.

Indeed, one could argue that the second and third pitfalls should rather be seen as the horns of a dilemma: either these inadequate theories avoid the interesting questions, or they show themselves up, and hence have to expend more and more energy defending themselves against the charge of irrelevancy. Behaviourism offers the classical example. The original popular experimental design, running rats in mazes, in fact screened out the interesting phenomena of insightful learning. Once these are put on the agenda, behaviourism enters its long decline, moving through phase after phase of special pleading. Something similar seems to be emerging with theories purporting to explain intelligent performance on a model based on the digital computer. Artificial Intelligence programs tend to do rather well on very explicitly structured tasks, like playing chess, and even more checkers, and become more and more manifestly inadequate the more they call on implicit know-how. (I have tried to draw the boundary between the areas where a mechanistic psychology can be useful and those where it must fail in volume 1 chapter 5.)

What is striking about this family of theories is their reductive nature; they are all trying to avoid recognizing some important and obtrusive aspect of human life, and purport to explain the phenomena we normally understand in terms of this aspect by other factors. Behaviourism, which was the target of my *Explanation of Behaviour*,[1] tried to ignore purpose and intentionality, indeed, even to side-step consciousness. Computer-influenced theories ignore what I call 'significance' in volume 1 chapter 8, the fact that we are beings to whom things matter. The atomist theories which I discuss in volume 2 chapter 1 have no place for the common meanings which are embedded in our institutions and practices; they see political culture as a question of the 'orientations' of individuals.

But this diversity in the aspect ignored raises the question whether my targets really form a family. The theories I want to attack take issue explicitly with each other on this matter of reduction. For instance, the theories of cognitive psychology were partly devised to cope with the manifest inadequacies of behaviourism. One of their strongest talking points was that they could cope with the phenomena of intelligence which behaviourism was committed to deny.

But I think that for all the diversity of these reductionisms they form a family nonetheless. What they have in common is a certain metaphysical motivation. Defining this has been in a sense the next item on my agenda after the polemic against them. In fact the motivation is many-faceted, but one way of defining it is via the paradigm status accorded to the natural sciences as the models for the sciences of man. In a certain sense of the term, this family of theories shares an allegiance to 'naturalism', by which I mean not just the view that man can be seen as part of nature – in one sense or other this would surely be accepted by everyone – but that the nature of which he is a part is to be understood according to the canons which emerged in the seventeenth-century revolution in natural science. One of the most important of these is that we must avoid anthropocentric properties (what I call in the first section of volume 1 chapter 2 'subjective' properties), and give an account of things in absolute terms. 'Anthropocentric' properties are those which things have only within the experience of agents of a certain kind – the classical example in the seventeenth-century discussion are the 'secondary' qualities; while 'absolute' properties (I borrow the term from Bernard Williams in his

---

[1] London and New York, 1964.

Descartes)[2] are supposedly free of any such relativity. This requirement can be more or less stringently interpreted and can be applied at different levels, which accounts, I believe, for the variety of reductionist views, but it underlies all of them.

But naturalism is more than a view about the language of science. It ramifies also into an understanding of agency. This too can be described first negatively, in terms of what its reductionist temper ignores. What it fails to recognize is a crucial feature of our ordinary understanding of human agency, of a person or self.

One way of getting at this feature is in terms of the notion of self-interpretation. A fully competent human agent not only has some understanding (which may be also more or less *mis*understanding) of himself, but is partly constituted by this understanding. This is a thesis of post-Heideggerian hermeneutics, which I have tried to develop in a number of papers (especially volume 1 chapter 1 and volume 2 chapter 1). But it still does not capture the crucial point. This is that our self-understanding essentially incorporates our seeing ourselves against a background of what I have called 'strong evaluation'. I mean by that a background of distinctions between things which are recognized as of categoric or unconditioned or higher importance or worth, and things which lack this or are of lesser value. I discuss what is involved in this kind of distinction in volume 1 chapters 1 and 2.

In other terms, to be a full human agent, to be a person or a self in the ordinary meaning, is to exist in a space defined by distinctions of worth. A self is a being for whom certain questions of categoric value have arisen, and received at least partial answers. Perhaps these have been given authoritatively by the culture more than they have been elaborated in the deliberation of the person concerned, but they are his in the sense that they are incorporated into his self-understanding, in some degree and fashion. My claim is that this is not just a contingent fact about human agents, but is essential to what we would understand and recognize as full, normal human agency.

But if this is so, then the programme of naturalism as I define it above is severely limited in principle. For there can be no absolute understanding of what we are as persons, and this in two obvious respects. A being who exists only in self-interpretation cannot be understood absolutely; and one who can only be understood against the background of distinctions of worth cannot be captured by a scientific language which essentially

---

[2] Harmondsworth, 1978.

aspires to neutrality. Our personhood cannot be treated scientifically in
exactly the same way we approach our organic being. What it is to possess
a liver or a heart is something I can define quite independently of the space
of questions in which I exist for myself, but not what it is to have a self or
be a person.

In any case, it is this thesis about the self that I aspire to make clearly
and convincingly. I wish I could flatter myself that I had already done so,
but it is something I am still working on. It is, however, what I am
struggling towards in the papers that make up the first section of volume
1. While the second section of the first volume, and the first of the second
volume, are largely taken up with the polemic against naturalistic
theories in different domains, it is in this section on agency and the self
that I have tried to move further in my agenda towards the underlying
views of the nature of agency itself.

But this involves more than just making the negative point above, that
naturalism cannot cope with our understanding of the self. A critic of
naturalism from a hermeneutical standpoint, like myself, owes his opponent more. He has to give an account of his adversary's motivation in
hermeneutical terms. It is not just that the final challenge that this kind of
account ought to meet is to explain the opponent's error, that is, to
explain why people are attracted by naturalism. It is also that the very
nature of the claim I am putting forward, that we all as human agents
define ourselves against a background of distinctions of worth, requires
that we explain in these terms what people are doing who espouse a
naturalist outlook. For it surely could not be that naturalists are somehow exceptions to this rule, just because they do not *recognize* that they
are constituted by strongly evaluative self-interpretations. If the theory is
right, we ought to be able to give an account of what tempts naturalists to
adopt their thin theory of the self in terms of our richer theory.

Now I believe not only that this requirement can be met, but that it is
very illuminating to meet it. Because behind and supporting the impetus
to naturalism I mentioned above, viz. the understandable prestige of the
natural science model, stands an attachment to a certain picture of the
agent. This picture is deeply attractive to moderns, both flattering and
inspiring. It shows us as capable of achieving a kind of disengagement
from our world by objectifying it. We objectify our situation to the extent
that we can overcome a sense of it as what determines for us our paradigm
purposes and ends, and can come to see it and function in it as a neutral
environment, within which we can effect the purposes which we
determine out of ourselves. In a sense, the great shift in cosmology which

occurred in the seventeenth century, from a picture of the world-order based on the Ideas to one of the universe as mechanism, was the founding objectification, the source and inspiration for the continuing development of a disengaged modern consciousness.

The ideal of disengagement defines a certain – typically modern – notion of freedom, as the ability to act on one's own, without outside interference or subordination to outside authority. It defines its own peculiar notion of human dignity, closely connected to freedom. And these in turn are linked to ideals of efficacy, power, unperturbability, which for all their links with earlier ideals are original with modern culture.

The great attraction of these ideals, all the more powerful in that this understanding of the agent is woven into a host of modern practices – economic, scientific, technological, psychotherapeutic, and so on – lends great weight and credence to the disengaged image of the self. The liberation through objectification wrought by the cosmological revolution of the seventeenth century has become for many the model of the agent's relation to the world, and hence sets the very definition of what it is to be an agent.

My claim is that it is this image of agency which offers crucial support to the naturalist world-view. Despite its own pretensions, naturalism is not mainly powered by epistemological or scientific considerations. Looked at dispassionately, the scientific theories it encourages us to espouse are extremely implausible, in the ways I described above. In the papers in volume 1, section II, and volume 2, section I, as well as in a host of other writings, I have been trying to make this case. But after engaging long and hard in the debate within any one of the sciences of man, there comes a moment when one is led to stand back and question the significance of it all. Why is one spending this immense effort to show the inadequacy of what in the end is a wildly implausible view?

To take what is admittedly an extreme case, once one has broken out from the world-view of a very narrow form of naturalism, it seems almost unbelievable that anyone could ever have taken a theory like behaviourism seriously. It takes a very powerful metaphysical set of preconceptions for one to ignore or over-ride so much that is so intuitively obvious about human life, for no valid scientific or explanatory reason. Behaviourism is out of fashion, so many readers may agree with my sentiments on this case. But I think that the situation is not all that different with the contemporary fashion of computer-modelled explanations. Their neglect of what I call (in volume 1 chapter 8) the 'significance feature' is so flagrant, and so bizarre, that only very strong preconceptions could mask it.

What generates these preconceptions? If the scientific and epistemological arguments are so poor, what gives them their strength? I believe that they derive their force from the underlying image of the self, and that this exercises its hold on us because of the ideal of disengagement and the images of freedom, dignity and power which attach to it. More specifically, the claim is that the more we are led to interpret ourselves in the light of the disengaged picture, to define our identity by this, the more the connected epistemology of naturalism will seem right and proper to us. Or otherwise put, a commitment to this identity generates powerful resistances against any challenges to the naturalist outlook. In short, its epistemological weaknesses are more than made up for by its moral appeal.

But what I am offering here is an account of the appeal of naturalism within the terms of the hermeneutical theory. I am saying that it is the hold of a particular set of background distinctions of worth, those of the disengaged identity, which leads people to espouse what are ultimately rather implausible epistemological doctrines. And this explanation is flagrantly at odds with the one naturalism offers of itself. For it does not allow any account at all in terms of identity and self-interpretation, and it deems its epistemological grounds sufficient. To be able to make this hermeneutical account plausible would thus be to make the final refutation of naturalism, to show that its opponents understand it better than it does itself, that indeed the phenomenon of people believing in naturalism was only adequately explicable in terms of a rival, incompatible theory.

And so my own agenda draws me on, as it were, to try a proof of this kind, partly because the very nature of the hermeneutical theory seems to make this demand of me, as I said above; and partly because the long experience of polemic against naturalist views on the epistemological level of the philosophy of science, the sense of futility when one fails to carry conviction against what seem ultimately absurd views, convinces me that the real issue lies elsewhere.

Of course, this is not at all uncharted terrain. A number of influential accounts have been put forth explaining the hold of the scientific outlook in terms of the appeal of a certain moral self-understanding. The most famous, or notorious, author of such a theory was Nietzsche, and in a sense all those in the twentieth century who have developed such have been influenced to some degree by him. These include Scheler, Heidegger, the writers of the Frankfurt school, Foucault, and various varieties of French 'post-structuralism', to mention the best known. But I confess to being very dissatisfied with most of these theories. They generally share two great drawbacks: they are often underdemonstrated, indeed, rather impressionistically argued for; and they also tend to be hostile and dismissive towards the scientific outlook and the disengaged identity. But this latter stance is both uncalled for, and in the end inauthentic. That is, the disengaged identity is far from being simply wrong and misguided, and besides, we are all too deeply imbued with it to be able really and authentically to repudiate it. The kind of critique we need is one that can free it of its illusory pretensions to define the totality of our lives as agents, without attempting the futile and ultimately self-destructive task of rejecting it altogether.

So for all these reasons the case for the ultimately moral grounding of modern naturalism needs to be made again, with more convincing argument and with finer moral discrimination. Having said this, I cannot claim to be very advanced in this task. Some beginnings of it are made in volume 1 chapter 4, but only the very first moves. But I think I see better than in the past what such a case would involve.

Apart from the negative side of the argument, the case that naturalism makes a bad philosophy of science (which I think has been very powerfully made), the positive thesis can only be established in an historical account. This would have to show how, through the whole course of the development of the modern identity, the moral motivation has been intertwined with the epistemological, how the latter has never been a sufficient motive force but has always been seconded by the former, but how paradoxically the very nature of this modern identity has tended to make us reluctant to acknowledge this moral dimension. The very ideal of disengagement militates against it. This would mean placing the history of our scientific and philosophical consciousness in relation to the whole development of modern culture, and particularly of the underlying interpretations of agency and the self. What would ultimately carry conviction would be an account of this development which illuminated it and made more sense of it than its rivals, and particularly than naturalistic ones. As for any hermeneutic explanation, interpretive plausibility is the ultimate criterion.

Michel Foucault has in a sense been engaged in an account of this kind, and I touch on some of the things it would require in my paper on his work (volume 2 chapter 6); I also sketch some of the themes it would have to deal with in the discussion of contemporary 'legitimation crisis' (volume 2 chapter 10). But I am basically at the beginning. I am now trying to write a larger work which will come to grips with this kind of historical account, and do at least something to meet this demand which I see as weighing on a position like mine, to explain plausibly the spiritual roots of naturalism.

So what I have to offer here is, alas, mainly promissory notes. But there are yet further items on my tightly knit agenda where I have some modest progress to report. I mentioned above that the ideal account of the spiritual basis of modern naturalism should not only be very convincing as interpretation, but should also allow us to discriminate sensitively what we want to affirm and what we want to reject. But even before such an account has been worked out we can try to define more clearly the features of the modern identity, and the ideals which help constitute it, and offer a critique of them.

One of the most negative of these features is atomism. The disengaged identity and its attendant notion of freedom tend to generate an understanding of the individual as metaphysically independent of society. Of course, it can allow for views which see the individual as shaped by his social environment; and these are the views generally espoused today – the early atomism of the seventeenth century seems incredible to us. But what it hides from view is the way in which an individual is constituted by the language and culture which can only be maintained and renewed in the communities he is part of. The community is not simply an aggregation of individuals; nor is there simply a causal interaction between the two. The community is also constitutive of the individual, in the sense that the self-interpretations which define him are drawn from the interchange which the community carries on. A human being alone is an impossibility, not just *de facto*, but as it were *de jure*. Outside of the continuing conversation of a community, which provides the language by which we draw our background distinctions, human agency of the kind I describe above would be not just impossible, but inconceivable. As organisms we are separable from society – although it may be hard in fact to survive as a lone being; but as humans this separation is unthinkable. On our own, as Aristotle says, we would be either beasts or Gods.

Because of the ascendancy of the modern identity, this dimension of our existence is constantly being lost from sight. It is not that moderns are attracted to theories which really portray human beings as independent of society, in the manner of seventeenth-century contract theory. It is rather that, however tightly the dependence is conceived, it is seen in causal terms, and not as touching our very identity. Bringing this back into view is therefore a perpetually necessary philosophical task, both in order to attain a more valid conception of the nature of social science, and in order to purge our key normative notions – freedom, justice, rights – of their atomist distortions.

I have tried to do something to the first purpose in some of the papers in volume 2, section I (notably chapter 1); and something to the second in the papers of volume 2, section II (especially chapters 7, 8 and 11).

Obviously, from here my 'agenda' ramifies in a number of directions, some of which I have followed up. For instance, once one accepts a hermeneutical conception of the sciences of man, a number of further questions arise. I have tried to deal with some of the more insistent, such as: the nature of the contrast between human and natural sciences (volume 2 chapter 3); what is involved in explaining/understanding a quite different culture (volume 2 chapter 4); and the issue of relativism (volume 2 chapter 5).

But I would like to say something here about a rather different direction, which is in a way more fundamental. That is the philosophy of language. Obviously a view of human life as constituted by self-understanding is one in which the philosophy of language will play a central role. Heidegger's philosophical development illustrates this strikingly. And obviously, too, the conception of language will be rather different from those which develop out of naturalist views. This will emerge, among other places, in their theories of meaning. A number of views on linguistic meaning have been put forward during the history of modern philosophy from the standpoint of what I have been calling the disengaged modern identity. The earlier views, those of Hobbes or Locke for instance, saw language as an instrument, and understood meaning in terms of designation. Discovering the meaning of words is finding what ideas or things they stood for. We are much more sophisticated in the twentieth century, and especially in the English-speaking philosophical world, which has been through the Fregean revolution. But some of the basic ideas of that Hobbes–Locke tradition still survive in transposed form. With truth-conditional theories of meaning, for instance, we still have the basic notion that meaning is to be understood in terms of the things language is used to talk about. The crucial unit is now the sentence and not the word, and relations like 'making true' and 'satisfying' replace the earlier emphasis on designation (or 'signifying', in seventeenth-century parlance), but meaning is still being explicated by some notion of representation: the meaning of a word is to be explained by the way it can be used to *depict* the world.

By contrast, a hermeneutical view requires a very different conception. If we are partly constituted by our self-understanding, and this in turn can be very different according to the various languages which articulate for us a background of distinctions of worth, then language does not only serve to *depict* ourselves and the world, it also helps *constitute* our lives. Certain ways of being, of feeling, of relating to each other are only possible given certain linguistic resources. Without a certain articulation of oneself and of the highest, it is neither possible to *be* a Christian ascetic, nor to *feel* that combination of one's own lack of worth and high calling (the 'grandeur et misère' of Pascal), nor to be *part* of, say, a monastic order.

In order to understand this, we need a rather different theory of meaning, more in line with those developed in the Romantic period, which explore how language not only depicts, but also articulates and makes things manifest, and in so doing helps shape our form of life. The original figures in this expressive-constitutive line of thought are, I believe, Herder and Humboldt. Their work contains seminal insights which need further development. This is what I am trying to argue in the papers in volume 1, section III. In volume 1 chapter 9 I sketch the historical development of both the designative and expressive views on meaning, and try to define the contrast between them; in volume 1 chapter 10 I explore some of the features of the Herder–Humboldt view by showing the kind of critique one can make of the truth-conditional theories from their standpoint.

Of course, here again one seems to be trespassing on terrain that is already well occupied. Structuralist and especially 'post-Structuralist' thinkers have already allegedly made the critique of purely designative views. The latter seem to have gone Frege one better; while he shifted the crucial unit of meaning from the word to the sentence, they have gone further and identified the text as an indissociable whole. And their rejection of depictive theories seems all the more radical in that they refuse to allow any relation to a reality outside the text to serve as our key to understanding it.

There is, of course, an important line of historical filiation between Herder and Humboldt and twentieth-century structuralist theories. For instance, Saussure's privileging of the code over the individual item within it is prefigured in Humboldt's image of language as a web. But nevertheless it seems to me that the current vogue, say, of Derrida's later writings (admittedly largely outside philosophical circles) is something close to an unmitigated disaster for this tradition. A good case is being discredited by obscurity, posturing and dramatic over-statement.

A critique of what can be called 'subjectivism' is, indeed, one of the central themes of the Herder–Humboldt line of thought. They saw that the disengaged identity and the designative account of meaning it gravitates toward centres everything on the subject, and exalts a quite unreal model of self-clarity and control. The ultimate absurdity into which the designative view can fall is the voluntarism parodied in Lewis Carroll's Humpty Dumpty. The speaking agent is in fact enmeshed in two kinds of larger order, which he can never fully oversee, and can only punctually and marginally refashion. For he is only a speaking agent at all as part of a language community, as I argued above, and the meanings and illocutionary forces activated in any speech act are only what they are against the background of a whole language and way of life. In the light of this, certain models of transparent consciousness and clairvoyant control are shown to be not only unrealizable but destructive.

But this point is more parodied than articulated by playful rhetoric about the end of subjectivity, or about texts with nothing outside to relate to. If any general position emerges from all this, it points to a view of the code as ultimate, dominating the supposedly autonomous agent. But this makes just as much sense as, and no more than, the equal and opposite error of Humpty Dumpty subjectivism. A position like this can only make itself remotely plausible by claiming that the only alternative to it is some such wildly extreme subjectivism. And so it has a vested interest in muddying the waters, and obscuring all the interesting insights which must necessarily lie in the space between these two absurd theses. Like a debate between, say, an orthodox Cartesian and a vulgar Marxist, this one will be rich in histrionics, but a waste-land intellectually.

This is the more to be regretted in that there is a genuinely interesting frontier to be explored beyond modern subjectivism through the philosophy of language. Heidegger, and later Gadamer, have tried to open this up. I do not know how clear I can be about this at the present stage, but perhaps I can gesture towards the question in this way: if one of the fundamental uses of language is to articulate or make manifest the background of distinctions of worth we define ourselves by, how should we understand *what* is being manifested here? Is what we are articulating ultimately to be understood as our human response to our condition? Or is our articulation striving rather to be faithful to something beyond us, not explicable simply in terms of human response? In the philosophy of the late Heidegger, the first alternative is seen as the quintessential expression of modern subjectivism. It belongs to the 'humanism' he is trying to get beyond. He seemed to be exploring variations of the second answer. Which shows how far removed he is from the contemporary theories of self-enclosed texts for all their immense debt to him.

I would dearly like to be able to cut through the clutter and confusion that we all labour under so as to be able to explore this question, but I have to admit that I am far away from this at present. I need, among other things, to be much clearer about language and meaning. Once more, in these last paragraphs, my discussion has been leading up to another promissory note (this one with a rather remote maturity).

But if this question could be tackled, it would greatly help with another issue, which stands more urgently on the agenda. Let my definition of this be my last promissory note. If, as I said above, the ultimate basis of naturalism turns out to be a certain definition of agency and the background of worth, does the critique terminate with the proof that this is so (supposing I finally bring it off), or is there a way we can go on and rationally assess this and other definitions of worth? This is, in fact, a particular way of putting the general question: what are the capacities of practical reason? Is it quite helpless before such basic differences in spiritual outlook, like that between the disengaged identity and its opponents? Or is there, at least in principle, a way in which this kind of question can be rationally arbitrated? I am fiercely committed to the latter view, and I recognize that the onus is on me to come up with a good argument. I am working on it, and I hope at not too remote a date to be able to publish something convincing (at least to some) on this.

But for the moment, let this collection serve as a kind of fragmentary and provisional exploration of aspects of this much more ambitious project.

PART I

AGENCY AND THE SELF

CHAPTER ONE

WHAT IS HUMAN AGENCY?

I

I

I would like to explore in this paper what is involved in the notion of a self, of a responsible human agent. What is it that we attribute to ourselves as human agents which we would not attribute to animals?

This question takes us very far indeed, and into several issues of capital importance in philosophy. I am not even going to try to sound them all. But I'd like to make a preliminary exploration of the terrain, using as my guide a key notion which has been introduced recently by Harry Frankfurt, in order to see how well the territory of the self may be mapped with its aid.

The key notion is the distinction between first- and second-order desires which Frankfurt makes in his 'Freedom of the will and the concept of a person'.[1] I can be said to have a second-order desire when I have a desire whose object is my having a certain (first-order) desire. The intuition underlying Frankfurt's introduction of this notion is that it is essential to the characterization of a human agent or person, that is to the demarcation of human agents from other kinds of agent. As he puts it,

Human beings are not alone in having desires and motives, or in making choices. They share these things with members of certain other species, some of which even appear to engage in deliberation and to make decisions based on prior thought. It seems to be peculiarly characteristic of humans, however, that they are able to form ... second order desires ...[2]

Put in other terms, we think of (at least higher) animals as having desires, even as having to choose between desires in some cases, or at least as inhibiting some desires for the sake of others. But what is distinctively

---

[1] H. Frankfurt, 'Freedom of the will and the concept of a person', *Journal of Philosophy*, 67:1 (Jan. 1971), pp. 5–20.　　[2] *Ibid.*, p. 6.

human is the power to *evaluate* our desires, to regard some as desirable and others are undesirable. This is why 'no animal other than man … appears to have the capacity for reflective self-evaluation that is manifested in the formation of second-order desires'.[3]

I agree with Frankfurt that this capacity to evaluate desires is bound up with our power of self-evaluation, which in turn is an essential feature of the mode of agency we recognize as human. But I believe we can come closer to defining what is involved in this mode of agency if we make a further distinction, between two broad kinds of evaluation of desire.

Thus someone might be weighing two desired actions to determine the more convenient, or how to make different desires compossible (for instance, he might resolve to put off eating although hungry, because later he could both eat and swim), or how to get the most overall satisfaction. Or he might be pondering to see which of two desired objects attracts him most, as one ponders a pastry tray to see if one will take an éclair or a mille feuilles.

But what is missing in the above cases is a qualitative evaluation of my desires; the kind of thing we have, for instance, when I refrain from acting on a given motive − say, spite, or envy − because I consider it base or unworthy. In this kind of case our desires are classified in such categories as higher and lower, virtuous and vicious, more and less fulfilling, more and less refined, profound and superficial, noble and base. They are judged as belonging to qualitatively different modes of life: fragmented or integrated, alienated or free, saintly, or merely human, courageous or pusillanimous and so on.

Intuitively, the difference might be put in this way. In the first case, which we may call weak evaluation, we are concerned with outcomes; in the second, strong evaluation, with the quality of our motivation. But just put this way, it is a little too quick. For what is important is that strong evaluation is concerned with the qualitative *worth* of different desires. This is what is missing in the typical cases where, for example, I choose a holiday in the south rather than the north, or choose to go to lunch at the beach rather than eat now in town. For in these cases, the favoured alternative is not selected because of the worth of the underlying motivation. There is 'nothing to choose' between the motivations here.

But this does not mean (a) that in weak evaluation the motivations are homogeneous. We may not be weighing two objects of the same desire, or put somewhat differently, two outcomes with the same desirability

[3] *Ibid.*, p. 7.

characterization. Take the example of someone who is hesitating between taking a holiday in the south or in the north. What the holiday in the north has going for it is the tremendous beauty of the wild, the untracked wastes, etc.; what the south has going for it is the lush tropical land, the sense of well-being, the joy of swimming in the sea, etc. Or I might put it to myself that one holiday is more exhilarating, the other is more relaxing.

The alternatives have different desirability characterizations; in this sense they are qualitatively distinct. But what is missing in this case is a distinction between the desires as to worth, and that is why it is not a strong evaluation. I ultimately opt for the south over the north not because there is something more worthy about relaxing than being exhilarated, but just because 'I feel like it'.

It follows *a fortiori* (b) that weak evaluations are not simply quantitative either. That is, the alternatives cannot necessarily be expressed in some common units of calculation and in this sense rendered commensurable. This has often been obscured by the recurring ambition of our rationalist civilization to turn practical reflection as much as possible into calculation, an ambition whose major expression has been the doctrine of utilitarianism.

The bent of utilitarianism has been to do away with qualitative distinctions of worth on the grounds that they represent confused perceptions of the real bases of our preferences which are quantitative. The hope has been that once we have done away with strong evaluation we will be able to calculate. Utilitarianism has, I believe, been wrong on both counts. For decisions between alternatives which are not distinguished as to worth are not necessarily amenable to calculation – for instance, the choice between the two holidays above is clearly not so amenable, or only in part (or *some* of the considerations relevant to my choice of holiday might be quantifiable in a strict sense, for example, cost). Nor is there any calculation when I stare at the pastry tray and try to decide whether to have an éclair or a mille feuilles.

All these weak evaluations are only 'quantitative' in the weak sense that they do not involve qualitative distinctions of worth. We sometimes explain our choices of this kind by saying that one alternative was 'more fun', or 'better value'; but there is no genuine quantification behind these expressions; they are just cover terms for 'preferred'. Utilitarians are certainly right from their own standpoint in rejecting strong evaluation, for doing away with this is a necessary condition of reducing practical reason to calculation. But it is far from being a sufficient condition.

Nor can we say (c) that weak evaluation is only concerned with outcomes, and never with desires; that all cases of second-order desires are
strong evaluations. For I can have what Frankfurt calls 'second-order
volitions' on the basis of weak evaluations. I have a second-order volition
when I want certain first-order desires to be the ones which move me to
action. So I can want the desire to lunch-and-swim-later to be prepotent,
because I know that I will have a better time all things considered, though
I fear that I will break down since you are offering me lunch now. And I
can have second-order desires on the same kind of basis: I might want my
addiction to rich desserts to abate so that I can control my weight. But in
both of these cases by hypothesis the alternatives would not be distinguished in that one of the desires was unworthy or base, or alienating,
or trivial, or dishonourable, or something of the sort; in short there would
be no qualitative distinction of the worth of the motivations.

And just as one can desire not to have a desire one has on the basis of
weak evaluation, so one can desire a desire one has not got. Roman
banqueters had and acted on this kind of second-order desire when they
went to the vomitorium, so as to restore appetite and be able to go on
eating with pleasure. This contrasts sharply with the case where I aspire to
a desire out of a strong evaluation, where I see it as admirable, for
instance, as when I want to be capable of a great and single-minded love
or loyalty.[4]

The distinction between the two kinds of evaluation, then, doesn't
simply turn on that between quantitative and qualitative evaluation, or
on the presence or absence of second-order desires. It concerns rather
whether desires are distinguished as to worth. And for this we can perhaps
set out two interlocking criteria.

(1) In weak evaluation, for something to be judged good it is sufficient
that it be desired, whereas in strong evaluation there is also a use of 'good'
or some other evaluative term for which being desired is not sufficient;
indeed some desires or desired consummations can be judged as bad, base,
ignoble, trivial, superficial, unworthy, and so on.

It follows from this that (2) when in weak evaluation one desired

---

[4] We might add a fourth reservation and protest that strong evaluation is generally not of
desires or motivations, but of qualities of action. I eschew some action because that is a
cowardly way to *behave*, or a base *action*. The point is well taken if we mean that we are
not speaking of desires alone, but we are seriously mistaken if we think that what is
evaluated here are actions *as distinct from* motivations. Cowardly or other kinds of base
behaviour are such partly in virtue of their motivation. So that strong evaluation necessarily involves a qualitative distinction of desires.

alternative is set aside, it is only on grounds of its contingent in-compatibility with a more desired alternative. I go to lunch later, although hungry now, because then I shall be able to lunch and swim. But I should be happy to have the best of both worlds: if the pool were open now, I could assuage my immediate hunger as well as enjoying a swim at lunch-time.

But with strong evaluation this is not necessarily the case. Some desired consummation may be eschewed not because it is incompatible with another, or if because of incompatibility this will not be contingent. Thus I refrain from committing some cowardly act, although very tempted to do so, but this is not because this act at this moment would make any other desired act impossible, as lunching now would make swimming impossible, but rather because it is base.

But of course there is also a way in which we could characterize this alternative which would bring out incompatibility. If we examine my evaluative vision more closely, we shall see that I value courageous action as part of a mode of life; I aspire to be a certain kind of person. This would be compromised by my giving in to this craven impulse. Here there is incompatibility. But this incompatibility is no longer contingent. It is not just a matter of circumstances which makes it impossible to give in to the impulse to flee and still cleave to a courageous, upright mode of life. Such a mode of life *consists* among other things in withstanding such craven impulses.

That there should be incompatibility of a non-contingent kind here is not adventitious. For strong evaluation deploys a language of evaluative distinctions, in which different desires are described as noble or base, integrating or fragmenting, courageous or cowardly, clairvoyant or blind, and so on. But this means that they are characterized contrastively. Each concept of one of the above pairs can only be understood in relation to the other. No one can have an idea what courage is unless he knows what cowardice is, just as no one can have a notion of 'red', say, without some other colour terms with which it contrasts. It is essential to both 'red' and 'courage' that we understand with what they are contrasted. And of course with evaluative terms, as with colour terms, the contrast may not just be with one other, but with several. And indeed, refining an evalua-tive vocabulary by introducing new terms would alter the sense of the existing terms, even as it would with our colour vocabulary.

This means that in strong evaluation, we can characterize the alterna-tives contrastively; and indeed, it can be the case that we must do so if we are to express what is really desirable in the favoured alternative. But this is not so with weak evaluation.[5] Of course, in each case, we are free to express the alternatives in a number of ways, some of which are and some of which are not contrastive. Thus I can describe my first issue above as between going to lunch *now* and going to lunch *later*; and this is a contrastive description in that it is essential to the identity of one of these alternatives that it not be the other. This is because the term 'now' only has sense through contrast with other terms like 'later', 'earlier', 'tomorrow', and so on. Indeed given the context (e.g., that one cannot decide to lunch in the past), and the contrastive background necessary to 'now', it would be enough to pose my issue to ask myself, 'shall I lunch now?' (or perhaps, 'had I better lunch later?').

But if I want to identify the alternatives in terms of their desirability, the characterization ceases to be contrastive. What lunching now has going for it is that I am hungry, and it is unpleasant to wait while one is hungry and a great pleasure to eat. What eating later has going for it is that I can swim. But I can identify the pleasures of eating quite independently from those of swimming; indeed, I may have enjoyed eating long before swimming entered my life. Not being contrastively described, these two desired consummations are incompatible, where they are, only contingently and circumstantially.

Reciprocally, I can describe the issue of my strong evaluations non-contrastively. I can say that the choice is between saving my life, or perhaps avoiding pain and embarrassment, on one hand, and upholding my honour on the other. Now certainly I can understand preserving my life, and what is desirable about it, without any acquaintance with honour, and the same goes for avoiding pain and embarrassment. And even if the reverse is not quite the case, no one could understand 'honour' without some reference to our desire to avoid death, pain, or embarrassment; for while one preserves honour, among other things, by a certain stance towards such things, even so saving one's honour is not simply contrastively defined with saving one's own life, avoiding pain and so on; there are many cases where one can save one's life without any taint to honour, indeed without the question even arising.

And this non-contrastive description may even be the most apposite for

---

[5] It might be objected that utilitarians too make use of a qualitative contrast, i.e., that between pleasure and pain. But this is precisely not a qualitative contrast of *desires* of desired consummations, which is what we are considering here. Only pleasure is what is desired, according to utilitarian theory; pain we are averse to. Of course, we might want to contrast the *avoidance of pain*, which in one sense of the term we desire, and pleasure. It is exactly this contrast which utilitarians have notoriously failed to make.

certain purposes. Since there are certainly contingent conditions underlying my being faced with this dread choice of death or dishonour – if only
the colonel had not sent me to the front line at just that moment when the
enemy were attacking – it is indeed in virtue of a contingent set of circumstances that I must now risk my life to avoid dishonour. But if I focus
again on what makes the alternative to be rejected undesirable, that is
that running away is in this case incompatible with honour, the incompatibility is no longer a contingent one: honourable conduct just
consists in standing in face of such threat to life when this kind of issue is
at stake. Or to put it in one word, running is to be eschewed because it is
'cowardly', a word which carries the sense of a non-contingent conflict
with honourable conduct.

Thus while another pair of alternatives can be described either contrastively or non-contrastively, when we come to the desirability (or
undesirability) characterizations in virtue of which one alternative is
rejected, the alternatives in strong evaluation must be contrastively described. For in strong evaluation, where we deploy a language of evaluative distinctions, the rejected desire is not so rejected because of some
mere contingent or circumstantial conflict with another goal. Being
cowardly does not compete with other goods by taking up the time or
energy I need to pursue them, and it may not alter my circumstances in
such a way as to prevent my pursuing them. The conflict is deeper; it is not
contingent.[6]

2

The utilitarian strand in our civilization would induce us to abandon the
language of qualitative contrast, and this means, of course, abandoning
our strong evaluative languages, for their terms are only defined in contrast. And we can be tempted to redefine issues we are reflecting on in this
non-qualitative fashion.

For instance, let us say that I am addicted to over-eating. I find it hard to
resist treating myself to rich desserts. As I struggle with this issue, in the
reflection in which I determine that moderation is better, I can be looking
at the alternatives in a language of qualitative contrast. I can be reflecting
that someone who has so little control over his appetites that he would let
his health go to pot over cream-cake is not an admirable person. I yearn to

---

[6] I am indebted for the present formulation of this point to the vigorous objections of Anne
Wilbur Mackenzie against the whole enterprise of distinguishing strong from weak
evaluation.

be free of this addiction, to be the kind of person whose mere bodily appetites respond to his higher aspirations, and don't carry on remorselessly and irresistibly dragging him to incapacity and degradation.

But then I might be induced to see my problem in a quite different light. I might be induced to see it as a question of quantity of satisfaction. Eating too much cake increases the cholesterol in my blood, makes me fat, ruins my health, prevents me from enjoying all sorts of other desired consummations; so it isn't worth it. Here I have stepped away from the contrastive language of strong evaluation. Avoiding high cholesterol content, obesity, ill health, or being able to climb stairs, and so on, can all be defined quite independently from my eating habits. Someone might even invent some drug which would allow me to go on eating rich desserts and also enjoy all those other goods, whereas no drug would allow me to eat my cake and attain the dignity of an autonomous, self-desciplined agent which I pined after on my first reading of the issue.

It may be that being talked around to see things in this non-qualitative light will help me solve my problem, that somehow it was too deeply disturbing when I put it in terms of dignity versus degradation, and now I can come to grips with it. But this is a separate question from deciding which way of putting it is more illuminating and true to reality. This is a question about what our motivation really is, how we should truly characterize the meaning things have for us.

This is a conflict of self-interpretations. Which one we adopt will partly shape the meanings things have for us. But the question can arise which is more valid, more faithful to reality. To be in error here is thus not just to make a misdescription, as when I describe a motor-vehicle as a car when it is really a truck. We think of misidentification here as in some sense distorting the reality concerned. For the man who is trying to talk me out of seeing my problem as one of dignity versus degradation, I have made a crucial misidentification. But it is not just that I have called a fear of too high cholesterol content by the name 'degradation'; it is rather that infantile fears of punishment or loss of parental love have been irrationally transferred to obesity, or the pleasures of eating, or something of the sort (to follow a rather vulgar-Freudian line). My experience of obesity, eating, etc. is shaped by this. But if I can get over this 'hang-up' and see the real nature of the underlying anxiety, I will see that it is largely groundless, that is I do not really incur the risk of punishment or loss of love; in fact there is quite another list of things at stake here: ill health, inability to enjoy the outdoor life, early death by heart-attack, and so on.

So might go a modern variant of the utilitarian thrust, trying to reduce our qualitative contrasts to some homogeneous medium. In this it would be much more plausible and sophisticated than earlier variants which talked as though it were just a matter of simple misidentification, that what people sought who pined after honour, dignity, integrity, and so on were simply other pleasurable states to which they gave these high-sounding names.

There are of course ripostes to these attempts to reduce our evaluations to a non-qualitative form. We can entertain the counter-surmise that the rejection of qualitative distinctions is itself an illusion, powered perhaps by an inability to look at one's life in the light of some of the distinctions, a failure of moral nerve, as it were; or else by the draw of a certain objectifying stance towards the world. We might hold that the most hard-bitten utilitarians are themselves moved by qualitative distinctions which remain unadmitted, that they admire the mode of life in which one calculates consciously and clairvoyantly as something higher than the life of self-indulgent illusion, and do not simply elect it as more satisfying.

We cannot resolve this issue here. The point of introducing the distinction between strong and weak evaluation is to contrast the different kinds of self that each involves. In examining this it will, I think, become overwhelmingly plausible that we are not beings whose only authentic evaluations are non-qualitative as the utilitarian tradition suggests.

A subject who only evaluates weakly – that is, makes decisions like that of eating now or later, taking a holiday in the north or in the south – such a subject we might call a simple weigher of alternatives. And the other, who deploys a language of evaluative contrasts ranging over desires, we might call a strong evaluator.

Now we can concur that a simple weigher is already reflective in a minimal sense, in that he evaluates courses of action, and sometimes is capable of acting out of that evaluation as against under the impress of immediate desire. And this is a necessary feature of what we call a self or a person. He has reflection, evaluation and will. But in contrast to the strong evaluator he lacks something else which we often speak of with the metaphor of 'depth'.

The strong evaluator envisages his alternatives through a richer language. The desirable is not only defined for him by what he desires, or what he desires plus a calculation of consequences; it is also defined by a qualitative characterization of desires as higher and lower, noble and base, and so on. Reflection is not just a matter, where it is not calculation of consequences, of registering the conclusion that alternative A is more attractive to me, or draws me more than B. Rather the higher desirability of A over B is something I can articulate if I am reflecting as a strong evaluator. I have a vocabulary of worth.

In other words, the reflection of the simple weigher terminates in the inarticulate experience that A is more attractive than B. I am presented with the pastry tray, I concentrate on it, hesitate between an éclair and a mille feuilles. It becomes clear to me that I feel more like an éclair now, so I take it. Of course, one can say a lot more about the attractiveness of the alternatives in other cases of simple weighing. For instance, when I was choosing between a holiday in the north and one in the south, I talked about the tremendous beauty of the north, of the wild, the sense of untracked wastes, etc., or the lush tropical land, the sense of well-being, the joys of swimming in the sea, etc. All this can be expressed. What cannot be expressed is what makes the south, my ultimate choice, superior.

Thus faced with incommensurables, which is our usual predicament, the simple weigher's experiences of the superiority of A over B are inarticulable. The role of reflection is not to make these articulate, but rather to step back from the immediate situation, to calculate consequences, to compensate for the immediate force of one desire which might not be the most advantageous to follow (as when I put off lunch to swim-with-lunch later), to get over hesitation by concentrating on the inarticulate 'feel' of the alternatives (do I really feel like an éclair or a mille feuilles?).

But the strong evaluator is not similarly inarticulate. There is the beginning of a language in which to express the superiority of one alternative, the language of higher and lower, noble and base, courageous and cowardly, integrated and fragmented, and so on. The strong evaluator can articulate superiority just because he has a language of contrastive characterization.[7]

So within an experience of reflective choice between incommensurables, strong evaluation is a condition of articulacy, and to acquire a

---

[7] It is because the alternatives are characterized in a language of qualitative contrast that strong evaluative choices show the feature we mentioned above, that the rejected alternative is not rejected because of some merely contingent or circumstantial conflict with the goal chosen. To have a language of qualitative contrast is to characterize the noble essentially as in contrast to the base, the courageous to the cowardly, and so on.

With this in mind we can see right away how the holiday preference could become articulate, too. We might decide to go south rather than north because we will have a more humanly meaningful or uplifting experience in visiting some ancient civilization than in being away from any traces of man. With this example we can also see that languages of strong evaluation do not have to be exclusively ethical, as one might have surmised from the examples above; they can also be aesthetic and of other kinds as well.

strongly evaluative language is to become (more) articulate about one's preferences. I cannot tell you perhaps very volubly why Bach is greater than Liszt, say, but I am not totally inarticulate: I can speak of the 'depth' of Bach, for instance, a word one only understands against a corresponding use of 'shallow', which, unfortunately, applies to Liszt. In this regard I am way ahead of where I am in articulating why I now prefer that éclair to the mille feuilles; about this I can say nothing (not even that it tastes better, which I could say, for instance, in explaining my preference for éclairs over brussels-sprouts; but even this is on the verge of inarticulacy – compare our replying above that Bach 'sounds better'). And I am also way ahead of where I might be if I had never aquired any language to talk about music, if it were a quite inarticulable experience for me (of course, it would then be a very different experience).

To be a strong evaluator is thus to be capable of a reflection which is more articulate. But it is also in an important sense deeper.

A strong evaluator, by which we mean a subject who strongly evaluates desires, goes deeper, because he characterizes his motivation at greater depth. To characterize one desire or inclination as worthier, or nobler, or more integrated, etc. than others is to speak of it in terms of the kind of quality of life which it expresses and sustains. I eschew the cowardly act above because I want to be a courageous and honourable human being. Whereas for the simple weigher what is at stake is the desirability of different consummations, those defined by his *de facto* desires, for the strong evaluator reflection also examines the different possible modes of being of the agent. Motivations or desires do not only count in virtue of the attraction of the consummations but also in virtue of the kind of life and kind of subject that these desires properly belong to.[8]

[8] To be a strong evaluator is thus to see desires in an additional dimension. And this is in fact essential to our important evaluative distinctions. It has been remarked for instance that the criteria of a courageous act cannot be given simply in terms of external achievement in a given context. Someone may rush the machine-guns out of stupidity, or drunk with frenzy, or because he has had too much of life. It is not sufficient just that he see the danger, a condition which is met in the last two cases. Or suppose a man is driven with some uncontrollable lust, or hatred, or desire for revenge, so that he runs out into danger. This is not courage either, so long as we see him as *driven*.

Courage requires that we face danger, feel the fear which is appropriate, and nevertheless over-rule the impulse to flee because we in some sense dominate it, because we are moved by something higher than mere impulse or the mere desire to live. It may be glory, or the love of country, or the love of some individuals we are saving, or a sense of our own integrity. Implicit in all of these is that the courageous man is moved by what we can at least think of as seen by him to be higher. If someone for instance thought that there was nothing higher than life and the avoidance of pain, and believed that no one could sanely and responsibly think otherwise, he would have no place in his vocabulary for physical

But this additional dimension can be said to add depth, because now we are reflecting about our desires in terms of the kind of being we are in having them or carrying them out. Whereas a reflection about what we feel like more, which is all a simple weigher can do in assessing motivations, keeps us as it were at the periphery; a reflection on the kind of beings we are takes us to the centre of our existence as agents. Strong evaluation is not just a condition of articulacy about preferences, but also about the quality of life, the kind of beings we are or want to be. It is in this sense deeper.

And this is what lies behind our ordinary use of the metaphor of depth applied to people. Someone is shallow in our view when we feel that he is insensitive, unaware or unconcerned about issues touching the quality of his life which seem to us basic or important. He lives on the surface because he seeks to fulfil desires without being touched by the 'deeper' issues, what these desires express and sustain in the way of modes of life; or his concern with such issues seems to us to touch on trivial or unimportant questions, for example, he is concerned about the glamour of his life, or how it will appear, rather than the (to us) real issues of the quality of life.

The compleat Utilitarian would be an impossibly shallow character, and we can gauge how much self-declared Utilitarians really live their ideology by what importance they attribute to depth.

3

Thus the strong evaluator has articulacy and depth which the simple weigher lacks. He has, one might say, articulacy about depth. But where there is articulacy there is the possibility of a plurality of visions which there was not before. The simple weigher may hesitate, as before the éclair and mille feuilles, and his momentary preference may go back and forth. But we would not say that he envisages his situation of choice now one way, now another. With strong evaluation, however, there can be and often is a plurality of ways of envisaging my predicament, and the choice may be not just between what is clearly the higher and the lower, but between two incommensurable ways of looking at this choice.

Let us say that at the age of 44 I am tempted to pack up, abandon my job and go to some other quite different job in Nepal. One needs to renew the sources of creativity, I tell myself, one can fall into a deadening routine,

---

courage. Any act that might appear to qualify for this title would have to be classified by him as foolhardy, mad, or moronically insensitive to reality, or something of the kind. If we can think of gangsters as being heroic it is because in this post-Romantic age we see something admirable in people living some grand design to the ultimate end, whatever it be.

go stale, simply go through the motions of teaching the same old courses; this way is premature death. Rather rejuvenation is something one can win by courage and decisive action; one must be ready to make a break, try something totally new; and so on, and so on. All this I tell myself when the mood is on me. But then at other moments, this seems like a lot of adolescent nonsense. In fact nothing in life is won without discipline, hanging in, being able to last through periods of mere slogging until something greater grows out of them. One has to have a long breath, and standing loyalties to a certain job, a certain community; and the only meaningful life is that which is deepened by carrying through these commitments, living through the dead periods in order to lay the foundations for the creative ones; and so on.

We see that, unlike the choice between éclairs and mille feuilles, or the vacations north and south, where we have two incommensurable objects attracting us, we have here 'objects' – courses of action – which can only be characterized through the qualities of life they represent, and characterized contrastively. It is part of the desirability characterization of each that it has an undesirability story to tell about the other. But the struggle here is between two such characterizations, and this introduces a new incommensurability. When I am feeling that the break to Nepal is the thing, my desire to stay is a kind of pusillanimity, a weary enmiring in routine, the growing action of a sclerosis that I can only cure by 'splitting'. It is far from being the quietly courageous loyalty to an original line of life, hanging in during the dry period to permit a fuller flowering. And when I am for staying, my trip to Nepal looks like a lot of adolescent nonsense, an attempt to be young again by just refusing to act my age, hardly great liberation, renewal and all that.

We have here a reflection about what to do which is carried on in a struggle of self-interpretations, like our example above of the man struggling against his addiction to rich desserts. The question at issue concerns which is the truer, more authentic, more illusion-free interpretation, and which on the other hand involves a distortion of the meanings things have for me. Resolving this issue is restoring commensurability.

II

I

Starting off from the intuition that the capacity for second-order desires, or evaluating desires, is essential to human agency, I have tried to distinguish two kinds of such evaluation. I hope the discussion has also served to make this basic intuition more plausible, if indeed it lacked any plausibility at the outset. It must be clear that an agent who could not evaluate desires at all would lack the minimum degree of reflectiveness which we associate with a human agent, and would also lack a crucial part of the background for what we describe as the exercise of will.

I should also like to add, but with perhaps less certainty of universal agreement, that the capacity for strong evaluation in particular is essential to our notion of the human subject; that without it an agent would lack a kind of depth we consider essential to humanity, without which we would find human communication impossible (the capacity for which is another essential feature of human agency). But I will not try to argue this case here. The question would revolve around whether one could draw a convincing portrait of a human subject to whom strong evaluation was quite foreign (is Camus' Meursault such a case?), since in fact the human beings we are and live with are all strong evaluators.

But for the remainder of this paper, I should like to examine another avenue of the self, that of responsibility, with the aid of the key notion of second-order desire. For we think of persons as responsible as well, in a way that animals are not, and this too seems bound up with the capacity to evaluate desires.

There is one sense of responsibility which is already implicit in the notion of will. A being capable of evaluating desires may find that the upshot of such evaluation is in conflict with the most urgent desire. Indeed, we might think of it as a necessary feature of the capacity to evaluate desires that one be able to distinguish the better one from the one that presses most strongly.

But in at least our modern notion of the self, responsibility has a stronger sense. We think of the agent not only as partly responsible for what he does, for the degree to which he acts in line with his evaluations, but also as responsible in some sense for these evaluations.

This sense is even suggested by the word 'evaluation', which belongs to the modern, one might almost say post-Nietzschean, vocabulary of moral life. For it relates to the verb 'evaluate', and the verb here implies that this is something we do, that our evaluations emerge from our activity of evaluation, and in this sense are our responsibility.

This active sense is conveyed in Frankfurt's formulation where he speaks of persons as exhibiting 'reflective self-evaluation that is manifested in the formation of second-order desires'.

Or we might put the suggestion another way. We have certain *de facto*, first-order desires. These are given, as it were. But then we form evaluations, or second-order desires. But these are not just given, they are also endorsed, and in this sense they engage our responsibility.

How are we to understand this responsibility? An influential strand of thought in the modern world has wanted to understand it in terms of choice. The Nietzschean term 'value', suggested by our 'evaluation', carries this idea that our 'values' are our creations, that they ultimately repose on our espousing them. But to say that they ultimately repose on our espousing them is to say that they issue ultimately from a radical choice, that is, a choice which is not grounded in any reasons. For to the extent that a choice is grounded in reasons, these are simply taken as valid and are not themselves chosen. If our 'values' are to be thought of as chosen, then they must repose finally on a radical choice in the above sense.

This is, of course, the line taken by Sartre in L'Être et le Néant, where he argues that the fundamental project which defines us reposes on a radical choice. The choice, Sartre puts it with his characteristic flair for striking formulae, is 'absurde, en ce sens, qu'il est ce par quoi ... toutes les raisons viennent à l'être'.[9] This idea of radical choice is also defended by an influential Anglo-Saxon school of moral philosophers.

But in fact we cannot understand our responsibility for our evaluations through the notion of radical choice – not if we are to go on seeing ourselves as strong evaluators, as agents with depth. For a radical choice *between* strong evaluations is quite conceivable, but not a radical choice *of* such evaluations.

To see this we might examine a famous Sartrian example, which turns out, I believe, to illustrate the exact opposite of Sartre's thesis, the example in L'Existentialisme est un Humanisme of the young man who is torn between remaining with his ailing mother and going off to join the Resistance. Sartre's point is that there is no way of adjudicating between these two strong claims on his moral allegiance through reason or the reliance on some kind of over-reaching considerations. He has to settle the question, whichever way he goes, by radical choice.

Sartre's portrayal of the dilemma is very powerful. But what makes it plausible is precisely what undermines his position. We see a grievous moral dilemma because the young man is faced here with two powerful moral *claims*. On the one hand his ailing mother may well die if he leaves her, and die in the most terrible sorrow, not even sure that her son still lives; on the other hand is the call of his country, conquered and laid waste by the enemy, and not only his country, for this enemy is destroying

---

[9] J. P. Sartre, L'Être et le Néant (Paris, 1943), p. 559.

the very foundation of civilized and ethical relations between men. A cruel dilemma, indeed. But it is a dilemma only because the claims themselves are not created by radical choice. If they were the grievous nature of the predicament would dissolve, for that would mean that the young man could do away with the dilemma at any moment by simply declaring one of the rival claims as dead and inoperative. Indeed, if serious moral claims were created by radical choice, the young man could have a grievous dilemma about whether to go and get an ice cream cone, and then again he could decide not to.

It is no argument against the view that evaluations do not repose on radical choice that there are moral dilemmas. Why should it even be surprising that the evaluations we feel called upon to assent to may conflict, even grievously, in some situations? I would argue that the reverse is the case, that moral dilemmas become inconceivable on the theory of radical choice.

Now in this hypothetical case the young man has to resolve the matter by radical choice. He simply has to plump for the Resistance or for staying at home with his mother. He has no language in which the superiority of one alternative over the other can be articulated; indeed, he has not even an inchoate sense of the superiority of one over the other; they seem quite incommensurable to him. He just throws himself one way.

This is a perfectly understandable sense of radical choice. But then imagine extending this to all cases of moral action. Let us apply it to the case where I have an ailing mother and no rival obligation. Do I stay, or do I go for a holiday on the Riviera? There is no doubt I should stay. Of course, I *may* not stay. In this sense, there is also a 'radical choice' open: whether to do what we ought or not (although here I might put forward all sorts of rationalizations for going to the Côte d'Azur: I owe it to myself, after all I have faithfully taken care of her all these years while my brothers and sisters have gone off, and so on). But the question is whether we can construe the determination of what we ought to do here as issuing from a radical choice.

What would this look like? Presumably, we would be faced with the two choices, to stay with my mother or go to the south. On the level of radical choice these alternatives have as yet no contrastive characterization, that is, one is not the path of duty, while the other is that of selfish indulgence, or whatever.

This contrastive description will be created by radical choice. So what does this choice consist in? Well, I might ponder the two possibilities, and then I might just find myself doing one rather than another. But this brings us to the limit where choice fades into non-choice. Do I really choose if I just start doing one of the alternatives? And above all, this kind of resolution has no place for the judgement 'I owe it to my mother to stay', which is supposed to issue from the choice.

What is it to have this judgement issue from radical choice? Not that on pondering the alternatives, the sense grows more and more strongly that this judgement is *right*, for this would not be an account of radical choice, but rather of our coming to see that our obligation lay here. This account would present obligations as issuing not from radical choice but from some kind of vision of our moral predicament. This choice would be grounded. What is it then for radical choice to issue in this judgement? Is it just that I find myself assenting to the judgement, as in the previous paragraph I found myself doing one of the two actions? But then what force has 'assenting to the judgement'? I can certainly just find myself saying 'I owe it to my mother', but this is surely not what it is to assent. I can, I suppose, find myself feeling suddenly, 'I owe this to my mother'; but then what grounds are there for thinking of this as a choice?

In order for us to speak of choice, we cannot just find ourselves in one of the alternatives. We have in some sense to experience the pull of each and give our assent to one. But what kind of pull do the alternatives have here? What draws me to the Côte d'Azur is perhaps unproblematic enough, but what draws me to stay with my mother cannot be the sense that I owe it to her, for that *ex hypothesi* has to issue from the choice. It can only be a *de facto* desire, like my desire for the sun and sea of the Côte d'Azur. But then the choice here is like the choice of the two holidays in the previous section. I feel the attraction of these two incommensurable alternatives, and after I ponder them I find that one begins to become prepotent, it draws me more. Or perhaps, the matter obstinately refuses to resolve itself, and I say at one moment, 'what the hell, I'll stay'.

The agent of radical choice has to choose, if he chooses at all, like a simple weigher. And this means that he cannot properly speaking be a strong evaluator. For all his putative strong evaluations issue from simple weighings. The application of a contrastive language which makes a preference articulate reposes on fiat, a choice made between incommensurables. But then the application of the contrastive language would be in an important sense bogus. For by hypothesis the experience on which the application reposed would be more properly characterized by a preference between incommensurables; the fundamental experience which was supposed to justify this language would in fact be that of the simple weigher, not of the strong evaluator. For again by hypothesis, what leads him to call one alternative higher or more worthy is not that in his experience it appears to be so, for then his evaluations would be judgements, not choices; but rather that he is led to plump for one rather than the other after considering the attractiveness of both alternatives.

But of course, even this account of choice would not be acceptable to the theorist of radical choice. He would refuse the assimilation of these choices to such decisions as whether to go south or north for my holiday. For these choices are not supposed to be simply the registration of my preferences, but radical choices. But what is a radical choice which is not even a registration of preference? Well, it may be that I just decide, just throw myself one way rather than another. I just say, 'what the hell, I'll stay'. But this, of course, I can do in the holiday choice case, where, for instance, I cannot seem to make up my mind which is preferable. This does not distinguish the two cases.

Perhaps then it is that in radical choice I do not consult preferences at all. It is not that I try to see which I prefer, and then failing to get a result, I throw myself one way or the other; but rather, this kind of choice is made quite without regard to preferences. But then with regard to what is it made? Here we border on incoherence. A choice made without regard to anything, without the agent feeling any solicitation to one alternative or the other, or in complete disregard of such solicitation: is this still choice? What could it be? Well, suddenly he just goes and takes one of the alternatives. Yet, but this he could do in a fit of abstraction. What makes it a choice? It must be something to do with what he is thinking out of which this act comes. But what could that be? Can it just be that he is thinking something like 'I must take one of them, I must take one of them', repeating it to himself in a fever? Surely not. Rather he must be pondering the alternatives, be in some way considering their desirability, and the choice must be in some way related to that. Perhaps he judges that A is by all criteria more desirable, and then he chooses B. But if this is a choice and not just an inexplicable movement, it must have been accompanied by something like: 'damn it, why should I always choose by the book, I'll take B'; or maybe he just suddenly felt that he really wanted B. In either case, his choice clearly relates to his preference, however suddenly arising and from whatever reversal of criteria. But a choice utterly unrelated to the desirability of the alternatives would not be intelligible as a choice.

The theory of radical choice in fact is deeply incoherent, for it wants to maintain both strong evaluation and radical choice. It wants to have strong evaluations and yet deny their status as judgements. And the result is that on close examination, it crumbles; in order to maintain its coherence the theory of radical choice in fact mutates into something quite different. Either we take seriously the kinds of consideration which weigh in our moral decisions, and then we are forced to recognize that these are for the most part evaluations which do not issue from radical choice; or else we try at all costs to keep our radical choice independent of any such evaluations, but then it ceases to be a choice of strong evaluations, and becomes a simple expression of preference, and if we go farther and try to make it independent even of our *de facto* preferences, then we fall ultimately into a criteria-less leap which can not properly be described as choice at all.

In fact the theory maintains a semblance of plausibility by surreptitiously assuming strong evaluation beyond the reach of radical choice, and that in two ways. First, the real answer to our attempted assimilation of radical moral choice to the mere preference of a simple weigher is that the choices talked about in the theory are about basic and fundamental issues, like the choice of our young man above between his mother and the Resistance. But these issues are basic and fundamental not in virtue of radical choice; their importance is given, or revealed in an evaluation which is constated, not chosen. The real force of the theory of radical choice comes from the sense that there are different moral perspectives, that there is a plurality of moral visions, as we said in the previous section, between which it seems very hard to adjudicate. We can conclude that the only way of deciding between these is by the kind of radical choice that our young man had to take.

And this in turn leads to a second strong evaluation beyond the reach of choice. If this is the predicament of man, then it is plainly a more honest, more clairvoyant, less confused and self-deluding stance to be aware of this and take the full responsibility for the radical choice. The stance of 'good faith' is higher, and this not in virtue of radical choice, but in virtue of our characterization of the human predicament in which radical choice has such an important place. Granted this is the moral predicament of man, it is more honest, courageous, self-clairvoyant, hence a higher mode of life, to choose in lucidity than it is to hide one's choices behind the supposed structure of things, to flee from one's responsibility at the expense of lying to oneself, of a deep self-duplicity.

When we see what makes the theory of radical choice plausible we see how strong evaluation is something inescapable in our conception of the agent and his experience; and this because it is bound up with our notion of the self. So that it creeps back in even where it is supposed to have been excluded.

We can see this from a different angle if we consider another way of showing the theory of radical choice to be wrong. I mentioned in the last section that strong evaluators can be called deep because what weighs with them are not only the consummations desired but also what kind of life, what quality of agent they are to be. This is closely connected with the notion of identity.

By 'identity' I mean that use of the term where we talk about 'finding one's identity', or going through an 'identity crisis'. Now our identity is defined by our fundamental evaluations. The answer to the question 'What is my identity?' cannot be given by any list of properties of other ranges, about my physical description, provenance, background, capacities, and so on. All these can figure in my identity, but only as assumed in a certain way. If my being of a certain lineage is to me of central importance, if I am proud of it, and see it as conferring on me membership in a certain class of people whom I see as marked off by certain qualities which I value in myself as an agent and which come to me from this background, then it will be part of my identity. This will be strengthened if I believe that men's moral qualities are to a great extent nourished by their background, so that to turn against one's background is to reject oneself in an important way.

So my lineage is part of my identity because it is bound up with certain qualities I value, or because I believe that I must value these qualities since they are so integrally part of me that to disvalue them would be to reject myself. In either case, the concept of identity is bound up with that of certain strong evaluations which are inseparable from myself. This either because I identify myself by my strong evaluations, as someone who essentially has these convictions; or else because I see certain of my other properties as admitting of only one kind of strong evaluation by myself, because these properties so centrally touch what I am as an agent, that is, as a strong evaluator, that I cannot really repudiate them in the full sense. For I would be thereby repudiating myself, inwardly riven, and hence incapable of fully authentic evaluation.

Our identity is therefore defined by certain evaluations which are inseparable from ourselves as agents. Shorn of these we would cease to be ourselves, by which we do not mean trivially that we would be different in the sense of having some properties other than those we now have – which would indeed be the case after any change, however minor – but that shorn of these we would lose the very possibility of being an agent who evaluates; that our existence as persons, and hence our ability to adhere as persons to certain evaluations, would be impossible outside the horizon of these essential evaluations, that we would break down as persons, be incapable of being persons in the full sense.

Thus, if I were forced by torture or brainwashing to abandon these convictions by which I define my identity, I would be shattered, I would no longer be a subject capable of knowing where I stood and what the meanings of things were for me, I would suffer a terrifying breakdown of precisely those capacities which define a human agent. Or if, to take the other example, I were somehow induced to repudiate my lineage, I would be crippled as a person, because I would be repudiating an essential part of that out of which I evaluate and determine the meanings of things for me. Such repudiation would both be itself inauthentic and would make me incapable of other authentic evaluations.

The notion of identity refers us to certain evaluations which are essential because they are the indispensable horizon or foundation out of which we reflect and evaluate as persons. To lose this horizon, or not to have found it, is indeed a terrifying experience of disaggregation and loss. This is why we can speak of an 'identity-crisis' when we have lost our grip on who we are. A self decides and acts out of certain fundamental evaluations.

This is what is impossible in the theory of radical choice. The agent of radical choice would at the moment of choice have *ex hypothesi* no horizon of evaluation. He would be utterly without identity. He would be a kind of extensionless point, a pure leap into the void. But such a thing is an impossibility, or rather could only be the description of the most terrible mental alienation. The subject of radical choice is another avatar of that recurrent figure which our civilization aspires to realize, the disembodied ego, the subject who can objectify all being, including his own, and choose in radical freedom. But this promised total self-possession would in fact be the most total self-loss.

3

What then is the sense we can give to the responsibility of the agent, if we are not to understand it in terms of radical choice? Do we have to conclude that we are not in any sense responsible for our evaluations?

I think not. For there is another sense in which we are responsible. Our evaluations are not chosen. On the contrary they are articulations of our sense of what is worthy, or higher, or more integrated, or more fulfilling, and so on. But as *articulations*, they offer another purchase for the concept of responsibility. Let us examine this.

Much of our motivation – our desires, aspirations, evaluation – is not simply given. We give it a formulation in words or images. Indeed, by the fact that we are linguistic animals our desires and aspirations cannot but be articulated in one way or another. Thus we are not simply moved by psychic forces comparable to such forces as gravity or electro-magnetism, which we can see as given in a straightforward way, but rather by psychic 'forces'[10] which are articulated or interpreted in a certain way.

Now these articulations are not simply descriptions, if we mean by this characterizations of a fully independent object, that is, an object which is altered neither in what it is, nor in the degree or manner of its evidence to us by the description. In this way my characterization of this table as brown, or this line of mountains as jagged, is a simple description.

On the contrary, articulations are attempts to formulate what is initially inchoate, or confused, or badly formulated. But this kind of formation or reformulation does not leave its object unchanged. To give a certain articulation is to shape our sense of what we desire or what we hold important in a certain way.

Let us take the case above of the man who is fighting obesity and who is talked into seeing it as a merely quantitative question of more satisfaction, rather than as a matter of dignity and degradation. As a result of this change, his inner struggle itself becomes transformed, and is now quite a different experience.

The opposed motivations – the craving for cream cake and his dissatisfaction with himself at such indulgence – which are the 'objects' undergoing rediscription here, are not independent in the sense outlined above. When he comes to accept the new interpretation of his desire to control himself, the desire itself has altered. True, it may be said on one level to have the same goal, that he stop eating cream cake, but since it is no longer understood as a seeking for dignity and self-respect it has become quite a different kind of motivation.

Of course, even here we often try to preserve the identity of the objects undergoing redescription – so deeply rooted is the ordinary descriptive model. We might think of the change, say, in terms of some immature sense of shame and degradation being detached from our desire to resist over-indulgence, which has now simply the rational goal of increasing

---

[10] I put the expression in quotes here because the underlying motivation which we want to speak of in terms of psychic 'forces' or 'drives' is only accessible through interpretation of behaviour or feeling. The line here between metaphor and basic theory is very hard to draw. Cf. Paul Ricoeur, *De L'Interprétation* (Paris, 1965) and my 'Force et sens' in G. Madison (ed.), *Sens et Existence* (Paris, 1975).

over-all satisfaction. In this way we might maintain the impression that the elements are just rearranged while remaining the same. But on a closer look we see that on this reading, too, the sense of shame does not remain self-identical through the change. It dissipates altogether, or becomes something quite different.

We can say therefore that our self-interpretations are partly constitutive of our experience. For an altered description of our motivation can be inseparable from a change in this motivation. But to assert this connection is not to put forward a causal hypothesis: it is not to say that we alter our descriptions and then *as a result* our experience of our predicament alters. Rather it is that certain modes of experience are not possible without certain self-descriptions. The particular quality of experience in the obesity case where I approach the alternative purely as a balance of utility, where I am free from the menace of degradation and self-contempt, cannot be without my characterizing the two rival desires in this 'deflated' way, as two different kinds of advantage. This deflated description is part of the objectifying, calculative way I now experience the choice. We can say that it is 'constitutive' of this experience, and this is the term I shall use for this relation.

But the fact that self-interpretations are constitutive of experience says nothing about how changes in both descriptions and experience are brought about. It would appear in fact that change can be brought about in two different ways. In some circumstances we are led to reflect, on our own or in exchange with others, and can sometimes win through to a new way of seeing our predicament, and hence a change in our experiences. But more fundamentally, it would apear that certain descriptions of experience are unacceptable or incomprehensible to some people because of the nature of their experience. To someone who strongly experiences the fight against obesity in terms of degradation, the 'deflated' descriptions appear a wicked travesty, a shameless avoidance of moral reality – rather as we react to the hiding of political crime through Orwellian language, for example renaming mass murder a final 'solution'.

That description and experience are bound together in this constitutive relation admits of causal influences in both directions: it can sometimes allow us to alter experience by coming to fresh insight; but more fundamentally it circumscribes insight through the deeply embedded shape of experience for us.

Because of this constitutive relation, our descriptions of our motivations, and our attempts to formulate what we hold important, are not simple descriptions in that their objects are not fully independent. And yet they are not simply arbitrary either, such that anything goes. There are more or less adequate, more or less truthful, more self-clairvoyant or self-deluding interpretations. Because of this double fact, because an articulation can be *wrong*, and yet it shapes what it is wrong about, we sometimes see erroneous articulations as involving a distortion of the reality concerned. We do not just speak of error but frequently also of illusion or delusion.

We could put the point this way. Our attempts to formulate what we hold important must, like descriptions, strive to be faithful to something. But what they strive to be faithful to is not an independent object with a fixed degree and manner of evidence, but rather a largely inarticulate sense of what is of decisive importance. An articulation of this 'object' tends to make it something different from what it was before.

And by the same token a new articulation does not leave its 'object' evident or obscure to us in the same manner or degree as before. In the fact of shaping it, it makes it accessible and/or inaccessible in new ways. This is in fact well illustrated by our example of the man fighting obesity.

Now our articulations, just because they partly shape their objects, engage our responsibility in a way that simple descriptions do not. This happens in two related ways which correspond to the two directions of causal influence mentioned above.

First, because our insights into our own motivations and into what is important and of value are often limited by the shape of our experience, failure to understand a certain insight, or see the point of some moral advice proffered, is often taken as a judgement on the character of the person concerned. An insensitive person, or a fanatic, cannot see what he is doing to others, the kind of suffering he is inflicting on them. He cannot see, for instance, that this act is a deep affront to someone's sense of honour, or perhaps deeply undermines his sense of worth. He is proof to all remonstrating on our part.

He cannot listen to us because he has closed off all sensitivity to questions of honour, or perhaps to the sense of personal worth, in himself, say; and this might in turn be related to earlier experiences which he has undergone. These earlier experiences account for a shape of his current experience in which these issues figure as specious and of no account, and this current shape makes it impossible for him to allow the insights we are pressing on him. He cannot admit them without his whole stance towards these matters crumbling; and this stance may be motivationally of deep importance to him.

But in his kind of case we take the limits of the man's insight as a judgement on him. It is because of what he has become – perhaps indeed, in response to some terrible strain or difficulty, but nevertheless what he has become – that he cannot see certain things, cannot understand the point of certain descriptions of experience. In the sense of 'responsibility' where we only attribute it to people in relation to outcomes that they can presently encompass or avoid, we should not speak of responsibility here. And even if we take account of what the agent could have done differently in the past, the responsibility in this sense may be very attenuated, for example when people have been marked by truly harrowing early experiences.

But in another sense of 'responsibility', one older than our modern notions of moral agency, we hold them responsible in that we judge them morally on the basis of what they see or do not see. So that a man may condemn himself by giving his sincerely held view on the nature of experience that he or others are living through, or on what is of importance to himself or what he sees as important to men in general.

This is one sense in which we think of people as responsible for their evaluations, and in a way which has nothing to do with the theory of radical choice. But we also think of ourselves as responsible for them in a more straightforward 'modern' sense.

This has to do with the other direction of causal influence in which we can sometimes alter ourselves and our experience by fresh insight. In any case, our evaluations would always be open to challenge. Because of the character of depth which we saw in the self, our evaluations are articulations of insights which are frequently partial, clouded and uncertain. But they are all the more open to challenge when we reflect that these insights are often distorted by our imperfections of character. For these two reasons evaluation is such that there is always room for re-evaluation.

Responsibility falls to us in the sense that it is always possible that fresh insight might alter my evaluations and hence even myself for the better. So that within the limits of my capacity to change myself by fresh insight, within the limits of the first direction of causal influence, I am responsible in the full direct, 'modern' sense for my evaluations.

What was said about the challengeability of evaluations applies with greatest force to our most fundamental evaluations, those which provide the terms in which other less basic ones are made. These are the evaluations which touch my identity in the sense described in the previous section. There I spoke of the self as having an identity which is defined in terms of certain essential evaluations which provide the horizon or foundation for the other evaluations one makes.

Now precisely these deepest evaluations are the ones which are least clear, least articulated, most easily subject to illusion and distortion. It is those which are closest to what I am as a subject, in the sense that shorn of them I would break down as a person, which are among the hardest for me to be clear about.

Thus the question can always be posed: ought I to re-evaluate my most basic evaluations? Have I really understood what is essential to my identity? Have I truly determined what I sense to be the highest mode of life?

Now this kind of re-evaluation will be radical; not in the sense of radical choice, however, that we choose without criteria; but rather in the sense that our looking again can be so undertaken that in principle no formulations are considered unrevisable.

What is of fundamental importance for us will already have an articulation, some notion of a certain mode of life as higher than others, or the belief that some cause is the worthiest that can be served; or the sense that belonging to this community is essential to my identity. A radical re-evaluation will call these formulations into question.

But a re-evaluation of this kind, once embarked on, is of a peculiar sort. It is unlike a less than radical evaluation which is carried on within the terms of some fundamental evaluation, when I ask myself whether it would be honest to take advantage of this income-tax loophole, or smuggle something through customs. These latter can be carried on in a language which is out of dispute. In answering the questions just mentioned the term 'honest' is taken as beyond challenge. But in radical re-evaluations by definition the most basic terms, those in which other evaluations are carried on, are precisely what is in question. It is just because all formulations are potentially under suspicion of distorting their objects that we have to see them all as revisable, that we are forced back, as it were, to the inarticulate limit from which they originate.

How, then, can such re-evaluations be carried on? There is certainly no metalanguage available in which I can assess rival self-interpretations, such as my two characterizations above of my ambition to go to Nepal. If there were, this would not be radical re-evaluation. On the contrary, the re-evaluation is carried on in the formulae available but with a stance of attention, as it were, to what these formulae are meant to articulate and with a readiness to receive any gestalt shift in our view of the situation, any quite innovative set of categories in which to see our predicament, that might come our way in inspiration.

Anyone who has struggled with a philosophical problem knows what this kind of enquiry is like. In philosophy typically we start off with a question, which we know to be badly formed at the outset. We hope that in struggling with it, we shall find that its terms are transformed, so that in the end we will answer a question which we could not properly conceive at the beginning. We are striving for conceptual innovation which will allow us to illuminate some matter, say an area of human experience, which would otherwise remain dark and confused. The alternative is to stick stubbornly to certain terms and try to understand reality by classifying it in these terms (are these propositions synthetic or analytic, is this a psychological question or a philosophical question, is this view monist or dualist?).

The same contrast can exist in our evaluations. We can attempt a radical re-evaluation, in which case we may hope that our terms will be transformed in the course of it; or we may stick to certain favoured terms, insist that all evaluations can be made in their ambit, and refuse any radical questioning. To take an extreme case, someone can adopt the utilitarian criterion and then claim to settle all further issues about action by some calculation.

The point has been made again and again by non-naturalists, existentialists, and others, that those who take this kind of line are ducking a major question: should I really decide on the utilitarian principle? But this does not mean that the alternative to this stance is a radical choice. Rather it is to look again at our most fundamental formulations, and at what they were meant to articulate, in a stance of openness, where we are ready to accept any categorical change, however radical, which might emerge. Of course we will actually start thinking of particular cases, for instance where our present evaluations recommend things which worry us, and try to puzzle further. In doing this we will be like the philosopher and his initially ill-formed question. But we may get through to something deeper.

In fact this stance of openness is very difficult. It may take discipline and time. It is difficult because this form of evaluation is deep in a sense, and total in a sense, that other less than radical ones are not. If I am questioning whether smuggling a radio into the country is honest, or judging everything by the utilitarian criterion, then I have a yardstick, a definite yardstick. But if I go to the radical questioning, then it is not exactly that I have no yardstick, in the sense that anything goes, but rather that what takes the place of the yardstick is my deepest unstructured sense of what is important, which is as yet inchoate and which I am trying to bring to definition. I am trying to see reality afresh and form more adequate categories to describe it. To do this I am trying to open myself, use all of my deepest, unstructured sense of things in order to come to a new clarity.

Now this engages me at a depth that using a fixed yardstick does not. I am in a sense questioning the inchoate sense that led me to use the yardstick. And at the same time it engages my whole self in a way that judging by a yardstick does not. This is what makes it uncommonly difficult to reflect on our fundamental evaluations. It is much easier to take up the formulations that come most readily to hand, generally those which are going the rounds of our milieu or society, and live within them without too much probing. The obstacles in the way of going deeper are legion. There is not only the difficulty of such concentration, and the pain of uncertainty, but also all the distortions and repressions which make us want to turn away from this examination: and which make us resist change even when we do re-examine ourselves. Some of our evaluations may in fact become fixed and compulsive, so that we cannot help feeling guilty about X, or despising people like Y, even though we judge with the greatest degree of openness and depth at our command that X is perfectly all right, and that Y is a very admirable person. This casts light on another aspect of the term 'deep', as applied to people. We consider people deep to the extent, inter alia, that they are capable of this kind of radical self-reflection.

This radical evaluation is a deep reflection, and a self-reflection in a special sense: it is a reflection about the self, its most fundamental issues, and a reflection which engages the self most wholly and deeply. Because it engages the whole self without a fixed yardstick it can be called a personal reflection (the parallel to Polanyi's notion of personal knowledge is intended here); and what emerges from it is a self-resolution in a strong sense, for in this reflection the self is in question; what is at stake is the definition of those inchoate evaluations which are sensed to be essential to our identity.

Because this self-resolution is something we do, when we do it, we can be called responsible for ourselves; and because it is within limits always up to us to do it, even when we do not – indeed, the nature of our deepest evaluations constantly raises the question whether we have them right – we can be called responsible in another sense for ourselves, whether we undertake this radical evaluation or not.

4

I have been exploring some aspects of a self or human agent, following the key notion that a crucial feature of human agency is the capacity for second-order desires or evaluation of desires. In the course of the discussion, it will have become more and more plausible, I hope, that the capacity for what I have called strong evaluation is an essential feature of a person.

I think that this has helped to cast light on the sense in which we ascribe reflection, will and also responsibility to human agents. But our conception of human agency is also of crucial importance to any potential science of the human subject, in particular to psychology.

In concluding, I would like to sketch a few of the consequences for the study of psychology of this conception. First, it evidently means that a concept like 'drive', used in motivational theory as a psychic force operating in abstraction from any interpretation, cannot find a fruitful application. The idea of measuring drive like a force in natural science is in principle misguided. Instead we would have to accept that those branches of psychology which attempt to account for fully motivated behaviour must take account of the fact that the human animal is a self-interpreting subject. And this means that these branches of the discipline must be 'hermeneutical' sciences.

I have discussed some of what is involved in this elsewhere.[11] But one consequence, which has been touched on in this symposium, is for the study of personality. For if we take the view that man is a self-interpreting animal, then we will accept that a study of personality which tries to proceed in terms of general traits alone can have only limited value. For in many cases we can only give their proper significance to the subject's articulations by means of 'idiographic' studies, which can explore the particular terms of an individual's self-interpretations. Studies exclusively in terms of general traits can be empty, or else end up with baffling inconsistencies. I believe that there is some common ground here with a point made by W. and H. Mischel in a very stimulating paper[12] that such functions as self-control are carried out more discriminatively than we can account for in terms of something like 'a unitary trait entity of conscience or honesty'.

But perhaps the most valuable fruits of a more fully developed conception of the self on the above lines, which avoided the reductiveness of drive theory, would come in dialogue with those strands in psychoanalysis which are particularly concerned with the development of the

---

[11] Chapter 5 below.

[12] W. Mischel and H. N. Mischel, 'Self-control and the self', in T. Mischel (ed.), *The Self* (Oxford, 1977), pp. 31–64.

self, of which a paper by Ernest Wolf gives an extremely interesting account.[13] For evidently any theory of the ontogenesis of the self, and any identification of its potential breakdowns, must also both draw and draw from, implicitly or explicitly, a portrait of the fully responsible human agent. The attempt to explore our underlying notion of responsibility could therefore both help and be helped by a study of the growth and pathologies of the self.

Thus I believe that there are links between the rather groping remarks about identity in this paper and the much more fully developed notion of a 'cohesive self' that Kohut and Ernest Wolf have introduced. These links would greatly repay further exploration. They are made all the closer in that Kohut and Wolf are not working with a drive or psychic 'force' view of motivation. Thus sexual libido is not seen as a constant factor, but rather sexual desire and excitability have a very different impact on a cohesive self than on one which has lost its cohesion.[14]

The prospect of psychoanalytic theory which could give an adequate account of the genesis of full human responsibility, without recourse to such global and reified mechanisms as the super-ego, and with a truly plausible account of the shared subjectivity from which the mature cohesive self must emerge, is a very exciting prospect indeed.

---

[13] Cf. E. S. Wolf, 'Irrationality in a psychoanalytic psychology of the self', in T. Mischel (ed.), *The Self* (Oxford, 1977), pp. 203–23.

[14] *Ibid.*; see also, for example, Heinz Kohut, *The Restoration of the Self* (New York, 1977).

CHAPTER TWO

SELF-INTERPRETING ANIMALS

I

Human beings are self-interpreting animals. This is a widely echoing theme of contemporary philosophy. It is central to a thesis about the sciences of man, and what differentiates them from the sciences of nature, which passes through Dilthey and is very strong in the late twentieth century. It is one of the basic ideas of Heidegger's philosophy, early and late. Partly through his influence, it has been made the starting point for a new skein of connected conceptions of man, self-understanding and history, of which the most prominent protagonist has been Gadamer. At the same time, this conception of man as self-interpreting has been incorporated into the work of Habermas, the most important successor of the post-Marxist line of thought known somewhat strangely as critical theory.

And one could go on. Through all this cross-talk about 'hermeneutics', the question of what one means by this basic thesis, that man is a self-interpreting animal, and how one can show that it is so, may still go unanswered. These are of course tightly related questions; and I would like to try to fumble my way towards an answer to them.

It may turn out to be a mistake, but I am tempted to try to put together the full picture that this thesis means to convey by stages; to lay out, in other words, a series of claims, where the later ones build on the earlier ones, and in that sense form a connected picture. But to talk of claims implies that what is said at each stage is controversial, and that it will have to be established against opposition. So before starting it may be useful to say a word about who or what is opposing, or what the argument is all about.

The thesis that man is a self-interpreting being cannot just be stated flatly, or taken as a truism without argument, because it runs against one of the fundamental prejudices or, to sound less negative, leading ideas of modern thought and culture. It violates a paradigm of clarity and objectivity.

According to this, thinking clearly about something, with a view to arriving at the truth about it, requires that we think of it objectively, that is, as an object among other objects. This means that we avoid attributing to it properties, or describing it in terms of properties, which are 'subjective' in the sense that they are only properties of the object in our experience of it.

This was one of the basic components of the seventeenth-century revolution in scientific thought, which we still see rightly as the foundation of modern science, and indeed of modern thought in general. And perhaps the best illustrative example to take is that paradigm of the seventeenth-century discussion, the distinction between primary and secondary qualities.

Secondary qualities could not be integrated into a science of nature in the same way as the primary, because they were subjective in the above sense. That is, they were properties of the objects concerned only in our experience of them. Only in the experience of creatures endowed with the particular form of sensibility we call sight can things be coloured. Should these creatures cease to exist, the light that objects give off would indeed go on being of a certain wave-length, but there would no longer be what we think of as colour. Secondary properties were sometimes objected to on the grounds that they were variable, or not susceptible to inter-subjective validation – the water that feels cold to me now may feel warm later, or warm to you now. But the ultimate ground of objection was that they were subjective. Even if we were somehow guaranteed in fact against variations in our perceptions over time and between persons, such properties were still suspect because they cannot make good a claim to be independently part of the furniture of things. The assurance against variation could always only be *de facto*, because these properties are in their nature dependent on our sensibility.

The distinction could be put in terms of a contemporary science-fiction fable if we say that the primary, the objective, is what we could agree about with Alpha Centaurans, who as everybody knows are large gaseous clouds, somehow endowed with sapience, but unrecognizable by us as living beings, lacking what we think of as sense organs, lacking our notion of individuality (they agglomerate and redivide in all sorts of ways). When we finally managed to establish communication with them, and learnt each other's conventions of measurement, we could presumably come to agreement with them in attributing wave-lengths to the light reflecting off different objects. But what we experience as colour would remain quite incommunicable. With Alpha Centaurans, we shall have to be completely Democritean: by convention, coloured and sweet; by nature, atoms, quarks, pi-mesons, and wave-lengths.

Following this line of thought, colour, sweetness, felt heat, and so on, are not banished altogether – how could they be considered as nothing? But they are placed ontologically not in things but in our sensibility, or in our experience of things. And this was one of the roots of the notorious theory of perception as made up of 'ideas' or 'impressions', which has wreaked such havoc in philosophical psychology down the centuries. This theory of experience has turned out to be an embarrassment for everyone, and in recent times this same basic objectivist orientation rather expresses itself in the perspective of a reductive explanation of human action and experience in physiological and ultimately in physical and chemical terms. In this way we shall be able to treat man, like everything else, as an object among other objects, characterizing him purely in terms of properties which are independent of his experience – in this case, his self-experience; and treat the lived experience of, for example, sensation as epiphenomenon, or perhaps as a misdescription of what is really a brain-state.

This view gets a little incoherent around the edges; but I do not want to argue that now. I wanted only to articulate somewhat the standard of clarity and objectivity, that is, of a clear account of what things objectively are, against which the conception of man as self-interpreting must contend all the way. For it essentially resists the reduction of experience to a merely subjective view on reality, or an epiphenomenon, or a muddled description. On the contrary, the claim is that our interpretation of ourselves and our experience is constitutive of what we are, and therefore cannot be considered as merely a view on reality, separable from reality, nor as an epiphenomenon, which can be by-passed in our understanding of reality.

II

I

With the background established, I turn to the claims. The first is that many of our feelings, emotions, desires, in short much of our experienced motivation, are such that saying properly what they are like involves expressing or making explicit a judgement about the object they bear on.

This point has often been made in contemporary philosophy in the form of a thesis that (to put it in capsule form) emotions are essentially related to certain objects. To experience fear is to experience some object as terrifying or dangerous; to experience shame is to experience some object or situation as shameful or humiliating, and so on.

The obvious counter-examples that one is tempted to bring forward to this thesis serve to entrench it and at the same time to clarify it. People are tempted to invoke as an objection such 'objectless' emotions as nameless dread, or unfocussed anxiety. But the point about these, one might reply, is just that there is no object where there should be one. The very structure of fear is that it is of something; what marks out nameless fear, or in a different way, unfocussed anxiety, is that we cannot designate an object. But this does not show that the emotions are not essentially related to objects; for it is not just that there is no object here, rather there is a felt absence of object. The empty slot where the object of fear should be is an essential phenomenological feature of this experience. But an essential phenomenological feature of an *experience* is equivalent to an essential feature of it *tout court*.

To put the point in different terms, to have a sense of nameless dread is to have a sense of threat for which I can not find any (rational) focus in this situation. The inability to find a focus is itself an aspect of my sense of my situation. But even in this unfocussed way, the sense I have is one of *threat*, or that something *harmful* is impending, that something terrible might *happen*. Without something of this range, it cannot be *dread* that we experience. The emotion is not 'objectless' *simpliciter*, because it is of something terrible impending; it is just that I cannot say what. But perhaps for this reason, it is better not to put the point in terms of an essential relation to objects, and speak rather of these emotions as essentially involving a sense of our situation. They are affective modes of awareness of situation. And we can rephrase our first claim and say that describing properly what these emotions are like involves making explicit the sense of the situation they essentially incorporate, making explicit some judgement about the situation which gives the emotion its character.

We could put it this way: that experiencing a given emotion involves experiencing our situation as being of a certain kind or having a certain property. But this property cannot be neutral, cannot be something to which we are indifferent, or else we would not be moved. Rather, experiencing an emotion is to be aware of our situation as humiliating, or shameful, or outrageous, or dismaying, or exhilarating, or wonderful; and so on.

Each of these adjectives defines what I would like to call an import, if I can introduce this as a term of art. By 'import' I mean a way in which something can be relevant or of importance to the desires or purposes or aspirations or feelings of a subject; or otherwise put, a property of something whereby it is a matter of non-indifference to a subject.

But the 'whereby' in the previous clause is meant in a strong sense. In identifying the import of a given situation we are picking out what in the situation gives the grounds or basis of our feelings, or what could give such grounds, or perhaps should give such grounds, if we feel nothing or have inappropriate feelings. We are not just stating in other terms that we experience a certain feeling in this situation.

That is, it could not be a sufficient condition of our ascribing what I am calling an import to a given situation that we experience a certain feeling or desire in it or relative to it. Some predicates do have this logic. Louis XV was 'le bien aimé' just because he was in fact loved by many of his subjects. A situation is painful, just because we feel pain in it. A certain place at the table is much coveted just because many people desire it. But we are saying something different when we say that someone is lovable, or that a position is enviable. Whether these properties are correctly ascribed does not turn on whether many love the person or envy the position, although their being popular or much sought after can be good evidence for the ascription.

But imports have a different logic. And my first claim, therefore, can be put this way: that experiencing a given emotion involves experiencing our situation as bearing a certain import, where for the ascription of the import it is not sufficient just that I feel this way, but rather the import gives the grounds or basis for the feeling. And that is why saying what an emotion is like involves making explicit the sense of the situation it incorporates, or, in our present terms, the import of the situation as we experience it.

Thus it is essential to an emotion like fear or shame that we experience it as a response to the situation's bearing the relevant import – its being menacing or shameful. These emotions are defined by the imports they relate to: fear is the affective response to the menacing, anger to the provoking, indignation to the flagrantly wrongful, and so on. We might say: fear is the affect which belongs to our experience of our situation as menacing; and so on for the other emotions.

That is why we can experience emotions like shame and fear mistakenly or unwarrantedly, whereas we cannot in the same sense love mistakenly – although we can love unwisely, which is quite a different matter – nor, for instance, feel pain mistakenly. And, for the same reason, it is possible to feel shame or fear irrationally, where for instance, we are intellectually convinced that the situation is not menacing or shameful, but we cannot help feeling afraid or ashamed. There would be no room for the notion of irrationality, if we were not in some sense affirming the import in feeling the emotion that we are intellectually agreeing to deny. There can be no irrational pain.

But in what sense affirming it?

It cannot simply be that experiencing the emotion is ascribing the import. Because a prominent feature of those situations we consider as paradigmatic of irrational emotion is where the person sees and admits that the import does not apply, but goes on feeling that way anyway. I feel ashamed, even though I see perfectly that it's absurd, that there is nothing shameful in having succumbed to a bout of anger in such trying circumstances. So having the feeling plainly is not equivalent to ascribing the import, particularly if we think of this as equvalent to making the judgement that the situation bears the import. For in the case I am imagining, I am precisely withholding the intellectual assent which is essential to my being said to have judged that p. It is just that I cannot help going on feeling ashamed.

So the relation is not one of simple equivalence, where feeling the emotion is ascribing the import. But nor can it be true that there is no relation at all, as with physical pain. Rather it is that experiencing the emotion is experiencing our situation as bearing a certain import, where this is compatible in some cases with recognizing that the situation does not bear this import, and withholding intellectual assent from the judgement that it does.

Saying what an emotion is like therefore involves making explicit the import-ascription, a judgement which is not thereby affirmed, it is true, but experienced as holding the sense of the situation which it incorporates.

This first claim does not sit well with the modern conception of objectivity. That is, emotions understood as having this logical structure do not fit easily into an account of men and human behaviour as objects among objects. Such an account should be able to explain what men do in terms of objective factors in the meaning of this term sketched above, that is, in terms of factors which are not experience-dependent. Properties are experience-dependent when they hold of things only in human experience (or the experience of other sentient beings), like the secondary properties of the classical distinction.

Thus we should be able to explain human motivation in terms, say, of certain underlying physiological states, which are certainly identifiable in terms independent of experience. In addition to this a role is certainly played by the environment, but this can surely be coped with if we can characterize this 'input' to the system itself in experience-independent terms: either as 'receptor impulses', or in terms of physical features of our field.

Of course, the ideally simple theory of this objective kind would be a behaviourist one, where we would correlate physical features of the environment with movements of the organism; and this helps account for the strange continuing obsession with this wildly implausible approach to the science of man. But once this breaks down, and one has to admit some inner motivational states, the least disturbing are those, like physical pain, which involve no import-ascription at all. Someone moves his finger on the blackboard, and I wince and shudder. This is a bit of experienced motivation which involves no judgement or import-ascription at all. It is sufficient that I take in the squeak for me to react. The same can be said for the leap and curse that escape me in the dentist's chair when he touches a nerve suddenly.

But what I have called imports are quite essentially experience-dependent properties, or appear to be. For they characterize things in their relevance to our desires and purposes, or in their role in our emotional life. If we now claim that reference to an import is essential to making clear what is involved in certain emotions, and if in turn we have recourse to these emotions in order to explain the behaviour they motivate, then the ideal of an objective account will have been breached.

That is why those who aim for an objective account would rather propose reductive explanations of our emotions. One can do this, presumably, through an account of human behaviour at a neurophysiological level, by-passing the psychological level altogether. But we are very far from even the beginnings of such a theory of neurophysiological function, let alone any idea of how to characterize the 'input' of, say, humiliating or threatening situations in physiological terms.

The hope for a reductive account must surely lie in another direction. And one can see another possibility: that one can give an objective account of the imports involved. To take a plausible example, when we are physically afraid we experience our situation as importing menace to life and limb. A tiger is prowling in the garden, or a hostile mob seems about to attack. Now presumably we could give an account of what this import involves in objective terms. We fear, you might say, injury which will cause severe pain, or malfunction of our limbs or organs, or death. For all of these states, we can set out the conditions in a medical language which invokes only experience-independent properties. However difficult it may be to define bone fracture, and especially the distinction life/death, in medical terms, the difficulties surely do not arise from our having to use experience-dependent terms. The heart's ceasing, or the decay of certain brain cells, can be characterized in a language which does not depend for its meaning on our experiencing things the way we do. We could presumably communicate about these distinctions with Alpha Centaurans, even though they might have some trouble understanding how it was that our function as sapient beings depended on the condition of these brain cells.

Now the import of a menacing situation could be defined in terms of these medically defined states: it would be a situation which in virtue of well-understood causal mechanisms had a certain probability of bringing about one of these states; hungry tigers are likely to sink their teeth in nearby flesh, angry human beings in the mass are likely to beat whoever provokes them unrelentingly. Our model of human beings as capable of experiencing fear would then see them as beings capable of recognizing situations with these causal properties, that is correlated with a high degree of probability with the negative medically defined states. And there seems to be no obstacle in principle to our giving an objective account of a system capable of such recognition. We could imagine building a machine, with receptors attached to a computer and memory-bank, which could presumably recognize a tiger, search in the bank for facts about tigers, and recognize danger accordingly.[1]

On recognizing danger, the machine could print out instructions to some locomotion mechanism to take evasive action. We would then have, it seems, a complete structural analogue of fear, including the import-recognition of danger and the flight. What would be missing would be the actual feeling of fear, and indeed the sense of self-awareness itself. But this, as we have seen, has to be treated as epiphenomenon in an objective account. Whether it is ultimately coherent to treat it so, I very much doubt. But I do not want to pursue that now. The whole enterprise has another flaw.

The crucial flaw with this as a general formula for a reductive account of emotions is that it breaks down for the key cases in its first step: the objective explication of the import. And this is the substance of my second claim.

The explication seemed to work well enough for the physically

---

[1] Actually this is much more problematic than it sounds, as work on the limitation of computers – especially H. L. Dreyfus, *What Computers Can't Do* (New York, 1979) – has shown; but I want to set this aside for the sake of the discussion here.

menacing. But let us look at the shameful. Shame is an emotion that a subject experiences in relation to a dimension of his existence as a subject. What we can be ashamed of are properties which are essentially properties of a subject. This may not be immediately evident, because I may be ashamed of my shrill voice, or my effeminate hands. But of course it only makes sense to see these as objects of shame if they have for me or my culture an expressive dimension: a shrill voice is (to me, to my culture) something unmanly, betokens hysteria, not something solid, strong, macho, self-contained. It does not radiate a sense of strength, capacity, superiority. Effeminate hands are – effeminate. Both voice and hands clash with what I aspire to be, feel that my dignity demands that I be, as a person, a presence among others.

These properties are thus only demeaning for a subject for whom things can have this kind of meaning. But things can have this kind of meaning only for a subject in whose form of life there figures an aspiration to dignity, to be a presence among men which commands respect.

In a world in which there were no beings of this kind the concept 'shameful' could not be given a sense. But a subject with this kind of aspiration must be a subject of awareness, of experience. This is not to say that I am always aware of what is shameful in my life. I may be lamentably insensitive to it. The point is rather that a subject with this aspiration must be capable of experiencing the whole range of imports connected with shame, dignity, respect, however insensitive he may be in certain cases. A world without beings capable of this kind of experience would be one without any aspiration to dignity. In this kind of world – say, to take an extreme case, a world without sentient beings – the concept 'shameful' could get no grip whatever.

Thus the import shameful can be explicated only by reference to a subject who experiences his world in a certain way. And in this the shameful is quite unlike the physically menacing which we discussed earlier.

What is emerging here is not the banal truism that nothing has the import shameful except for a subject for whom there are imports. This is a tautology, valid for any import, including the physically menacing. Rather the point is that the term 'shameful' has no sense outside of a world in which there is a subject for whom things have certain (emotional) meanings. For the (linguistic) meaning of 'shameful' can only be explicated with reference to a subject for whom these (emotional) meanings have weight, and if there were no such subjects, the term itself would lack sense.

We could put the point in this way: the import term 'shameful' only has sense in a world in which there are subjects who experience it as an import. For we can explicate the term only with reference to such subjects and their experience. By contrast the physically menacing can be given a sense quite independent of any subject's experience of it. It can be given a meaning even for animate beings who have no sense of it, and could be given a meaning even if all animate beings lacked such a sense. We can give its meaning, we argued above, in purely medical terms. That is why the Alpha Centaurans could understand what we meant by menacing, but they will never be able to grasp this human business of shame and humiliation.

To go into this further, an import defines a way in which our situation is of relevance to our purposes or desires, or aspirations. Consequently, no sense can be given to an import term except in a world in which there are beings which are taken to have purposes. (These may be external purposes, like the purposes our instruments have in our lives; so that there can be imports for my car: sand in the petrol is a menace; or they may be 'internal' purposes, those of animate organisms.) But it may still be that some of these imports can be explicated independently of the experience, if any, of animate beings. This seemed to be the case with our medically defined states of danger to life and limb.

An objectifying science would even aspire to define the crucial properties – for example, the heart's beating/stopping – independently of their status as imports (as Alpha Centaurans would understand it: they would be able to see that the heart stopped, but they would not quite understand why it mattered).

But with the shameful, this pattern of explication breaks down. For the shameful is not a property which can hold of something quite independent of the experience subjects have of it. Rather, the very account of what shame means involves reference to things – like our sense of dignity, of worth, of how we are seen by others – which are essentially bound up with the life of a subject of experience.

I should like to call properties of which this is true, like shameful, 'subject-referring' properties. These are properties which can only exist in a world in which there are subjects of experience, because they concern in some way the life of the subject *qua* subject.

Subject-referring properties are experience-dependent, since these properties are what they are only in relation to the experience of subjects. The relation may not be a simple one, as is that of secondary qualities, viz., that they are only what they are in the ordinary experience of human subjects. It may be something that is presupposed by this experience, or gives it its shape; like an aspiration to dignity or, even less immediately, one to integrity, or wholeness, or fulfilment, about which we can only speculate or offer controvertible interpretations. But in either case we are dealing with factors which can only be explicated with reference to human experience, and hence for all of these a reductive account along the lines of the physically menacing above is impossible.

That is why, as has frequently been noticed for emotion terms like shame, an explication cannot be found which does not invoke other meanings for the subject. Why is this situation shameful? Because something shows me up to be base, or to have some unavowable and degrading property, or to be dishonourable. In this account, however long we carry it on, other words appear, like 'base', 'dishonourable', 'degrading', or a host of moral terms: 'cheat', 'liar', 'coward', 'fraud', which involve other meanings that things have for us. We cannot escape from these terms into an objective account, because in fact shame is about an aspect of the life of the subject *qua* subject.

Subject-referring properties do not fit into an objectivist's view of the world. This allows for an account of things in terms of objective properties, and then also perhaps for a subjective reaction to or view of things on the part of the subject. Emotions like shame do not fit into either slot. They cannot take a place, unamended, in the objective account of things, because they can only be explicated in experience-dependent terms. But nor can they just be classed as a subjective view on things. To feel shame is related to an import-ascription, in the way described above. But to ascribe an import is to make a judgement about the way things are, which cannot simply be reduced to the way we feel about them, as we saw earlier. Beyond the question whether I feel ashamed is the question whether the situation is really shameful, whether I am rightly or wrongly, rationally or irrationally, ashamed.

It is this quality of the shameful, like the other crucial imports of our emotional life, which will not fit into the objectivist's grid. According to the logic of the concept, there is a truth of the matter, what is shameful, irreducible to me or you feeling this or that way about it. But the truth of this matter has no place in the objectivist's ontology.

This is the kind of matter, to return to our fable, that one could not explain to the Alpha Centaurans. But we could not blame them for not understanding the fuss we humans make about shame, dignity, and the like. For all this relates to our lives *qua* subjects, and the kind of subjects that we are. We can only explicate these things in terms which again only make sense to us. With Alpha Centaurans, we shall have a radical communication gap. But this is hardly surprising; on these matters, we have quite a communication gap among ourselves, when we come from different cultures, and sometimes even when we are from the same culture. For our human experience differs, and this helps shape the language that will be meaningful to us in this area.

2

There are two further points, before going on. The first is that it is this irreducibility of our emotion terms which is essentially linked to their playing the role they do in our language. For one of the things they do is to enable us to characterize our feelings in a richer way. One way we can characterize our feelings is in terms of the things we want to do or have or experience, the consummations desired: I want to eat, to sleep, to be at home again. These provide alternative ways of saying that I am hungry, sleepy, home-sick (but the equivalence fails in the last case).

But we can sometimes go deeper into our feelings, make more articulate what is involved in our desires, if we can express the imports which underlie them and give them their point. When I am ashamed, I want to hide, or conceal, or perhaps undo what is shameful. But the vocabulary of shame and the shameful allows us to articulate to a considerable degree what it is which makes me want to hide. I could try to say what I feel purely in terms of a consummation desired, by saying something like: 'I want my pride back', or 'I want my self-respect back'. But these terms would not be understood, either, without a grasp of the import which is articulated in the whole vocabulary of shame, the shameful, dignity, pride, respect.

A language which enables us to talk of imports as well allows a much fuller and richer articulation of feelings than one which only deals with consummations desired. Our understanding of the consummations we desire is deepened by our grasp of the imports things have for us, and vice versa, and a language in which we can speak of both enables us to be more articulate.

Now our emotion vocabulary describes our experience of the import things have for us, and of the consummations we correspondingly desire. Where we are dealing with an import which is objectively specifiable, we can say what is involved in language which makes no reference to experience, as we saw above, that is in language other than that of feeling and emotion. But where the meaning of the import is bound up with the nature of our experience, we can only articulate import and consummation in emotion language. Thus, to return to our fable again, we could explain the imports and goals involved in our fear for our physical safety to Alpha Centaurans, but not our outrage at our wounded dignity. Our emotion language is indispensable precisely because it is irreducible. It becomes an essential condition of articulacy; and import and goal, the language of feelings and consummations desired, form a skein of mutual referrals, from which there is no escape into objectified nature.

3

The second point concerns the use of the term 'subject-referring'. The choice of this term, as well as the examples above – shame and wounded dignity – may mislead. But subject-referring does not necessarily mean self-referring. The shameful or humiliating is subject-referring, because something is only humiliating for me by virtue of the way I understand myself – or better (as I hope to expound below), because of the way I see myself and aspire to appear in public space. Something only offends my dignity because it upsets or challenges the way I present, project or express myself in this public space. So one might gather from these examples that subject-referring imports only arise in connection with emotions which are self-concerned, not to say self-absorbed; that only our narcissistic side is engaged in this analysis.

But what about the experience of coming across someone in trouble and feeling called on to help, the experience the good Samaritan had (and presumably also the priest and the Levite, but they somehow rationalized it away)? Here the import surely does not concern the self. We see the man lying bleeding in the road, and feel that we cannot pass by on the other side, but must bind his wounds. The import concerns the needs of this wounded man, not ourselves. Indeed, we may feel that there is something morally inferior, and tainted, about a motivation here which is self-regarding.

We are always painfully reminded that self-regarding motivations are all too possible even in this kind of situation. We go to help because we will look bad otherwise. What will others say? Or perhaps, more subtly, because we have a certain self-image we must keep up. But we are usually aware that such 'narcissistic' motivations reflect badly on us, and that the truly good man is focussed on the needs of the wounded person.

What of his motivation? This too is subject-referring in the above sense, even though not self-regarding. It is subject-referring, because the full recognition of this import involves reference to a subject. Of course, in this example, there is also irrelevantly reference to a subject because the being in need of help is a human being. But this is not the point I am making; and we could alter the example to exclude it: I might feel an obligation to succour animals, or to leave the world-order as it ought to be.

The crucial reference to the subject is, however, to the addressee of this felt obligation. For I do not just feel desire to help this man. Indeed, I might feel no such desire in the usual sense of the term. But I feel called upon to help him. And I feel called upon *qua* rational being, or moral being, or creature made by God in his image, in other words capable of responding to this like God, that is, out of agape. The obligation does not lie on an animal nor, in another way, on an idiot, nor on an infant.

In other words, implicit in this import is a reference to the subject; because the import this situation bears is that it lays an obligation of strong kind on me – what we call a moral obligation or an obligation of charity. And a full understanding of what this means involves reference to the kind of being on whom this obligation is laid. The situation bears this import for me, in virtue of the kind of being I am; and this is a logical truth, internal to the meaning of the import.

For the import is not just that the situation provokes some impulse to go help. This would indeed happen, if it did, in virtue of the kind of being I am – a truism of the flattest. But that I am a being of the appropriate kind would not be part of the meaning of the import. But in this case, the import is that we are *called upon* to act. And we are called upon in virtue of being a certain kind of creature. Even though we may not be very sure in virtue of what we are called on, we know that the obligation lies on us, not on animals, stones, or idiots. The kind of being we are enters into the definition of this import.

It is true, of course, that the needs of the wounded man could be accounted for in objective terms. The import of the situation for him is perhaps objectively accountable. He needs to have his wounds bound. To explain this we need consider him only as a living being, not as a human subject (but this would not allow very satisfactory treatment, as we know, alas, from the many doctors who relate in this way to their patients). But to explain the import for us, we have to bring in the notion of an obligation; and this involves reference to the subject as proper addressee.

Hence the class of subject-referring imports is much wider than that of self-referring or self-regarding imports. To speak of subject-referring imports is not to see all motivation as narcissistic. On the contrary, these imports can have a very different structure, very different foci of attribution, as it were.

4

I can sum up the first two claims in the jargon I have developed in these pages:

1. that some of our emotions or experienced motivations involve import-ascriptions, and
2. that some of these imports are subject-referring.

Jointly, these two claims run very much against the bent of the objectivist ideal in that they show our important motivations to be irreducible to an objective account. This helps to account for the great resistance which the view incorporating these two claims encounters. But it seems to me clear nevertheless that these claims are valid. For these claims alone seem to make sense of our emotions as we live them, or, otherwise put, to be compatible with the logic of our language of the emotions.

III

1

Our subject-referring emotions are especially worth examining. For since they refer us to the life of the subject *qua* subject, they offer an insight into what this life amounts to.

In speaking of subject-referring emotions, I include all those which involve ascribing imports which are subject-referring, our sense of shame, of dignity, of guilt, or pride, our feelings of admiration and contempt, or moral obligation, of remorse, of unworthiness and self-hatred, and (less frequently) of self-acceptance, certain of our joys and anxieties. But we might also include some feelings which are not import-ascribing, at least which we do not understand to be such, but where we have some reason to believe that any adequate explanation of why we experience them would involve subject-referring imports. It may seem that our finding a given landscape, or someone's style, attractive, or our being sexually attracted to some people and not to others, are all examples of what we might call immediate reactions, and involve no import-ascription. We might be tempted therefore to class them with our fingernail-on-blackboard example, or the stab of pain in the tooth. But when we examine them more closely, it appears more than plausible that these feelings are related to, or shaped by, a host of subject-referring imports, of which we are only partially aware. Indeed, part of what is involved in growing insight is coming to see more clearly what these are. With time and greater self-understanding we can sometimes come to see what it is that draws us to certain places and people. A great number of our seemingly immediate desires and feelings are nevertheless partially constituted by a skein of subject-referring imports, which resonate through our psychic life.

Now all of these offer potential insight into our lives as subjects. They incorporate a sense of what is important to us *qua* subjects, or to put it slightly differently, of what we value, or what matters to us, in the life of the subject. We also value other things, for instance going on living, which pertain to us *qua* living organisms. But our feelings of shame, remorse, pride, dignity, moral obligations, aspirations to excel, just because the imports they involve are essentially those of a subject, all incorporate a sense of what is important for us in our lives as subjects.

If we think of this reflexive sense of what matters to us as subjects as being distinctively human – and it is clearly central to our notion of ourselves that we are such reflexive beings; this is what underlies the traditional definition of man as a rational animal – we could say that our subject-referring feelings incorporate a sense of what it is to be human, that is, of what matters to us as human subjects.

Now I want to claim – and this is my third claim – that this sense is crucial to our understanding of what it is to be human. This might not be immediately evident, because we also see ourselves as being aware of what is important to us as humans in other ways. Our society and tradition present us with moral rules, standards of excellence, pictures of good and bad life-forms, which go beyond, may even run against, what we sense in our feelings of shame, remorse, pride, aspiration, etc. We should distinguish what we feel as important or valuable, we often are led to say, from what we know rationally to be so.

But putting the distinction this way is misleading. If I want to say that I know certain things to be truly important: that one should be generous even to blackguards; or that the only thing one should really be ashamed of is being untrue to oneself; or that acting out of spite is always bad – even though my gorge rises at the thought of helping that cad, I feel ashamed at not making the football team, and I cannot resist lashing out at my successful rival – I am not just opposing feeling to reason. For I would not 'know' that one should be generous, and so on, unless I was moved in some way: perhaps I feel remorse when I have delivered myself of a spiteful attack; or feel self-contempt at my lack of autonomy when I allow myself to feel shame at not making the football team; or feel morally inspired by the ideal of universal generosity. If I were quite impervious to any such feelings, these norms and ideals would carry no weight with me; I would not even be tempted to subscribe to them, and I would not describe myself as 'knowing' that they were true/valid.

It is of course true that these insights can be 'recollected in tranquillity'. I may have a clear sense now that one should not be ashamed of any such unimportant thing, even though the insight is not now accompanied by any feeling; rather my only feeling at present is that ridiculous shame over not making the team. But I would not have this sense of the proper object of shame if I *never* felt any self-reproach, or self-contempt, or self-dissatisfaction, as a result of my continued unwarranted sense of humiliation. I have this sense of the proper object of shame through these feelings.

We often say 'I know that X, but I feel that Y', or 'I know that X, but I don't feel it'. But it would be wrong to conclude that knowing can be simply opposed to feeling. What I know is also grounded in certain feelings. It is just that I understand these feelings to incorporate a deeper, more adequate sense of our moral predicament. If feeling is an affective awareness of situation, I see these feelings as reflecting my moral situation as it truly is; the imports they attribute truly apply.

But are there not cases where our knowing is quite abstracted from feeling? Take this case, for instance. Someone is an instinctive racist, that is, he only feels a sense of moral solidarity with members of his own race; it is only towards them that he feels bound to act with respect, concerning them that he feels repugnance at killing or harming; in short, towards others he is like a contemporary carnivorous liberal towards animals. But then we reason with him, and argue that race should not make any difference; that what is to be valued and respected in people is nothing to do with race; and he is thus led to assent to the proposition that the respect for life and well-being ought to be extended to everyone. But we can easily imagine him saying that he knows this to be so, but does not feel it.

This does seem like a case of reasoning against feeling. But consider. What we built on was his sense of obligation to respect others, in his case, his compatriots. This sense is grounded in his feelings, for example, of repugnance at harming them. We then induced him to make explicit the sense of his compatriots that these feelings incorporate: what is it about them that gives them this claim to respect? We may not bring him so far as to accept some philosophical formulation, for instance that they are rational animals; but we bring him far enough to recognize that whatever it is race has nothing to do with it. He is thus forced to consent to our universalism.

Reasoning there certainly is here; but it is reasoning out of insight embedded in feeling, and in the absence of such feeling we could never have led our racist to the conclusion that he *ought* to respect all men. This is because our argument had to start from an awareness of import on his part. But there cannot be an awareness of subject-referring imports which is not grounded in feelings. This really flows from the point made in the previous section, that our subject-referring feelings attribute imports which cannot be reductively explained, but which involve reference to a subject who is aware of them. They are essentially imports for a subject. But this must mean a subject who has intuitive experience of them. For the awareness could not be exclusively that which comes from grasping an explanation of the imports; for in this case, *ex hypothesi* the subject-referring emotions would not exist at all prior to their being explained. But then they would never come to exist, since prior to the explanation there would be nothing to explain.

Now our direct, intuitive experience of import is through feeling. And thus feeling is our mode of access to this entire domain of subject-referring imports, of what matters to us *qua* subjects, or of what it is to be human. We may come to feel the force of some imports through having explained to us their relations to others, but these we must experience directly, through feeling. The chain of explanations must be anchored somewhere in our intuitive grasp of what is at stake.

It is only through our feelings that we are capable of grasping imports of this range at all. The fact that we are sometimes dispassionately aware of an import should not induce us to think that we could always be so aware. That supposition is absurd. This is a domain to which there is no dispassionate access.

But if feeling is our mode of access, the feelings are import-attributing. They incorporate a certain understanding of our predicament, and of the imports it bears. Thus we can feel entitled to say on the strength of certain feelings, or inferences from what we sense through certain feelings, that we know that X is right, or good, or worthy, or valuable; and this even when other feelings and reactions fail to concur, or even have an opposing purport! 'I know that X, but I feel that Y' does not oppose knowing to feeling, but rather reflects our conviction that what we sense through certain feelings is valid or adequate, while it devalues others as shallow, blind, distorting or perverse.

2

Our subject-referring feelings therefore open us on to the domain of what it is to be human; for we can have no dispassionate awareness of the human good; and the quality of our awareness of the good is a function of the alignment of our feelings. But if being divided we can know that certain feelings, for instance this remorse or that élan of aspiration, incorporate a deeper insight than others, for instance that sense of repulsion or this feeling of spite, it is because these feelings are articulated. That is, the sense of imports that they incorporate has been articulated into a picture of our moral predicament, according to which some goods are higher than others, while still others are false or illusory.

And this is where it begins to make sense to speak of man as a self-interpreting animal. For these articulations are in a sense interpretations. But it is not as though we started off with a raw material of repulsions and attractions, élans and uneases, which were then interpreted as higher and lower, élans towards some deep good, or uneases before some discreditable trait. On the contrary, human life is never without interpreted feeling; the interpretation is constitutive of the feeling.

That is, the feeling is what it is in virtue of the sense of the situation it incorporates. But a given sense may presuppose a certain level of articulacy, that the subject understand certain terms or distinctions. For example, a feeling cannot be one of remorse unless there is a sense of my having done wrong. Some understanding of right/wrong is built into remorse, is essential to its attributing the import that it does.

Thus certain feelings involve a certain level of articulation, in that the sense of things they incorporate requires the application of certain terms. But at the same time, they can admit of further articulation, in that the sense of things can yet be further clarified and made articulate. Thus while a feeling of remorse implies our sense that our act was wrong, and while it may be hard to imagine our having a feeling less articulate than this, which would only subsequently be clarified as one of remorse by our realizing that we see this act as wrong (though there are circumstances in which something like this could happen), it is quite a common experience for us to feel remorse without being able fully to articulate what is wrong about what we have done. In these cases we may seek to understand further. And if we succeed, our feelings may alter. The remorse may dissipate altogether, if we come to see that our sense of wrong-doing is unfounded; or it may alter in other ways, as we come to understand what is wrong; perhaps it will be more acute as we see how grave the offence was; perhaps it will be less as we see how hard it was to avoid.

Hence we can see that our feelings incorporate a certain articulation of our situation, that is, they presuppose that we characterize our situation in certain terms. But at the same time they admit of – and very often we feel that they call for – further articulation, the elaboration of finer terms permitting more penetrating characterization. And this further articulation can in turn transform the feelings.

On closer examination, we can see that these two sides, that feelings incorporate an articulation, and that they call for further articulation, are related. Our subject-referring feelings have to incorporate a certain degree of articulation in order to open us to the imports involved. For instance, as we saw above, remorse presupposes that we can apply the terms 'right' and 'wrong'; shame requires that we have terms like 'worthy' and 'unworthy' in our lexicon. These feelings are essentially articulated; that is, they cannot be without a certain degree of articulation.

But these feelings attribute imports, indeed they open us to the domain of what it is to be human. And because they are articulated they purport to give a characterization of these imports, and hence to offer insight into this domain. One might say, they ascribe a form to what matters to us. For example, in feeling remorse for some act of self-affirmation, I experience this act as a violation, or a betrayal, or as evil.

But in offering a characterization, these feelings open the question whether this characterization is adequate, whether it is not incomplete or distortive. And so from the very fact of their being articulated, the question cannot but arise whether we have properly articulated our feelings, that is, whether we have properly explicated what the feeling gives us a sense of.

In an important sense, this question once opened can never be closed. For unlike the non-subject-referring imports like physical danger, which can ultimately be grounded on external criteria, the articulations of these emotions have to be self-validating. The adequate insight would just show itself to be so by its intrinsic clarity and the access to reality it opens. There could be no appeal to some unchallengeable external mark.

That our feelings are thus bound up with a process of articulation is my fourth claim. And it is this feature on top of the other three which justifies our talking of self-interpretation. For the joint result of the first three claims is that our subject-referring emotions open us to the domain of what it is to be human. And now we see them as giving articulation to this domain.

But we can speak of these attempted articulations as interpretations; for although they are constitutive of our feelings, these cannot just be shaped at will by the account we offer of them. On the contrary, an articulation purports to characterize a feeling; it is meant to be faithful to what it is that moves us. There is a getting it right and getting it wrong in this domain. Articulations are like interpretations in that they are attempts to make clearer the imports things have for us.

But then we must speak of man as a self-interpreting being, because this kind of interpretation is not an optional extra, but is an essential part of our existence. For our feelings always incorporate certain articulations; while just because they do so they open us on to a domain of imports which call for further articulation. The attempt to articulate further is potentially a life-time process. At each stage, what we feel is a function of what we have already articulated and evokes the puzzlement and perplexities which further understanding may unravel. But whether we want to take the challenge or not, whether we seek the truth or take refuge in illusion, our self-(mis)understandings shape what we feel. This is the sense in which man is a self-interpreting animal.

Reference to 'articulation' poses the question of the role of language in our emotions, something which has been implicitly evoked in the above discussion. More should be said about this.

IV

But before saying more, I should like to examine something else which was implicit in the above discussion. Our subject-referring emotions open us to a sense of what it is to be human, and this sense, as we saw, involves our interpreting some of our feelings as offering valid insight into what really matters and others as shallow, or even blind and distorted. Our emotions make it possible for us to have a sense of what the good life is for a subject; and this sense involves in turn our making qualitative discriminations between our desires and goals, whereby we see some as higher and others as lower, some as good and others as discreditable, still others as evil, some as truly vital and others as trivial, and so on. This kind of discrimination is an essential part of the articulations of our emotions.

I should like briefly to examine this discrimination by means of the notion of strong evaluation. I want to speak of strong evaluation where we 'evaluate', that is, consider good/bad, desirable/despicable, our desires themselves. Of course, what we frequently articulate as good or bad are actions, or even ways of life. We condemn running away from the danger, or gross self-indulgence, or spiteful speech or action without utilitarian purpose; or else we condemn a slothful life-form. But to speak of strong evaluation as an evaluation of desires, or motivations, brings out something important here.

It is not just that these actions/ways of life incorporate as part of their definition certain motivations: the running away concerned is out of fear, the self-indulgence is only that if one is indulging in things desired for pleasure, spiteful action specifies its own motivation, and so on. It is also that the condemnation here is in spite of, or even sometimes because of, the motivation.

The essence of strong evaluation comes out when we consider what it is to condemn an act in spite of our motivation to it. For the fact that we desired to do it is at least an embryonic justification, a prima facie ground for calling it good, following the precedent of the ancients. To condemn the act is to over-ride the embryonic justification in the name of another good which is thus judged higher or more worthy. It is to introduce a class difference between motivations, here between that turned to the good sought in the condemned act and that turned to the more worthy end.

The man who flees seeks a good, safety. But we condemn him: he ought to have stood. For there is a higher good, the safety of the polis, which was here at stake. The judgement involves ranking goods, hence ranking motivations (since these are defined by their consummations, which is what we are calling 'goods' in this context).

It is because this involves ranking motivations that I speak of it as strong evaluation. It means that we are not taking our *de facto* desires as the ultimate in justification, but are going beyond that to their worth. We are evaluating not just objects in the light of our desires, but also the desires themselves. Hence strong evaluation has also been called 'second-order' evaluation.[2]

The dimension of strong evaluation is even more evident where we condemn the action not in spite of but because of the motivation. The spite case above is a good example. Acting out of that motivation is base, mean, unworthy. Indeed, a man is the better for not experiencing such a motivation at all, though being human we often find it hard not to, however successfully we may keep it from influencing our conduct. Here we have not just a comparative ranking of motivations, but the judging of one as intrinsically bad. Hence we have once more an evaluation of desires themselves, so strong evaluation, or 'second-order' evaluation.

In the cases of both comparison and intrinsic judgement we have a qualitative assessment of motivations, where some are judged higher or lower, others as intrinsically bad. Because it weighs motivations, hence

[2] Cf. Harry Frankfurt, 'Freedom of the will and the concept of a person', *Journal of Philosophy*, 67:1 (Jan. 1971), pp. 5–20.

ends, this kind of assessment bites deeper than one which might, for instance, condemn certain actions in the name of the desires they are meant to fulfil, as being inefficacious, or confused, or ill-directed, for instance.

I have spoken of these strong evaluations as assessments, but they are anchored in feelings, emotions, aspirations; and could not motivate us unless they were. Such are our moral and aesthetic intuitions about given acts and possibilities, our remorse or sense of worthiness, our longings to be good, noble, pure, or whatever. In giving the strongly evaluative assessment, we are giving the import to which the feeling relates. Our moral revulsion before an act of spite is our affective awareness of the act as having an import of moral baseness.

And this is where we connect with the topic of subject-referring feelings. Strong evaluations involve subject-referring imports because they involve discriminating our motivations as higher or lower, or intrinsically good or bad. They are thus, one might say, inherently reflexive, and explicating the imports concerned involves referring to the life of the subject. It involves, one might say, attributing to different motivations their place in the life of the subject. When I hold back a certain reaction, because it springs from spite, and I see this as base, petty, or bad; or when I feel remorse for not having held it back, or perhaps contempt or disapproval for you when you have acted spitefully; what is involved is a strong evaluation. And the tenor of this evaluation is perhaps something like this: that spite, revenge, returning evil for evil, is something we are prone to, but that there is a higher way of seeing our relations with others; which is higher not just in producing happier consequences – less strife, pain, bad blood – but also in that it enables us to see ourselves and others more broadly, more objectively, more truly. One is a bigger person, with a broader, more serene vision, when one can act out of this higher standpoint.

Implicit in this strong evaluation is thus a placing of our different motivations relative to each other, the drawing, as it were, of a moral map of ourselves; we contrast a higher, more clairvoyant, more serene motivation, with a baser, more self-enclosed and troubled one, which we can see ourselves as potentially growing beyond, if and when we can come to experience things from the higher standpoint. The drawing of a moral map puts us squarely in the domain of the subject-referring, since this touches quintessentially on the life of the subject *qua* subject. It is in fact an attempt to give shape to our experience.

This drawing a moral map of the subject is an intrinsic part of what I referred to earlier as discerning the good or higher life, or the shape of our aspirations, or the shape of our life as subject. It involves defining what it is we really are about, what is really important to us; it involves entering the problematic area of our self-understanding and self-interpretation. We can see from the above example how the strong evaluations which are woven into our emotional experience place us in this problematic domain, for they refer us to a map of our motivations which we have yet to draw clearly, and will never complete.

The only reminder we need in connection with the example above about spite is that strong evaluation involves all qualitative discriminations between motives or ends, not just those we call moral. We (almost) all have an important set of strong evaluations concerning what we could call personal style. Some people feel that it is more worthy, or dignified, or admirable, to be 'cool' in their style, for instance. But most of them would repudiate any suggestion that they were making a moral issue out of this. We also think that some people are more sensitive in their tastes and others more gross, and we unquestionably admire the first and are perhaps mildly contemptuous of the second; but our praise and blame are not moral. And so on. All this enters into the (unfinished) map of goals and motivations which defines what we have been calling the good life.

These strong evaluations involve, as we have seen, subject-referring imports, and reciprocally our subject-referring feelings are or involve strong evaluations. And this is why they refer us to the central issues about our lives as subjects.

V

I

Now we may return to the question posed above: what is the role of language in our subject-referring emotions? Following what was said in section III about articulations, it would seem to be absolutely central. For these articulations surely require language. Language would thus be essential to these emotions, indeed constitutive of them. This fits in with a common intuition, or prejudice. But some challenge this as species chauvinism. We think that we, the language animals, are the only ones to have feelings of shame, wounded dignity, even right and wrong. But we just assume this, it is said, because we neglect to examine other species.

But look at baboons. The top ones swagger around with a sense of – dignity? And they react with anger when this is challenged. All-too-human behaviour. Is there not at least a proto-sense of dignity?

One answer to this kind of challenge has been to question how one really can know whether the big baboon is experiencing indignation at his offended dignity or just anger, or indeed anything that we could give a sense to. For it is our being in the same community of discourse, potentially or actually, with people which allows us to make these judgements in their case, often with certainty.

But suppose we hold this point in suspense for a moment, and concede for the sake of argument that baboons have a sense of dignity. Nevertheless this must be *toto caelo* different from ours, because our sense of dignity, and shame, and moral remorse, and so on, are all shaped by language.

To see this we have to examine more closely what we barely invoked in section III.2, the way in which our feelings are shaped by articulations. Let us look at common experiences, and see how our experience of these emotions has been changed by our coming to accept different terms, or a new vocabulary, in which to talk about them. Thus consider someone who has been ashamed of his background. This is what we say (and also he says) retrospectively; at the time, this was not at all clear to him. He feels unease, lack of confidence, a vague sense of unworthiness. Then he is brought to reflect on this. He comes to feel that being ashamed for what you are, apologizing for your existence, is senseless. That on the contrary, there is something demeaning precisely about feeling such shame, something degrading, merely supine, craven. So he goes through a revolution like that expressed in the phrase 'black is beautiful'.

Now the shame disappears; or sinks to a merely residual unease like the craving for a cigarette after meals of the ex-smoker; and is judged as merely another such nagging emotional kink, not as a voice telling him something about his predicament. What he can now feel ashamed of is having felt such shame. At the same time, the various features of himself and his background which were formerly objects of shame undergo a transvaluation. They too are seen under different concepts and experienced differently. Let us say there is some property very common in his group, a kind of tenacity. This was formerly seen as a kind of stupid obstinacy, and was one of the objects of shame. Now it is seen as a kind of admirable tenacity, a courage of one's own convictions and right.

In this example of transvaluation, we can see two kinds of conceptual revolution going on. The first is when he comes to say to himself: 'What I am doing is apologizing for my own existence'; that is, he comes to see his set of attitudes as a personal stance towards himself, a kind of cringing. The second is the one involved in the transvaluation of the different typical features, like the tenacity above. Now it is clear that the changes in outlook connected with coming to see that the new concepts are appropriate (coming to see that I am apologizing for my existence, coming to see that this stubbornness really is tenacity) are essential to the transvaluation. In order to deny an essential, constitutive role for language, one would have to be able to envisage a non-conceptual analogue for such changes in outlook.

This is already quite hard to do; but another example might quite dispel the temptation even to try. Let us imagine that we are very drawn to someone, we have a kind of love–fascination–attraction to him – but precisely the right term is hard, because we are dealing with an emotion that has not yet become fixed. Then we come, perhaps under his influence, to think very highly of certain qualities or causes or achievements; and these are qualities which he exhibits, causes he has espoused, achievements he has realized. Our feeling now takes shape as admiration. And we come to be able to apply this term to it.

Here again we can see two phases. We come to recognize certain qualities, achievements, and so on; and this can often mean that we have a vocabulary we did not have before. Let us say we are taught by this man what a refined sensibility is. We did not really know before, as we might put it in retrospect. This is one change intrinsically related to language; not of course, our finding a use for the term 'refined sensibility', but our finding a sense for all the terms which, used in judgements about things, express such a sensibility. And the second change comes when we disambiguate our feeling for this person, at least partly, by seeing it as admiration. This recognition helps to shape the feeling itself.

Similar self-shaping recognitions come when one realizes, for example: I deeply love her; or, I am jealous; or, I don't really care.

Why should it be that coming to see (or feel) that certain terms properly describe our emotions often involves shaping (reshaping) those emotions? This is because our subject-referring feelings are given their character by the sense of the import they incorporate; when this sense alters in an important way, then the feeling changes. But because of the problematic nature of our self-understanding, a number of different accounts are possible; and these, by changing our understanding of the import, also change the emotions we can experience.

(Of course, this is not to say that we can change our emotions arbitrarily by applying different names to them. We are not talking about a process which could be arbitrarily undertaken. It is not just applying the name that counts, but coming to 'see–feel' that this is the right description; this is what makes the difference. Language is essential here because it articulates insight, or it makes insight possible.

It follows from this that our thesis here that language is constitutive of our subject-referring emotions says nothing about the order of causation. It is not a thesis to the effect that people change because their ideas about themselves change. Sometimes this is (part of) a good explanation, as in varying degrees in our two examples above. But it is also common experience that our insight grows or changes because of what we have suffered or what we have been forced to become. To say that language is constitutive of emotion is to say that experiencing an emotion essentially involves seeing that certain descriptions apply; or a given emotion involves some (degree of) insight. Nothing is said about how this emotion-insight comes into being or develops.)

This was what happened with our transvaluer above. And the same is also true of our admirer; only here the change is not a revolution negating the past, but rather the move from a confused, inchoate understanding of his imports to a clearer, more articulate view of the same. In both cases, the emotions themselves are transformed. We do not experience the same things, we do not have the same feelings. We can even say we cannot have the same feelings before and after such breaks.

To deny a role for language here is to want to claim that we can have such import-redefining revolutions without language. And this is just what our second group of cases is meant to show up as unbelievable. For here we have a move from the inchoate to the articulate. But this is precisely the change which language brings about. One might argue that it is this that only language (in the widest sense) can bring about. Language articulates our feelings, makes them clearer and more defined; and in this way transforms our sense of the imports involved; and hence transforms the feeling.

The reason why coming to recognize that 'I love her' or 'I'm jealous' alters the emotion is that this kind of self-articulacy is essential to *that* kind of love and jealousy. The avowal is constitutive of *this* feeling.

Thus the emotional lives of human beings from different cultures, who have been brought up with very different import vocabularies, differ very greatly. And even within one culture, people with different vocabularies have different experiences. Consider two people, one with a single love/lust dichotomy for the possible types of sexual feeling, the other with a very variegated vocabulary of different kinds of sexual relations. The experience of sexual emotions of these two men differs. And even if it is the case that one finds that his own vocabulary is distortive, and that the other's is much truer to his real experience, and so comes to adopt it, there will still be a change when he does, and comes to recognize and identify more clearly what he has been feeling, allegedly, all along.

Thus because our subject-referring import-attributing emotions are shaped by the way we see the imports, and the way we see the imports is shaped by the language we come to be able to deploy, language shapes these emotions. We can see this if we contrast them to our immediate feelings. What we experience in the dentist's chair, or when the fingernail is rubbed along the blackboard, is in a sense quite independent of language. That is, all sorts of terrible things we have learnt to be apprehensive about in our teeth can add to our panic. But we feel that this pain is language-independent; and we have no trouble imagining an animal having *this* experience.

Something similar might be said for non-subject-referring imports. Take fear. Here language can enter in because we may need to be apprised in language of the danger. But the import of physical danger is language-independent, in that different descriptions and understandings of the danger do not fundamentally alter for us the imports of bodily integrity or life. Thus we have the sense that there is something continuous here between what we felt before language, would feel without language, what animals feel, and what we feel now as fully developed language beings.

But with our subject-referring imports, the situation is different. As we articulate the imports, the emotions change. On this level, our experience is transformed by language.

What it is transformed by is the changed understanding of the imports which language makes possible. Our understanding of the imports that impinge on us is accepting a certain conception of ourselves. We are coming now once again to the point behind the claim that man is a self-interpreting animal. *Verstehen* is a *Seinsmodus*. We are language animals, we are stuck with language, as it were. And through the language we have come to accept, we have a certain conception of the imports that impinge on us. This conception helps constitute our experience; it plays an essential role in making us what we are. To say that man is a self-interpreting animal is not just to say that he has some compulsive tendency to form reflexive views of himself, but rather that as he is, he is always partly constituted by self-interpretation, that is, by his understanding of the imports which impinge on him.

But to finish first with the baboons: we can happily concede to the ape-protagonists that the baboons do have some analogue of human dignity. Only it cannot be the human experience, for reasons similar to, although multiplied by an untold factor, those which make it impossible for me to experience the emotions of a seventeenth-century Samurai who has just suffered an unanswerable affront, the emotions immediately preceding his decision to kill himself; or to share the experience of a Homeric hero which could be characterized poetically as having power breathed into him by a god. The fact that there are animal analogues should not obscure for us the language-dependence of what we experience.

But when this is said, there are some human imports for which even an analogue in animal life seems implausible, indeed puzzling. Take that of moral obligation; take the kind of experience of the man who sees the wounded victim lying in the road and feels called upon to help. Here the sense of being called on, quite distinct from desiring to help, though that may also be there, depends on a sense of the subject as a moral agent. For this demand is one that essentially is directed to him as an autonomous moral agent. In order to feel this range of emotions, for example, *Achtung* before the moral law, we have to have some idea of different dimensions in ourselves as subjects, that as moral subjects we have demands which are incomparable with those of desire.

But how could there be any such distinction without language? Of course, there do not need to be specific words in language meaning 'moral' or 'moral subject'. It can be that the distinction is carried in our language for something else, for instance deeds, or even in some of our ritual. This gets us into the wider question of what is language, which cannot be resolved here. But without some symbolic medium of expression, how could this distinction be articulated? How could it become a distinction for the agents concerned?

Does this necessity for language not apply to the whole range of strong evaluations? How can there be a sense of some goals or desires as higher and others as lower without a symbolic medium in which this can be articulated? For without this articulation, how can a higher (or more fulfilling, or moral, or worthy) desire be identified? What could discriminate it as higher, as against just stronger, or prepotent? And if it were not prepotent, what grounds would there be for calling it higher, except perhaps its functional importance?

What may obscure this for us is our experience of inarticulate emotion. We all know what it is like to have feelings which we only identify properly afterwards. Thus while it is clear that the *articulate understanding* of certain goals and desires as higher and others as lower depends on language, we may think of the pre-articulate sense as being language-independent. And thus we might be tempted to think of animals as experiencing inarticulately what we give names to.

But of course *our* pre-articulate sense of our feelings is *not* language-independent. For they are the feelings of a language being, who therefore can and does say something about them, for example, that he feels something disturbing and perplexing, which baffles him, and to which he cannot give a name. *We* experience our pre-articulate emotion as perplexing, as raising a question. And *this* is an experience that no non-language animal can have.

But it makes no sense to ascribe strong evaluation to a being who could not even have inarticulate emotion in our sense, for whom the question of what quality of feeling he is experiencing *could not arise*.

Thus for us language-animals our language is constitutive of our emotions, not just because *de facto* we have articulated some of them, but also *de jure* as the medium in which all our emotions, articulate and inarticulate, are experienced. Only a language-animal could have our emotions: and that means, inter alia, emotions which involve strong evaluations. This is my fifth claim.

What emerges from the five together is a picture of man as a self-interpreting animal. This is an animal whose emotional life incorporates a sense of what is really important to him, of the shape of his aspirations, which asks to be understood, and which is never adequately understood. His understanding is explicated at any time in the language he uses to speak about himself, his goals, what he feels, and so on; and in shaping his sense of what is important it also shapes what he feels.

But why does it ask to be understood? (This question can represent a real longing, a nostalgia, as the myths of the age of Kronos testify.) Because as language-animals we are already engaged in understanding it; we already have incorporated into our language an interpretation of what is really important. And it is this articulation, as we saw just a minute ago, which makes our inarticulate feelings into questions. Without language we could not have a sense of this distinction between what is really important and what we just from time to time desire. In our language we have already opened the issue by giving a first, fumbling answer.

It is language which lies behind the feature mentioned in section III.2, that our feelings are always open to further articulation just because they already involve articulation. It is because we are language-animals that we have articulated feelings, and hence that none of our subject-referring feelings can exist out of the range of articulation.

Because our language gives expression to qualitative distinctions, by which we can have a sense of higher goals, and hence have an emotional experience with strong evaluation, we open an issue which can never be definitively closed. Or otherwise put, man by his existence gives an answer to a question which *thereby* is posed and can never be finally answered. Our language is not just that in which we frame our answers, but that whereby there is a question about the truly worthy or good. Human language and language-constituted emotion opens this problematic area, which can never be decisively circumscribed because it can never be specified in objectified terms.

Now our attempted definitions of what is really important can be called interpretations, as we have suggested, and we can therefore say that the human animal not only finds himself impelled from time to time to interpret himself and his goals, but that he is always already in some interpretation, constituted as human by this fact. To be human is to be already engaged in living an answer to the question, an interpretation of oneself and one's aspirations.

The paradox of human emotions is that although only an articulated emotional life is properly human, all our articulations are open to challenge from our inarticulate sense of what is important, that is, we recognize that they ought to be faithful articulations of something of which we have as yet only fragmentary intimations. If one focusses only on the first point, one can believe that human beings are formed arbitrarily by the language they have accepted. If one focusses only on the second, one can think that we ought to be able to isolate scientifically the pure, uninterpreted basis of human emotion that all these languages are about. But neither of these is true. There is no human emotion which is not embodied in an interpretive language; and yet all interpretations can be judged as more or less adequate, more or less distortive. What a given human life is an interpretation of cannot exist uninterpreted; for human emotion is only what it is refracted as in human language.

Human emotion is interpreted emotion, which is nevertheless seeking its adequate form. This is what is involved in seeing man as a self-interpreting animal. It means that he cannot be understood simply as an object among objects, for his life incorporates an interpretation, an expression of what cannot exist unexpressed, because the self that is to be interpreted is essentially that of a being who self-interprets.

2

I want at the close to list in summary form my five claims. They are:

1. that some of our emotions involve import-ascriptions;

2.   that some of these imports are subject-referring;
3.   that our subject-referring feelings are the basis of our understanding of what it is to be human;
4.   that these feelings are constituted by the articulations we come to accept of them; and
5.   that these articulations, which we can think of as interpretations, require language.

Together these five claims, each of which builds on its predecessors, offer a picture of man as a self-interpreting being. This is a picture in which interpretation plays no secondary, optional role, but is essential to human existence. This is the view, I believe, which was adumbrated by Heidegger, and which has justly been immensely influential in contemporary thought.

CHAPTER THREE

HEGEL'S PHILOSOPHY OF MIND

As with any highly systematic body of thought, Hegel's philosophy of mind can be reconstructed from many perspectives. Each one gives us something, though some are more illuminating than others. But I believe that it is particularly illuminating to see Hegel's philosophy of mind through the perspective of his philosophy of action. This is, of course, hardly a surprising doctrine. Mind (*Geist*) for Hegel is thoroughgoing activity (*Tätigkeit*). But I think the insights from this perspective can be enlivened and made more penetrating if we relate Hegel's thought to a set of perennial issues that have been central to the philosophy of action in modern times. This is what I want to attempt in this paper.

At the same time, a study of this kind can be interesting in another way. Understanding Hegel's contribution to the developing modern debate on the nature of action helps us to understand the historical development of this debate. And this, I would like to argue, is important for understanding the debate itself.

I

We can perhaps identify one fundamental issue which has been left open in the philosophy of action in modern times. To do so, of course, requires some interpretation of the history of modern philosophy, and this as always can be subject to controversy. The precise question which defines this issue was not asked in the seventeenth or eighteenth century, and is rather one which is central to our twentieth-century debate. But I want to claim nevertheless that different answers to this question were espoused earlier, as one can see from a number of related philosophical doctrines which *were* expressly propounded, and which depend on these answers. I hope the plausibility of this reading will emerge in the course of the whole argument.

This being said, I will baldly identify my central issue in unashamedly contemporary terms: what is the nature of action? Or otherwise put, what distinguishes (human) action from other kinds of events? What are the peculiar features of action?

One family of views distinguishes actions by the kind of cause which brings them about. Actions are events which are peculiar in that they are brought about by desires, or intentions, or combinations of desires and beliefs. As events, actions may be described among other ways as physical movements. (Although one would have to be generous with the term 'physical movements', so as to include cases of non-movement, as for example with the action we would describe as 'He stood still'.) In this, they resemble a host of other events which are not actions. What distinguishes them is a peculiar type of psychological cause: that they are brought on by desires or intentions. Of course, to hold this is not necessarily to hold that psychological explanations are ultimate. One can also look forward to their reduction to some neurophysiological or physical theory. But in that case, the burden of distinguishing action from non-action would be taken over by antecedents differently described: perhaps some peculiar kind of firing in the cortex, which was found to be the basis for what we identify psychologically as desire.

A view of this kind seems to have been implicit in much of Donald Davidson's work.[1] But the basic conception goes back, I believe, at least to the seventeenth century. A conception of this kind was in a sense even more clearly at home in the basically dualist outlook common both to Cartesian and empiricist philosophies. *Qua* bodily movements actions resembled all other events. What distinguished them was their inner, 'mental' background. Within the bounds of this outlook, there was a clear ontological separation between outer event and inner background.

Against this, there is another family of views which sees action as qualitatively different from non-action, in that actions are what we might call intrinsically directed. Actions are in a sense inhabited by the purposes which direct them, so that action and purpose are ontologically inseparable. The basic intuition here is not hard to grasp, but it is difficult to articulate it very clearly. What is in any case clear is that this view involves a clear negation of the first: we cannot understand action in terms of the notions of undiscriminated event and a particular kind of cause; this is to explain it in terms of other primitive concepts. But for the second view, action is itself a primitive: there is a basic qualitative distinction

[1] D. Davidson, 'Actions, reasons and causes', *Journal of Philosophy*, 60:23 (1973), pp. 685–700, and 'Freedom to act', in Ted Honderich (ed.), *Essays on Freedom of Action* (London, 1973).

between action and non-action. To the extent that action can be further explicated in terms of a concept like 'purpose', this turns out not to be independently understandable. For the purpose is not ontologically separable from the action, and this means something like: it can only exist in animating this action; or its only articulation as a purpose is in animating the action; or perhaps a fundamental articulation of this purpose, on which all others depend, lies in the action.

This second view thus resists the basic approach of the first. We cannot understand action by first identifying it as an undifferentiated event (because it is qualitatively distinct), and then distinguishing it by some separably identifiable cause (because the only thing which could fill this function, the purpose, is not separably identifiable). One of the roots of this doctrine is plainly Aristotle's thesis of the inseparability of form and matter, and we can see that in contrast to Cartesianism and empiricism, it is plainly anti-dualist. This is not to say that proponents of the first view are necessarily dualist – at least not simply so; just that their conception permits of dualism, whereas the qualitative distinction thesis does not.

One of the issues which is thus bound up with that of the nature of action is the question of dualism. Another which I want briefly to mention here is the place of the subject. It is clear that the distinction between action and non-action is one that occurs to us as agents. Indeed, one can argue plausibly that a basic, not further reducible distinction between action and what just happens is indispensable and ineradicable from our self-understanding as agents.[2] That is, it is impossible to function as an agent at all unless one marks a distinction of this kind.

In this context, we can understand part of the motivation for the first, or causal, theory of action as lying in the aspiration to go beyond the subjective standpoint of the agent, and come to an understanding of things which is objective. An objective understanding in this sense would be one which was no longer tied to a particular viewpoint, imprisoned in the categories which a certain viewpoint imposes. If agency seems to impose the qualitative conception of action, then the causal one can appear as a superior analysis, an objective portrayal of the way things really stand, of the real components of action *an sich*. This drive for objectivity, or what Bernard Williams has called 'absolute' descriptions,[3] was one of the animating motives of both Cartesianism and empiricism.

---

[2] C. Taylor, 'Action as expression', in C. Diamond and J. Teichman (eds.), *Intention and Intentionality* (London, 1979).

[3] B. Williams, *Descartes* (London, 1978).

Now Hegel is clearly a proponent of the second, qualitative conception of action. And indeed, he emerges out of a climate in which this conception was staging a comeback after the ascendancy of Cartesian and empiricist views. In one sense, the comeback can be seen to start with Leibniz, but the tenor of much late-eighteenth-century thought in Germany was of this stamp. The reaction against dualism, the recovery of the subject, the rehabilitation of Aristotle-type inseparability doctrines – notably in the conception of the aesthetic object in Kant's *Third Critique* – all pushed towards, and indeed, articulated themselves through this understanding of action. I now want to develop its ramifications to show how central it is to Hegel's thought, and in particular his theory of mind.

II

The first important ramification of the qualitative theory is that it allows what I shall call agent's knowledge. The notion is that we are capable of grasping our own action in a way that we cannot come to know external objects and events. In other words, there is a knowledge we are capable of concerning our own action which we can attain as the doers of this action; and this is different from the knowledge we may gain of objects we observe or scrutinize.

This qualitative distinction in kinds of knowledge is grounded on the qualitative view of action. Action is distinct in that it is directed, aimed to encompass ends or purposes. And this notion of directedness is part of our conception of agency: the agent is the being responsible for the direction of action, the being for whom and through whom action is directed as it is. The notion of action is normally correlative to that of an agent.

Now if we think of this agent as identical with the subject of knowledge, then we can see how there can be different kinds of knowledge. One kind is gained by making articulate what we are doing, the direction we are already imprinting on events in our action. As agents, we will already have some sense, however dim, inarticulate or subliminal, of what we are doing; otherwise, we could not speak of directing at all. So agent's knowledge is a matter of bringing this sense to formulation, articulation or full consciousness. It is a matter of making articulate something we already have an inarticulate sense of.

This evidently contrasts with knowledge of other objects, the things we observe and deal with in the world. Here we are learning about things external to our action, which we may indeed act with or on, but which stand over against action.

Now the first, or causal view, cannot draw this contrast. To begin with, we can see why it was not concerned to: because the contrast is one which is evident from the agent's standpoint; agent's knowledge is available to the knower only *qua* agent, and thus from his standpoint. It cannot be recognized as knowledge from the absolute standpoint. Thus for the causal view, my action is an external event like any other, only distinct in having a certain kind of cause. I cannot claim to know it in some special way.

Of course, what I can claim 'privileged access' to is my desire, or intention – the cause of my action. And here we come closest to an analogous distinction within the causal view to that between agent's and observer's knowledge. In the original formulations of Cartesianism and empiricism, I am transparently or immediately aware of the contents of my mind. It may be accorded that I am immediately, even incorrigibly aware that I want to eat an apple, or that I intend to eat this apple. But of the consequences of this desire or intention, viz., my consuming the apple, I have knowledge like that of any other external event: I observe it.

We might then contrast the two views by noting that the causal view too recognizes two kinds of knowledge, but it draws the boundaries quite differently, between 'inner' and 'outer' reality. But we would have to add that this difference of location of the boundary goes along with a quite different view of what the knowledge consists of. The notion of immediate or incorrigible knowledge makes sense in the context of dualism, of a separate domain of inner, mental space, of which we can say at least that its *esse* entails its *percipi*. The contrast will be something like that between immediate and inferential knowledge, or the incorrigible and the revisable.

Once we draw the boundary in the way the qualitative theory does, there is no question of incorrigibility. We may never be without some sense of what we are doing, but coming to have knowledge is coming to formulate that correctly, and we may only do this in a partial or distorted fashion. Nor is this knowledge ever immediate; it is, on the contrary, mediated by our efforts at formulation. We have indeed a different mode of access to what we are doing, but it is questionable whether we should dub this access 'privileged'. Neither immediacy nor incorrigibility are marks of agent's knowledge.

In a sense this idea of agent's knowledge originates in modern thought with Vico. But since his work did not have the influence it deserved in the eighteenth century, we should perhaps see Kant as the important seminal figure. Not that Kant allowed a full-blooded notion of agent's knowledge.

Indeed, he shied away from using the word 'knowledge' in this context. But he made the crucial distinction between our empirical knowledge of objects on one hand, and the synthetic *a priori* truths which we can establish on the other about the mathematical and physical structure of things. In Kant's mind it is clear that we can only establish the latter with certainty because they are in an important sense our own doing.

Perceiving the world involves not just the reception of information, but crucially also our own conceptual activity, and we can know for certain the framework of empirical reality, because we ourselves provide it.

Moreover, in Kant's procedure of proof of these synthetic *a priori* truths, he shows them to be essential conditions of undeniable features of experience, such as that we mark a distinction between the objective and the subjective in experience, or that the 'I think' must be able to accompany all our representations. Later he will show the postulates of freedom, God and immortality as essential conditions of the practice of determining our action by moral precepts. If we ask what makes these starting points allegedly undeniable, I think the answer can only be that we can be sure of them because they are what we are *doing*, when we perceive the world, or determine our action on moral grounds.[4]

Kant thus brings back into the centre of modern epistemological debate the notion of activity and hence of agent's knowledge. Cartesian incorrigibility, the immediate knowledge I have of myself as a thinking substance, is set aside. In its place come the certainties which we do not have immediately, but can gain, concerning not some substance, or any object of knowledge whatever, but the structures of our own activity. What we learn by this route is only accessible by this route. It is something quite different from the knowledge of objects.

This has been an immensely influential idea in modern philosophy. One line of development from Kant lies through Schopenhauer, who distinguished our grasp of ourselves as representation and as will, and from this through Wittgenstein into modern British analytical philosophy, for example in Miss Anscombe's notion of 'non-observational knowledge'.[5]

But the line which interests us here passes through Fichte. Fichte's attempt to define subject–object identity is grounded on the view that agent's knowledge is the only genuine form of knowledge. Both Fichte and Schelling take up Kant's notion of an 'intellectual intuition', which

---

[4] I have argued this further in C. Taylor, 'The validity of transcendental arguments', *Proceedings of the Aristotelian Society* (1978–9), pp. 151–65.

[5] G. E. M. Anscombe, *Intention* (Oxford, 1957), pp. 13–15.

for Kant was the kind of agent's knowledge which could only be attributed to God, one through which the existence of the object itself was given (B72), or one in which the manifold is given by the activity of the self (*selbsttätig*, B68). But they make this the basis of genuine self-knowledge by the ego; and then of all genuine knowledge in so far as object and subject are shown to be identical.

The category of agent's knowledge has obviously taken on a central role, has exploded beyond the limits that Kant set for it; and is, indeed, the principal instrument by which these limits are breached and the realm of inaccessible noumena denied. But the extension of agent's knowledge obviously goes along with a redefinition of the subject. He is no longer simply the finite subject in general that figures in the *Critiques*, but is related in some way to a single infinite or cosmic subject.

Hegel is obviously the heir to this development. He takes up the task of demonstrating subject–object identity, and believes himself alone to be capable of demonstrating this properly. What is first seen as 'other' is shown to be identical with the self. It is crucial to this demonstration that the self cease to understand itself as merely finite, but see itself as part of spirit.

But the recognition of identity takes the form of grasping that everything emanates from spirit's activity. To understand reality aright is to understand it as 'actuality' (translating *Wirklichkeit*), that is, as what has been actualized. This is the crucial prerequisite of the final stage, which comes when we see that the agent of this activity is not foreign to us, but that we are identical to (in our non-identity with) spirit. The highest categories of the Logic, those which provide the entry into the absolute Idea, are thus those linked with agency and activity. We move from teleology into the categories of life, and then from knowledge to the good.

The recognition thus requires that we understand reality as activity, but it requires as well that we come to understand in a fuller way what we are doing up to the point of seeing what spirit is doing through us. Coming to this point, we see the identity of the world-activity with ours.

Thought thus culminates in a form of agent's knowledge. But this is not just a department of what we know alongside observer's knowledge, as it is for our ordinary understanding. Rather observer's knowledge is ultimately superseded. But the distinction is none the less essential to the system, since its crucial claim is that we only rise to the higher kind of knowledge through a supersession of the lower kind.

And this higher knowledge is far from immediate. On the contrary, it is only possible as mediated through forms of expression, among which the only adequate medium is conceptual thought. And this brings us to another ramification of the qualitative view, which is also of central importance for Hegel. On the qualitative view, action may be totally unreflecting; it may be something we carry out without awareness. We may then become aware of what we are doing, formulate our ends. So following on a conscious desire or intention is not an inescapable feature of action. On the contrary, this degree of awareness in our action is something we come to achieve.

In achieving this, we also transform our activity. The quality of consciously directed activity is different from that of our unreflected, semiconscious performance. This flows naturally from the second view on action: if action is qualitatively different from non-action, and this difference consists in the fact that action is directed, then action is also different when this direction takes on a crucially different character. And this it does when we move from unreflecting response, where we act in much the same manner as animals do, to conscious formulation of our purposes. Our action becomes directed in a different and stronger sense. To become conscious is to be able to act in a new way.

The causal theory does not allow for this kind of qualitative shift. Indeed in its original, dualist variant, it could not even allow for unreflecting action. Action is essentially caused by desire or intention, and on the original Cartesian–empiricist model our desires were essentially features of inner experience. To have a desire was to feel a desire. Hence, on this view, action was essentially preceded by a cause of which the agent was aware. This amounted in fact to making conscious action, where we are aware of our ends, the only kind of action. It left no place at all for totally unmonitored, unconscious activity, the kind of action animals engage in all the time, and we do much of the time.

And even when the causal theory is disengaged from its dualist or mentalist formulation, where the causes of action are seen as material, and hence quite conceivably largely unconscious, the theory still has no place for the notion that action is qualitatively transformed in becoming conscious. Awareness may allow us to intervene more effectively to control what comes about, but action remains essentially an undifferentiated external event with a certain kind of cause.

Now this offshoot of the qualitative view – that action is not essentially or originally conscious, that to make it so is an achievement, and that this achievement transforms it – is also crucial to the central doctrines of Hegel. I want to look at two of them here.

I

The first is what I have called elsewhere the 'principle of embodiment'.[6] This is the principle that the subject and all his functions, however 'spiritual' they may appear, are inescapably embodied. The embodiment is in two related dimensions: first, as a 'rational animal', that is, as a living being who thinks; and secondly, as an expressive being, that is, a being whose thinking is always and necessarily in a medium.

The basic notion here is that what passes in modern philosophy for the 'mental' is the inward reflection of what was originally external activity. Self-conscious understanding is the fruit of an interiorization of what was originally external. The seeming self-coincidence of thought where I am apparently immediately aware of my desires, aims and ideas, which is foundational to Cartesianism, is understood rather as an achievement, the overcoming of the externality of an unconscious, merely instinctive life. It is the fruit of a negation of what negates thought, not itself a positive datum. This understanding of conscious self-possession as the negation of the negation is grounded on the conception of action I have just been out-lining. In effect, it involves seeing our mental life fundamentally in the category of action. If we think of the constituents of mental life, our desires, feelings, ideas, as merely given, as the objects which surround us in the world are given, then it is plausible to think of our knowledge of them as privileged. They appear to be objects which we cannot but be aware of, if we are aware at all. Our awareness of them is something basic, assured from the start, since it is essentially involved in our being aware at all.

In order to understand mental life as something we have to achieve understanding of, so that self-transparency is a goal we must work to-wards, we have to abandon the view of it as constituted of data. We have to understand it as action, on at least one of two levels, if not both.

On one level, we have to see self-perception as something we do, some-thing we can bring off, or fail to bring off, rather than a feature of our basic predicament. This means that we see it as the fruit of an activity of formulating how things are with us, what we desire, feel, think, and so on. In this way, grasping what we desire or feel is something we can altogether fail to do, or do in a distorting or partial or censored fashion. If we think through the consequences of this, I believe we see that it requires that we conceive self-understanding as something that is brought off in a medium, through symbols or concepts, and formulating things in this medium as one of our fundamental activities.

[6] C. Taylor, *Hegel and Modern Society* (Cambridge, 1979), p. 18.

We can see this if we leap out of the Hegelian context and look at the quite different case of Freud. Here we have the most notorious doctrine of the non-self-transparency of the human psyche. But this is mediated through a doctrine of self-understanding through symbols, and of our (more or less distorted and screened) formulation of our desires, fears, and so on as something we do. For although these formulations occur without our wilful and conscious intent, they are nevertheless motivated. Displacements, condensations, and so on occur where we are strongly motivated to bring them off.

But on a second level, we may also see the features of ourselves that self-perception grasps not as simply givens but as themselves bound up with activity. Thus desires, feelings may not be understood as just mental givens, but as the inner reflection of the life-process that we are. Our ideas may not be conceived as simple mental contents, but as the precipitates of thinking. And so on.

Hegel understands mental life as activity on both these levels. In a sense, the first can be thought to represent the influence of Kant. It was Kant who defended the principle that there is no perception of any kind which is not constituted by our conceptual activity. Thus there is no self-awareness, as there is no awareness of anything else, without the active contribution of the 'I think'. It was the contribution of the new richer theory of meaning that arose in the wake of Romanticism to see that this constitutive thought required an expressive medium. Freud is, of course, via Schopenhauer, the inheritor both of this Kantian doctrine and of the expressivist climate of thought, and hence also through Schopenhauer of the idea that our self-understanding can be very different in different media, as well as distorted in the interests of deeper impulses that we barely comprehend.

The making activity central on the second level is also the fruit of what I want to call the expressivist climate of thought, which refused the distinctions between mind and body, reason and instinct, intellect and feeling, which earlier Enlightenment thought had made central. Thought and reason were to be understood as having their seat in the single life-process from which feeling also arose. Hence the new vogue for Aristotelian inseparability doctrines, of form and matter, of thought and expression, of soul and body.

Hegel's theory of mind is built on both these streams. Our self-understanding is conceived as the inner self-reflection of a life-process, which at the outset fails to grasp what it is about. We learn through a painful and slow process to formulate ourselves less and less inadequately. At the beginning, desire is unreflected, and in that condition aims simply for the incorporation of the desired object. But this is inherently unsatisfactory, because the aims of spirit are to recognize the self in the other, and not simply to abolish otherness. And so we proceed to a higher form of desire, the desire for desire, the demand for recognition. This too starts off in a barely self-conscious form, which needs to be further transformed. And so on.

In this theory, activity is made central on both levels: (a) on the second, more fundamental level, what is to be understood here, the desire, is not seen as a mere psychic given, a datum of mental life. On the contrary, it is a reflection (and at first an inadequate one) of the goals of a life-process which is now embodied and in train in the world. Properly understood, this is the life-process of spirit, but we are at the outset far from seeing that. So the active life-process is primary, even in defining the object of knowledge.

Then (b) on the first level, the achievement of more and more adequate understandings is something that comes about through our activity of formulating. This takes place for Hegel, as we shall see later, not only in concepts and symbols, but also in common institutions and practices. For example, the institution of the master–slave relationship is one 'formulation' (and still an inadequate one) of the search for recognition. Grasping things through symbols, establishing and maintaining practices, are things we do, are to be understood as activities, on Hegel's theory.

And so we have two related activities. There is a fundamental activity of Spirit, which it tries to grasp through the various levels of self-formulation. These two mutually conditional activities are at first out of phase, but they are destined in the end to coincide perfectly. That is because it will become clear at the end that the end of the whole life-process was that Spirit come to understand itself, and at the same time the life-process itself will be entirely transparent as an embodiment of this purpose.

But this perfect coincidence comes only at the end. And it only comes through the overcoming of non-coincidence, where what the pattern of activity is differs from what this pattern says. And so the distinction between these two dimensions is essential for the Hegelian philosophy: we could call them the effective and the expressive. Each life-form in history is both the effective realization of a certain pattern, and at the same time the expression of a certain self-understanding of man and hence also of Spirit. The gap between these two is the historical contradiction which moves us on.

And so for Hegel, the principle of embodiment is central. What we focus on as the mental can only be understood in the first place as the inner reflection of an embodied life-process; and this inner reflection is itself mediated by our formulations in an expressive medium. So all spiritual life is embodied in the two dimensions just described: it is the life of a living being who thinks; and his thinking is essentially expression. This double shift from Cartesianism, from a psychology of immediate self-transparency to one of achieved interiority, of the negation of the negation, is obviously grounded on the qualitative understanding of action, and the central role it plays here. The mental life has a depth which defies all immediate self-transparency, just because it is not merely self-contained, but is the reflection of a larger life-process; while plumbing this depth is in turn seen as something we do, as the fruit of the activity of self-formulation.

Once again, we see that the Hegelian understanding of things involves our seeing activity as all-pervasive. But the activity concerned is as it is conceived on the qualitative view.

2

We can thus see that this offshoot of the qualitative view, which sees action as first unreflecting, and reflective understanding as an achievement, underpins what I call the principle of embodiment in Hegel's thought. But we saw above that for this conception reflective consciousness transforms action. And this aspect too is crucial to Hegel's theory.

His conception is of an activity which is at first uncertain or self-defeating because its purposes are barely understood. The search for recognition is, properly understood, a demand for reciprocal recognition, within the life of a community. This is what our activity is in fact groping towards, but at first we do not understand it in this way. In a still confused and inarticulated fashion, we identify the goal as attaining one-sided recognition for ourselves from others. It follows that our practice will be confused in its purpose and self-defeating. For the essential nature of the activity is not altered by our inadequate understanding of it; the true goal of the search for recognition remains community. Our inadequacy of understanding only means that our action itself is confused, and that means that its quality as directed activity is impaired.

We can see this kind of confusion, for instance, at the stage where we seek to answer our need for recognition through an institution like that of slavery. We are already involved here with what will turn out to be the only possible solution to this quest, viz., community; because even the institution of the master–slave relation will typically be defined and mediated by law, a law which binds all parties, and which implicitly recognizes them as subjects of right. Within this framework, the relations of domination, of ownership of man by man, contradict the basic nature of law. If we think of our building and maintaining these institutions as an activity we are engaged in together, which is how Hegel sees it, then we can see that our activity itself is confused and contradictory. This is, indeed, why it will be self-defeating, and why this institutional complex will eventually undermine and destroy itself.

A new form of society will then arise out of the ruins of this one. But the practices of this new society will only be higher than previous ones to the extent that we have learnt from the previous error, and now have a more satisfactory understanding of what we are engaged in. Indeed, it is only possible to accede eventually to a practice which has fully overcome confusion and is no longer self-defeating if we finally come to an understanding which is fully adequate.

But throughout this whole development we can see the close relation which exists between the level of our understanding and the quality of our practice. On this view, our action itself can be more or less firmly guided, more or less coherent and self-consistent. And its being one or the other is related to the level of our self-understanding.

We are reminded here of a common conception of the Romantics, well expressed in a story of Kleist, that fully coherent action must either be totally unreflecting or the fruit of full understanding. The birth of self-consciousness on this view disrupts our activity, and we can only compensate for this disruption by a self-awareness which is total. Hegel takes up this conception with an important difference. The crucial activity is that of Spirit, and it aims for self-recognition. As a consequence, there is no such thing as the perfection of totally unreflecting activity. The earliest phases of human life are even then phases of Spirit, and the contradiction is present between their unconsciousness and what they implicitly seek.

In sum, we can see that this ramification of the qualitative theory of action involves a basic reversal in the order of explanation from the philosophy that Cartesianism and empiricism bequeathed to us. It amounts to another one of those shifts in what is taken as primitive in explanation, similar and related to the one we mentioned at the outset.

There I pointed out that for the Cartesian–empiricist view, action was something to be further explained, compounded out of undifferentiated events and a certain kind of cause. The cause here was a desire, or intention, a 'mental' event; and these mental occurrences are taken as primitives by this kind of theory, and part of the explanatory background of action.

But the qualitative view turns out to reverse this order. The 'mental' is not a primitive datum, but is rather something achieved. Moreover, we explain its genesis from action, as the reflective understanding we eventually attain of what we are doing. So the status of primitive and derived in explanation is reversed. One theory explains action in terms of the supposedly more basic datum of the mental; the other accounts for the mental as a development out of our primitive capacity for action.

III

The qualitative view also brings about another reversal, this time in the theory of meaning, which it is worth examining for its own sake, as well as for its importance to Hegel.

I said above that for this view becoming aware of ourselves, coming to self-consciousness, is something we do. We come to be able to formulate properly what we are about. But this notion of formulation refers us to that of an expressive medium.

One way to trace the connection is this: if we think of self-consciousness as the fruit of action, and we think of action as first of all unreflecting bodily practice, which only later comes to be self-understood; then the activity of formulating must itself conform to this model. That is, our formulating ourselves would be at first a relatively unreflective bodily practice, and would attain only later to the self-clarity required for full self-consciousness.

But this is just what we see in the new expressive theories of meaning which arose in the later eighteenth century, and which Hegel took over. First, the very notion of expression is that of self-revelation as a special kind of bodily practice. The Enlightenment theory of signs, born of the epistemological theories of the seventeenth century, made no fundamental distinction between expressive and any other form of self-revelation. You can see that I am afraid of a recession by the fact that I am selling short; you can see that I am afraid of you by the expression on my face; you can see that it is going to rain because the barometer is falling. Each of these was seen as a 'sign' which points beyond to something it designates or reveals. Enlightenment theorists marked distinctions between signs: some were by nature, some by convention. For Condillac, there were three kinds, accidental signs, natural signs, and signs by institution.

But the distinction they quite overlooked was the crucial one for an expressivist, that between 'signs' which allow you to infer to their 'designatum', like the barometer does to rain, and true signs which express something. When we make something plain in expression, we reveal it in public space in a way which has no parallel in cases of inference. The barometer 'reveals' rain indirectly. This contrasts with our perceiving rain directly. But when I make plain my anger or my joy, in facial or verbal expression, there is no such contrast. This is not a second best, the dropping of clues which enable you to infer. This is what manifesting anger or joy *is*. They are made evident not by or through the expression but in it.

The new theories of meaning, which start perhaps with Herder's critique of Condillac, involve a fundamental shift. They recognize the special nature of those human activities which reveal things in this special way. Let us call them expressive activities. These are bodily activities. They involve using signs, gestures, spoken or written words. And moreover, their first uses are relatively unreflecting. They aim to make plain in public space how we feel, or how we stand with eath other, or where things stand for us. It is a long slow process which makes us able to get things in clearer focus, describe them more exactly, and above all, become more knowledgeable about ourselves.

To do this requires that we develop finer and more discriminating media. We can speak of an embodiment which reveals in this expressive way as a 'medium'. Then the struggle for deeper and more accurate reflective self-understanding can be understood as the attempt to discover or coin more adequate media. Facial expressions do much to make us present to each other in our feelings and desires, but for self-understanding we need a refined and subtle vocabulary.

This amounts to another major reversal in theory. The Enlightenment account explained meaning in terms of the link of designation or 'signifying' between word and object. This was a link set up in thought. In Locke's theory, it was even seen as a link set up through thought, since the word strictly speaking signified the idea of the object. Meaning is explained here by thought, which once again is seen in the role of explanatory primitive. In this conception, expression is just one case of the signifying relation, which is seen as constituted in thought.

But for the expressive theory, it is expression which is the primitive. Thought, that is, the clear, explicit kind of thought we need to establish new coinages, new relations of 'signifying', is itself explained from expression. Both ontogenetically and in the history of culture, our first expressions are in public space, and are the vehicles of a quite unreflective awareness. Later we both develop more refined media, in concepts and images, and become more and more capable of carrying out some part of our expressive activity monologically; that is, we become capable of formulating some things just for ourselves, and hence of thinking privately. We then develop the capacity to frame some things clearly to ourselves, and thus even to coin new expressions for our own use. But this capacity, which the Enlightenment theory takes as a primitive, is seen here as a late achievement, a change we ultimately come to be able to ring on our expressive capacity. This latter is what is now seen as basic in the order of explanation.

In our day, a similar radical reversal was carried out in the theory of meaning by Ludwig Wittgenstein, who took as his target the theory which emerges out of modern epistemological theory, to which he himself had partly subscribed earlier. What I have called the Herderian theory is very reminiscent therefore of Wittgenstein's.

But Hegel wrote in the wake of the earlier expressive revolution. And one can see its importance for his thought by the crucial place in it of what I have called the notion of medium. The goal of spirit is clear, self-conscious understanding. But the struggle to attain this is just the struggle to formulate it in an adequate medium.

Thus Hegel distinguishes art, religion and philosophy as media, in ascending order of adequacy. The perception of the absolute is embodied in the work of art, it is presented there (*dargestellt*). But this is in a form which is still relatively inarticulate and unreflecting. Religious doctrine and cult bring us closer to adequacy, but are still clouded by images and 'representations' (*Vorstellungen*). The only fully adequate form is conceptual thought, which allows both transparency and full reflective awareness. But attaining our formulation in this medium is the result of a long struggle. It is an achievement; and one which builds on and requires the formulation in the other, less adequate media. Philosophy does not only build on its own past. For in earlier ages, the truth is more adequately presented in religion (e.g., the early ages of Christianity), or art-religion (at the height of the Greek polis). In coming to its adequate form, philosophy as it were catches up. True speculative philosophy has to say clearly what has been there already in the images of Christian theology.

Thus for Hegel too thought is the achievement whereby our expression is made more inward and clear. The attainment of self-understanding is the fruit of an activity which itself conforms to the basic model of action, that it is at first unreflecting bodily practice and only later attains self-clarity. This is the activity of expressing.

IV

I have been looking at how the qualitative theory of action and its ramifications underlie Hegel's philosophy of mind, for which in the end everything is to be understood in terms of the all-pervasive activity of Spirit. I have been arguing that we can only understand the kind of activity involved here if we have in mind the qualitative view.

But there are also some important features of human historical action on Hegel's view which only make sense against this conception. I want to mention two here.

I

The first is this: all action is not in the last analysis of individuals; there are irreducibly collective actions. The causal view was inherently atomist. An action was such because it was caused by desire, intention, some 'mental' state. But these mental states could only be understood as states of individuals. The mental is what is 'inner', which means within each one of us. And so action is ultimately individual. That is to say, collective actions ultimately amount to the convergent action of many individuals and nothing more. To say 'the X church did so-and-so', or 'the Y party did such-and-such' must amount to attributing converging action to clumps of individuals in each case. For what makes these events actions in each case is their having inner mental causes, and these have to occur or not occur discretely within individuals.

By contrast, the qualitative view does not tie action only to the individual agent. The nature of the agency comes clear to us only when we have a clear understanding of the nature of the action. This can be individual; but it can also be the action of a community, and in a fashion which is irreducible to individual action. It can even conceivably be the action of an agent who is not simply identical with human agency.

Hegel, of course, avails himself of both of these latter possibilities. In his conception of public life, as it exists in a properly established system of objective ethics (*Sittlichkeit*), the common practices or institutions which embody this life are seen as our doing. But they constitute an activity which is genuinely common to us; it is *ours* in a sense which cannot be analysed into a convergence of *mines*.

But for Hegel, there is a crucial level of activity which is not only more than individual, but even more than merely human. Some of what we do we can understand also and more deeply as the action of Spirit through us. In order to arrive at a proper understanding, we thus have to transcend our ordinary self-understanding; and to the extent that our common sense is atomist, we have to make two big transpositions: in the first, we come to see that some of our actions are those of communities; in the second, we see that some are the work of Spirit. It is in the *Phenomenology of Spirit* that we see these transitions being made. The first corresponds to the step from chapter V to chapter VI (here Hegel speaks of the community action by using the term 'Spirit'). The second is made as we move through the discussion in the third part of chapter VI into the chapter on Religion.

2

Following what I have said in earlier sections, human action is to be understood in two dimensions, the effective and the expressive. This latter dimension makes it even clearer how action is not necessarily that of the individual. An expression in public space may turn out to be the expression essentially of a common sentiment or purpose. That is, it may be essential to this sentiment or purpose that it be shared, and the expression may be the vehicle of this sharing.

These two features together – that action can be that of a community, and that it also exists in the expressive dimension – form the crucial background to Hegel's philosophy of society and history. The *Sittlichkeit* of a given society is not only to be seen as the action of a community, or of individuals only so far as they identify themselves as members of a community (an 'I' that is 'We', and a 'We' that is 'I');[7] it also embodies and gives expression to a certain understanding of the agent, his community and their relation to the divine. It is this latter which gives us the key to the fate of the society. For it is here that the basic incoherence underlying social practice will appear as contradiction, as we saw with the case of the slave-owning society above. Hegel's notion of historical development can only be properly stated if we understand social institutions in this way, as trans-individual action which also has an expressive dimension. By contrast, the causal view and its accompanying atomist outlook induces us to explain institutions in purely instrumental terms. And in these terms, Hegel's theory becomes completely unformulable. We cannot even begin to state what it is all about.[8]

---

[7] *Philosophy of Spirit* 140.

[8] I have developed this further in C. Taylor, 'Hegel's "Sittlichkeit" and the crisis of representative institutions', in Yirmiahu Yovel (ed.), *Philosophy of History and Action* (London and Jerusalem, 1978).

V

I have been arguing that we can understand Hegel against the background of a long-standing and very basic issue in modern philosophy about the nature of action. Hegel's philosophy of mind can be understood as firmly grounded on an option in favour of what I have been calling the qualitative view of action and against the causal view.

I have tried to follow the different ramifications of this qualitative view to show their importance to Hegel's thought. I looked first at the notion of agent's knowledge, and we saw that the system of philosophy itself can be seen as the integration of everything into a form of all-embracing agent's knowledge. I then followed another development of the qualitative view, which shows us action as primordially unreflecting bodily practice, which later can be transformed by the agent's achievement of reflective awareness. We saw that Hegel's conceptions of subjectivity and its development are rooted in this understanding. I then argued that the expressive revolution in the theory of meaning could be seen as an offshoot of this same view of action; and that Hegel is clearly operating within the expressive conception. Finally we can see that his theory of history supposes not just the expressive dimension but also the idea of irreducibly common actions, which only the qualitative view can allow.

One part of my case is thus that Hegel's philosophy of mind can be illuminated by making this issue explicit in all its ramifications. This is just in the way that we make any philosophy clearer by spelling out more fully some of its deepest assumptions. The illumination will be the greater the more fundamental and pervasive the assumptions in question are from the theory under study. Now my claim is that for Hegel the qualitative theory of action is very basic and all-pervasive, and the above pages have attempted to show this. Perhaps out of deference to Hegel's shade I should not use the word 'assumption', since for Hegel everything is ultimately demonstrated. But my claim stands that the thesis about action I have been describing here is quite central to his philosophy.

This is only one side of the gain that one can hope for in a study of this kind. The other, as I said at the outset, is that we should attain some greater understanding of the historical debate itself by situating Hegel in it. I think this is so as well, but I have not got space to argue it here.

What does emerge from the above is that Hegel is one of the important and seminal figures in the long and hard-fought emergence of a counter-theory to the long dominant epistemologically based view which the seventeenth century bequeathed to us. This can help explain why he has been an influential figure in this whole counter-movement. But what remains to be understood is why he has also often been ignored or rejected by major figures who have shared somewhat the same notions of action, starting with Schopenhauer but by no means ending there.

Perhaps what separates Hegel most obviously and most profoundly from those today who take the same side on the issue about action is their profoundly different reading of the same genetic view. For Heidegger, for example, the notion that action is first of all unreflected practice seems to rule out altogether as chimerical the goal of a fully explicit and self-authenticating understanding of what we are about. Disclosure is invariably accompanied by hiddenness; the explicit depends on the horizon of the implicit. The difference here is fundamental, but I believe that it too can be illuminated if we relate to it radically different readings of the qualitative view of action, which both espoused in opposition to the epistemological rationalism of the seventeenth century.

CHAPTER FOUR

THE CONCEPT OF A PERSON

I

In volume 2, chapters 3 and 4, I trace the conflict between two philosophies of social science. But the two underlying views do not just confront each other in social science. They also polarize the other sciences of man – psychology, for instance; and beyond that they inspire rival pictures of morality and human life. I want here to explore some of these deeper ramifications, by looking at two conceptions of what it is to be a person.

Where it is more than simply a synonym for 'human being', 'person' figures primarily in moral and legal discourse. A person is a being with a certain moral status, or a bearer of rights. But underlying the moral status, as its condition, are certain capacities. A person is a being who has a sense of self, has a notion of the future and the past, can hold values, make choices; in short, can adopt life-plans. At least, a person must be the kind of being who is in principle capable of all this, however damaged these capacities may be in practice.

Running through all this we can identify a necessary (but not sufficient) condition. A person must be a being with his own point of view on things. The life-plan, the choices, the sense of self must be attributable to him as in some sense their point of origin. A person is a being who can be addressed, and who can reply. Let us call a being of this kind a 'respondent'.

Any philosophical theory of the person must address the question of what it is to be a respondent. At the same time, it is clear that persons are a sub-class of agents. We do not accord personal status to animals, to whom we do, however, attribute actions in some sense. This poses a second question which any theory must answer: what is special about agents who are also persons?

With these questions in mind, I want to present, partly in summary, partly in reconstruction, two views of what it is to be a person, which I believe underpin a host of different positions and attitudes evident in modern culture. And clearly, our (perhaps implicit) notion of what it is to be a person will be determining for two *orders* of question: scientific ones – how are we to explain human behaviour? – and practical-moral ones – what is a good/decent/acceptable form of life?

The first view is rooted in the seventeenth-century, epistemologically grounded notion of the subject. A person is a being with consciousness, where consciousness is seen as a power to frame representations of things. Persons have consciousness, and alone possess it, or at least they have it in a manner and to a degree that animals do not. This answers the second question. But it also answers the first, the question of what makes a respondent. What makes it possible to attribute a point of view to persons is that they have a representation of things. They have the wherewithal to reply when addressed, because they respond out of their own representation of the world and their situation.

What this view takes as relatively unproblematic is the nature of agency. The important boundary is that between persons and other agents, the one marked by consciousness. The boundary between agents and mere things is not recognized as important at all, and is not seen as reflecting a qualitative distinction. This was so at the very beginning, where Descartes saw animals as complex machines; and it continues to be so today, where proponents of this first view tend to assume that some reductive account of living beings will be forthcoming. What marks out agents from other things tends to be identified by a performance criterion: animals somehow maintain and reproduce themselves through a wide variety of circumstances. They show highly complex adaptive behaviour. But understanding them in terms of performance allows for no distinction of nature between animals and machines which we have latterly designed to exhibit similarly complex adaptive behaviour.

We see this, for instance, with proponents of computer-based models of intelligence. They see no problem in offering these as explanations of animal performance. They only admit to puzzlement when it comes to relating consciousness to performance. We are conscious, but the machines which simulate our intelligent behaviour are not. But perhaps some day they might be? Speculation here is ragged and confused, the symptom of a big intellectual puzzle. By contrast, the reductive view of agency is subscribed to with serene confidence.

The second view I want to explore here does, by contrast, focus on the nature of agency. What is crucial about agents is that things matter to them. We thus cannot simply identify agents by a performance criterion, nor assimilate animals to machines.

To say things matter to agents is to say that we can attribute purposes, desires, aversions to them in a strong, original sense. There is, of course, a sense in which we can attribute purposes to a machine, and thus apply action terms to it. We say of a computing machine that it is, for example, 'calculating the payroll'. But that is because it plays this purpose in our lives. It was designed by us, and is being used by us to do this. Outside of this designer's or user's context, the attribution could not be made. What identifies the action is what I want to call here a derivative purpose. The purpose is, in other words, user-relative. If tomorrow someone else makes it run through exactly the same programme, but with the goal of calculating *pi* to the *n*th place, then *that* will be what the machine is 'doing'.

By contrast, animals and human beings are subjects of original purpose. That the cat is stalking the bird is not a derivative, or observer-relative fact about it. Nor is it a derivative fact about me that I am trying to explain two doctrines of the person.

Now one of the crucial issues dividing the first and second concepts of the person is what to make of this difference between original and derived purpose. If you take it seriously, then you can no longer accept a performance criterion for agency, because some agent's performances can be matched derivatively on machines. For the first view, the difference has to be relegated to the status of mere appearance. Some things (animals, ourselves) look to us to have purposes in a stronger, more original sense than mere machines.

But the second view does take it seriously, and hence sees the agent/thing boundary as being an important and problematic one. And it offers therefore a different answer to the question, what makes a respondent? This is no longer seen in terms of consciousness, but rather in terms of mattering itself. An agent can be a respondent, because things matter to it in an original way. What it responds out of is the original significance of things for it.

But then we have a very different conception from the first. The answers to the two questions are related in a very different way. The basic condition for being a respondent, that one have an original point of view, is something all agents fulfil. Something else needs to be said in answer to the question, what distinguishes persons from other agents?

And the answer to neither question can be given just in terms of a notion of consciousness as the power to frame representations. The answer to the respondent question clearly can not be given in these terms, because agents who have nothing like consciousness in the human sense have original purposes. Consciousness in the characteristically human form can be seen as what we attain when we come to formulate the significance of things for us. We then have an articulate view of our self and world. But things matter to us prior to this formulation. So original purpose can not be confused with consciousness.

Nor does the notion of consciousness as representation help to understand the difference between persons and animals, for two related reasons which it is worth exploring at some length.

The first is that built into the notion of representation in this view is the idea that representations are of independent objects. I frame a representation of something which is there independently of my depicting it, and which stands as a standard for this depiction. But when we look at a certain range of formulations which are crucial to human consciousness, the articulation of our human feelings, we can see that this does not hold. Formulating how we feel, or coming to adopt a new formulation, can frequently change how we feel. When I come to see that my feeling of guilt was false, or my feeling of love self-deluded, the emotions themselves are different. The one I now experience as a compulsive malaise rather than a genuine recognition of wrong-doing, the other as a mere infatuation rather than a genuine bent of my life. It is rare that the emotion we experience can survive unchanged such a radical shift in interpretation.

We can understand this, if we examine more closely the range of human feelings like pride, shame, guilt, sense of worth, love, and so on. When we try to state what is particular to each one of these feelings, we find we can only do so if we describe the situation in which we feel them, and what we are inclined to do in it. Shame is what we feel in a situation of humiliating exposure, and we want to hide ourselves from this; fear what we feel in a situation of danger, and we want to escape it; guilt when we are aware of transgression; and so on.

One could say that there is a judgement integral to each one of these emotions: 'this is shameful' for shame; 'there is danger' for fear, and so on. Not that to feel the emotion is to assent to the judgement. We can feel the emotion irrationally; and sometimes see that the judgement holds dispassionately. It is rather that feeling the emotion in question just is being struck by, or moved by, the state of affairs the judgement describes. We can sometimes make the judgement without being moved (the case of dispassionate observation); or we can feel very moved to assent to the judgement, but see rationally that it does not hold (irrational emotion). But the inner connection of feeling and judgement is attested in the fact that we speak here of 'irrational' emotion; and that we define and distinguish the feelings by the type of situation.

It follows from this that I can describe my emotions by describing my situation, and very often must do so really to give the flavour of what I feel. But then I alter the description of my emotions in altering the description I accept of my situation. But to alter my situation-description will be to alter my feelings, if I am moved by my newly perceived predicament. And even if I am not, the old emotion will now seem to me irrational, which itself constitutes a change in what I experience. So we can understand why, in this domain, our formulations about ourselves can alter what they are about.

We could say that for these emotions, our understanding of them or the interpretations we accept are constitutive of the emotion. The understanding helps shape the emotion. And that is why the latter cannot be considered a fully independent object, and the traditional theory of consciousness as representation does not apply here.

This might be understandable on the traditional theory if our formulations were not representative at all, that is, if there were no question of right and wrong here. It might be that thinking simply made it so, that how we sincerely describe our feelings just is how we feel, and that there is no point in distinguishing between the two. We might think that there are some domains of feeling where this is so. For instance, if on sincere introspection I come up with the verdict that I like blueberries, there is no further room here for talk of error or delusion.

But this is emphatically not the case with the emotions I described above. Here we can and do delude ourselves, or imperfectly understand ourselves, and struggle for a better formulation. The peculiarity of these emotions is that it is at one and the same time the case that our formulations are constitutive of the emotion, *and* that these formulations can be right or wrong. Thus they do in a sense offer representations, but not of an independent object. This is what makes the representative theory of consciousness inapplicable in this domain.

And so consciousness in this traditional sense does not seem to be the conception we need to capture the distinction between persons and other agents. The consciousness of persons, wherein they formulate their emotions, seems to be of another sort.

The second reason why representative consciousness cannot fill the bill here also comes to mind if we consider this range of human emotions. As long as we think of agents as the subjects of strategic action, then we might be inclined to think that the superiority of persons over animals lies in their ability to envisage a longer time scale, to understand more complex cause–effect relationships, and thus engage in calculations, and the like. These are all capacities to which the power to frame representations is essential. If we think merely in this strategic dimension, then we will tend to think that this representative power is the key to our evolution from animal to man.

But if we adopt the second view, and understand an agent essentially as a subject of significance, then what will appear evident is that there are matters of significance for human beings which are peculiarly human, and have no analogue with animals. These are just the ones I mentioned earlier, matters of pride, shame, moral goodness, evil, dignity, the sense of worth, the various human forms of love, and so on. If we look at goals like survival and reproduction, we can perhaps convince ourselves that the difference between men and animals lies in a strategic superiority of the former: we can pursue the same ends much more effectively than our dumb cousins. But when we consider these human emotions, we can see that the ends which make up a human life are *sui generis*. And then even the ends of survival and reproduction will appear in a new light. What it is to maintain and hand on a human form of life, that is, a given culture, is also a peculiarly human affair.

These human matters are also connected with consciousness in some sense. One could indeed argue that no agent could be sensitive to them who was not capable of formulating them, or at least of giving expression to them; and hence that the kind of consciousness which language brings is essential to them. We can perhaps see this if we take one example from the above list, being a moral agent. To be a moral agent is to be sensitive to certain standards. But 'sensitive' here must have a strong sense: not just that one's behaviour follow a certain standard, but also that one in some sense recognize or acknowledge the standard.

Animals can follow standards in the weaker sense. My cat will not eat fishmeal below a certain quality. With knowledge of the standard I can predict his behaviour. But there need be no recognition here that he is following a standard. This kind of thing, however, would not be sufficient to attribute moral action to an agent. We could imagine some animal who was systematically beneficent in his behaviour; what he did always redounded to the good of man and beast. We still would not think of him as a moral agent, unless there were some recognition on his part that in acting this way he was following a higher standard. Morality requires some recognition that there are higher demands on one, and hence the recognition of some distinction between kinds of goal. This has nothing to do with the Kantian diremption between duty and inclination. Even the holy will, which gladly does the good, must have some sense that this is the good, and as such worthy to be done.

Moral agency, in other words, requires some kind of reflexive awareness of the standards one is living by (or failing to live by). And something analogous is true of the other human concerns I mentioned. And so some kind of consciousness is essential to them. I think we can say that being a linguistic animal is essential to one's having these concerns; because it is impossible to see how one could make a distinction like the one above, between, for example, things one just wants to do, and things that are worthy to be done, unless one was able to mark the distinction in some way: either by formulation in language, or at least by some expressive ceremonial which would acknowledge the higher demands.

And so when we ask what distinguishes persons from other agents, consciousness in some sense is unquestionably part of the answer. But not consciousness understood as just representation. That can help explain some of the differences; for instance, the great superiority of man as strategic agent. But when we come to the peculiarly human concerns, the consciousness they presuppose cannot be understood just as the power to frame representations of independent objects. Consciousness – perhaps we might better here say language – is as it were the medium within which they first arise as concerns for us. The medium here is in some way inseparable from the content; which is why as we saw above our self-understanding in this domain is constitutive of what we feel.

We should try to gather the threads together, and show how the two conceptions square off against each other. They both start off with our ordinary notion of a person, defined by certain capacities: a person is an agent who has a sense of self, of his/her own life, who can evaluate it, and make choices about it. This is the basis of the respect we owe persons. Even those who through some accident or misfortune are deprived of the ability to exercise these capacities are still understood as belonging to the species defined by this potentiality. The central importance of all this for our moral thinking is reflected in the fact that these capacities form an important part of what we should respect and nourish in human beings. To make someone less capable of understanding himself, evaluating and choosing is to deny totally the injunction that we should respect him as a person.

What we have in effect are two readings of what these capacities consist of. The first takes agency as unproblematic. An agent is a being who acts, hence who has certain goals and endeavours to fulfil them. But this range of features is identified by a performance criterion, so that no difference of principle is admitted between animals and, say, complex machines, which also adaptively react to their surroundings so as to attain certain ends (albeit in a derivative way).

Along with agency, its ends too are seen as unproblematic. What is striking about persons, therefore, is their ability to conceive different possibilities, to calculate how to get them, to choose between them, and thus to plan their lives. The striking superiority of man is in strategic power. The various capacities definitive of a person are understood in terms of this power to plan. Central to this is the power to represent things clearly. We can plan well when we can lay out the possibilities clearly, when we can calculate their value to us in terms of our goals, as well as the probabilities and cost of their attainment. Our choices can then be clear and conscious.

On this view, what is essential to the peculiarly human powers of evaluating and choosing is the clarity and complexity of the computation. Evaluation is assessment in the light of our goals, which are seen ultimately as given, or perhaps as given for one part, and for the rest as arbitrarily chosen. But in either case the evaluation process takes the goal as fixed. 'Reason is and ought to be, the slave of the passions.' Choice is properly choice in the light of clear evaluation. To the human capacities thus conceived, the power of clear and distinct representation is obviously central.

So on one view, what makes an agent a person, a fully human respondent, is this power to plan. My interlocutor replies to me out of his power to make a life-plan and act on it. This is what I have to respect.

By contrast, the other view starts off quite differently. It raises the question of agency, and understands agents as in principle distinct from other things. Agents are beings for whom things matter, who are subjects of significance. This is what gives them a point of view on the world. But what distinguishes persons from other agents is not strategic power, that is, the capacity to deal with the same matter of concern more effectively. Once one focusses on the significance of things for agents, then what springs to view is that persons have qualitatively different concerns.

In other terms, once one raises the question of agency, then that of the ends of agents comes into view. And what is clear is that there are some peculiarly human ends. Hence the important difference between men and animals cannot simply consist in strategic power; it is also a matter of our recognizing certain goals. Consciousness is indeed essential to us. But this cannot be understood simply as the power to frame representations, but also as what enables us to be open to these human concerns. Our consciousness is somehow constitutive of these matters of significance, and does not just enable us to depict them.

This supports a quite different reading of the essentially personal capacities. The essence of evaluation no longer consists in assessment in the light of fixed goals, but also and even more in the sensitivity to certain standards, those involved in the peculiarly human goals. The sense of self is the sense of where one stands in relation to these standards, and properly personal choice is one informed by these standards. The centre of gravity thus shifts in our interpretation of the personal capacities. The centre is no longer the power to plan, but rather the openness to certain matters of significance. This is now what is essential to personal agency.

II

Naturally these conceptions ramify into very different views in both the sciences of man and the practical deliberations of how we ought to live. These are the two orders of questions I mentioned at the outset: how are we to explain human behaviour? and, what is a good life? We can for the sake of simplicity consider different doctrines in science and morals as consequences of these two underlying conceptions. But of course the motivation for our holding one or the other is more complex. We may be led to adopt one, because it relates to a certain approach to science, or goes with a certain style of moral deliberation, rather than adopting the approach or the style, because they are consequences of an already established core conception of the person.

In fact the order of motivation is mixed and varies from person to person. One can adopt a given core conception because its scientific ramifications strike him as valid, but only reluctantly accept what it entails about moral deliberation. Here it may rub against the grain of his intuitions, but because it seems true for what appear unanswerable reasons, he has no option but to endorse it. For another, it may be the moral consequences which make it plausible, and the scientific ones may be a matter of indifference. In fact, in talking about ramifications, I am also talking about possible motivations, although they may also be reluctant consequences of someone's vision of things.

In the remainder of my remarks, I would like to discuss the ramifications of these two conceptions, accounting for them for the sake of simplicity as motivations. I hope that this will make my rather abstract sketches somewhat fuller and more life-like, and that you might see these core conceptions actually at work in modern culture.

First, in the scientific domain. I am of course not neutral between them; and so the question that strikes me here is, what makes the first – let us call it the representation conception – so popular in our culture? I think an important part of the answer can be found in the prestige of the natural science model, which I discuss – and argue against – elsewhere.[1] Perhaps one of the key theses of the seventeenth-century revolution which inaugurates modern natural sciences is the eschewing of what one could call anthropocentric properties. Anthropocentric properties of things, but which they only have in so far as they are objects of experience. This was crucially at stake in the seventeenth-century distinction between primary and secondary properties. Secondary properties, like colour and felt heat, only applied to things in so far as they were being experienced. In a world without experiencing subjects, such properties could no longer be sensefully attributed to objects. They were therefore understood as merely subjective, as relative to us, not as absolute properties of things.

It was an important step in the development of modern natural science when these properties were distinguished and set aside. This distinction was a polemical instrumental in the struggle against the older conceptions of the universe as meaningful order. Such hypotheses, which explained features of the world in terms of their 'correspondences' against a background order of ideas, were condemned as mere projections. They concerned purely the significance of things for us, not the way things were.

This eschewal of anthropocentric properties was undoubtedly one of the bases of the spectacular progress of natural science in the last three centuries. And ever since, therefore, the idea has seemed attractive of somehow adapting this move to the sciences of man. We can see here, I think, one of the sources of that basic feature of the representation conception, its assimilating agency to things; or, otherwise put, its understanding agency by a performance criterion.

We are motivated to distinguish animals from machines which imitate their adaptive performance only if we take significance seriously, the fact that things matter to animals in an original way. But the significance of things is paradigmatically a range of anthropocentric properties (or in the case of other animals, properties which are relative to them; in any case, not absolute). So it can easily appear that a scientific approach to

---

[1] See volume 2, chapters 3 and 4.

behaviour which incorporates this important founding step of natural science would be one which gave no weight to significance.

Of course, we can admit that the distinction is in some way important for us. Things feel different inside to a human being, and to an animal; and there probably is nothing comparable in a machine. But all this has to do with the way things appear. It thus has no weight when we come to identifying the explanatory factors of a science of behaviour. Just as, analogously, we can admit that it really does appear that the sun goes below the horizon, but this must just be ignored when we want to establish a scientific theory of the movement of earth and the heavenly bodies.

Now if we follow out what is involved in a significance-free account, we shall come across themes that tend to recur in the modern sciences of man. We can see this if we return to my discussion above of our emotions, where I said that they incorporate in a sense a view of our situation. To experience an emotion is to be in a sense struck or moved by our situation being of a certain nature. Hence, I said, we can describe our emotions by describing our situation.

But this is only so because we describe our situation in its significance for us. We can usually understand how someone feels when he describes his predicament, because we normally share the same sense of significance. So someone says: 'imagine what I felt when he walked in just then and saw me'; and we can quite easily do so, because we share just this sense of embarrassment. Of course, it is a commonplace that between different cultures the sense of significance can vary, and then we can be quite baffled. Nothing comes across of how people feel from the simple narrative of events, or only something confused and perplexing.

So situation-description is only self-description because the situation is grasped in its significance. And in fact, we have a host of terms which operate in tandem with our emotion terms and which designate different significances a situation can have; such as, 'humiliating', 'exciting', 'dismaying', 'exhilarating', 'intriguing', 'fascinating', 'frightening', 'provoking', 'awe-inspiring', 'joyful', and so on. We can often describe our predicament with one of these, or alternatively we can give a sense of it by saying what it inclines us to do. Certain standard emotion terms are linked, as we saw, to standard situation-descriptions, as well as responses we are inclined to make. So fear is experienced at something dangerous, and inclines us to flee; shame at what is shameful or humiliating, and inclines us to do away with this, or at least to hide it; and so on.

Now our ordinary description/explanation of action in terms of our emotions and other motives is based on our sense of significance. That is, it either invokes this directly by using terms like the above, or it assumes it as the background which makes predicament descriptions intelligible as accounts of what we feel or want to do. The actions we are inclined to take are identified by their purposes, and frequently these are only intelligible against the background of significance. For instance, we understand the inclination to hide what is humiliating, only through understanding the humiliating. Someone who had no grasp of a culture's sense of shame would never know what constituted a successful case of hiding, or cover-up. We would not be able to explain to him even what people are inclined to do in humiliating predicaments in this culture, let alone why they want to do it.

What would it mean then to set about designing a significance-free account? Plainly what would remain basic is that people respond to certain situations, and perhaps also that they respond by trying to encompass certain ends. But if we had an account which really eschewed anthropocentric properties, and thus which did not have to draw on our background sense of significance for its intelligibility, it would characterize situation and end in absolute terms. In one way this might seem relatively easy. Any situation bears a great number, an indefinite number of descriptions. The predicament that I find humiliating is also one that can be described in a host of other ways, including some which make no reference to any significance at all. But of course the claim involved in this redescription would be that none of the important explanatory factors are lost from sight. It is that the explanatory relationship between situation and response can be captured in an absolute description; or that, in other words, the features picked out in the significance description are not essential to the explanation, but just concern the way things appear to us in ordinary life.

This kind of ambition has underlain various influential schools in academic psychology. At its most reductive, where there was a suspicion even of goal-seeking behaviour, as somehow tinged with anthropocentrism, we had behaviourism. Everything was to be explained in terms of responses to stimuli. But these were to be characterized in the most rigorously significance-free terms, as 'colourless movement and mere receptor impulse' in Hull's phrase. This school has passed its prime; the development of computing machines has shown how goal-behaviour can be accounted for in mechanistic terms, and so strategic action can now be allowed into the account. But the goal is to account for animate strategic action in the same terms as we explain the analogous behaviour of machines. And since for the latter case it is clear that the goal states have to be describable in absolute terms, this must also be true of the former, if the account is to succeed.

It seems to me then that this ambition to follow natural science, and avoid anthropocentric properties, has been an important motivation of the representation view. It gives us an important reason to ignore significance, and to accept a performance criterion for agency, where what matters is the encompassing of certain, absolutely identified ends. But the drive for absolute (i.e., non-anthropocentric) explanation can be seen not only in psychology. It is also at the origin of a reductive bent in social science. To see the connection here, we will have to follow the argument a little farther, and appreciate the limitations on this transposition into absolute terms.

These are evident when we return to what I called above the peculiarly human motivations, like shame, guilt, a sense of morality, and so on. Finding absolute descriptions which nevertheless capture the explanatory relevance of situation and goal is in principle impossible in this domain.

To see this, let us contrast one of these motives, shame, with one where the absolute transposition seems possible, say, physical fear. This latter is fear of physical danger, danger to life or limb. Now the significance of the situation here can perhaps be spelled out in medical terms: something in my predicament threatens to end my life in some particular way – say, I am likely to fall, and the impact would be lethal. Here we have a sense that we could describe the impending outcome in physiological terms, terms that made no reference to its importance to me, as we might describe the death of a sparrow, or any other process in nature.

And so we might think of a disengaged, absolute account that might be offered by my behaviour; where we would be told that this fall, and the resulting physiological changes occurring on impact, constituted a counter-goal for me; something I strove to avoid. And my behaviour could be explained strategically on this basis. Here we have an account of behaviour which we could imagine being matched on a machine. This too might become irreparably damaged on impact. And so we might design a machine to compute the likelihood of certain possible modes of destruction possible in its environment, and to take evasive action. What would be left out of account, of course, would be the subjective experience of the fear. This would survive in the account only as a direction of behaviour, a bent to avoidance. It would be a mere 'con-attitude' towards falling, and quite colourless. That is, the specific experienced difference between avoiding something out of fear, and avoiding it out of distaste, would fall away. This would be part of the subjective 'feel' of the lived experience which would be left outside the account. But we might nevertheless understand the claim here that all the really explanatory factors had been captured. We can presumably predict the behaviour of both machine and person, granted a knowledge of the situation described absolutely. What more could one want?

In fact, one might ask a lot more. But I do not want to argue this here. Let me concede the seeming success of the absolute transposition for this case of physical danger, in order to be able to show how impossible it is for shame. The corresponding task in this latter case would be to give an absolute account of a situation which was humiliating or shameful. This would be the analogue to the absolute description of danger above.

But this we cannot do. The reason lies in the reflexive nature of these motives, which I noted above. I can give sufficient conditions of a situation's being dangerous in absolute terms, because there are no necessary conditions concerning its significance. The fall will be lethal, however I or mankind in general regard it. This is a hard, culture-resistant fact. But a situation is not humiliating independent of all significance conditions. For a situation to be humiliating or shameful, the agent has to be of the kind who is in principle sensitive to shame.

This can perhaps become clearer if we reflect that shame involves some notion of standards. To feel shame is to sense that I fail on some standard. We can only get an adequate account of the shameful, if we can get clear on these standards. But built into the essence of these standards is that they are those of a being who is potentially sensitive to them. The subject of shame must be one who can be motivated by shame. It might appear that in certain cultures a sufficient condition of the shameful could be given in purely objective terms. For instance, defeat in battle might be shameful for the warrior. But what is forgotten here is that defeat is only shameful for the warrior, because he ought to have been so powerfully moved by the love of glory to have conquered, or at least to have died in the attempt. And the trudge back in the dust in chains is only humiliating because he is – or ought to be – a being who glories in power, in strutting over the earth as master.

We can see the essential place of significance conditions here when we note that shamelessness is shameful. In other words, there are conditions of motivation for avoiding shame, viz., that one be sensitive to shame. The one who does not care, who runs away without a scruple, earns the deepest contempt.

It is these significance conditions that make it the case that we cannot attribute shame to animals, let alone to machines. And this makes the contrast with danger. Just because this can be defined absolutely, we have no difficulty in envisaging animals as standing in danger in exactly the same sense as we can; and the extension to machines does not seem a very great step.

We can thus distinguish between motives which *seem* potentially capable of a significance-free account, and those which definitely are not. I emphasize 'seem' because, even for these, I have doubts on other grounds which I have no time to go into here. But they contrast with the peculiarly human in that these plainly are irreducible. These are the ones where the significance itself is such that we cannot explain it without taking into account that it is significant for us. These are the ones, therefore, where the variations occur between human cultures, that is, between different ways of shaping and interpreting that significance. So that what is a matter of shame, of guilt, of dignity, of moral goodness, is notoriously different and often hard to understand from culture to culture; whereas the conditions of medical health are far more uniform. (But not totally, which is part of my reason for doubt above, and my unwillingness to concede even the case of physical danger to a reductive account.)

This distinction underlies the reductive bent we see in much modern social science, towards accounts of human behaviour and society which are grounded in goals of the first type. The contemporary fad for sociobiology provides a good example. To explain human practices and values in terms of the goals of survival and reproduction is to account for things ultimately by explanatory factors which can be described in absolute terms. Survival, reproduction; these are conditions that can be predicated of animals as well, and could be extended analogously to machines, for that matter. The enterprise of giving a reductive account of culture in terms of these ends can thus appear as an answer to the demands of science, whereas anti-reductionist objections seem counsels of obscurity, or of despair of the scientific cause. The old requirement, that we eschew anthropocentric properties, is here working its way out, via the absolute transposition. The fact that it leads us into a blind alley in social science ought to make us reflect on the validity of this basic requirement, and hence of the natural science model. But that is a point I have sufficiently argued above.

But an absolute account would be a culture-free one, for reasons I have just touched on. It is the peculiarly human motivations which are reflexively constituted by our interpretations and therefore are deeply embedded in culture. The search for a 'materialist' account, as I interpret it here, is the search for an explanation in terms of ends which can be absolutely described. But this would not only meet the demands of 'science', it would at a stroke cut through the intractable difficulties of comparative social science. It would give us a truly neutral standpoint, from which we could survey all cultures without ethnocentricity. We have seen above that this is an illusion, but we can also appreciate how powerful an attraction it exercises in modern culture.

III

In the remaining pages, I would like to make a few remarks about the ramifications of the two conceptions of a person for our views about moral deliberation. Here too, the first conception has its attractions. If we understand ourselves in terms of certain absolutely defined ends, then the proper form of deliberation is strategic thinking. And this conception sees the superiority of man over animal as lying in greater strategic capacity. Reason is and ought to be primarily instrumental.

The pattern is familiar enough, but its attractions are insufficiently understood. There is, of course, the sense of control. The subject according to the significance perspective is in a world of meanings that he imperfectly understands. His task is to interpret it better, in order to know who he is and what he ought to seek. But the subject according to the representation view already understands his ends. His world is one of potential means, which he understands with a view to control. He is in a crucial sense disengaged. To understand things in the absolute perspective is to understand them in abstraction from their significance for you. To be able to look on everything, world and society, in this perspective would be to neutralize its significance, and this would be a kind of freedom – the freedom of the self-defining subject, who determines his own purposes, or finds them in his own natural desires.

Now I believe that the attractions of this freedom come from more than the sense of control that accompanies submitting nature and society to instrumental reason. They are also of spiritual origin, in a sense which is understandable from our Western religious tradition. In both its Greek and Christian roots (albeit a deviation in this latter stream), this has included an aspiration to rise above the merely human, to step outside the prison of the peculiarly human emotions, and to be free of the cares and the demands they make on us. This is of course an aspiration which also has analogous forms in Indian culture, and perhaps, indeed, in all human cultures.

My claim is that the ideal of the modern free subject, capable of objectifying the world, and reasoning about it in a detached, instrumental way, is a novel variant of this very old aspiration to spiritual freedom. I want to say, that is, that the motive force that draws us to it is closely akin to the traditional drive to spiritual purity. This is, of course, highly paradoxical, since the modern ideal understands itself as naturalistic, and thus as quite antithetical to any religious outlook. But I believe that in this it is self-deluded. This is one place where Nietzsche had more insight than most modern philosophers; he saw the connection between the modern scientific ideal of austere truth and the spiritual traditions of self-denial that come to us from the ancients. From this point of view, it is not surprising to see a modern naturalist like Hobbes denouncing vainglory with the vigour of an ancient moralist.

The analogy is that, in both cases, we have a place to stand outside the context of human emotions in order to determine what is truly important. In one case, that of the tradition, this is seen as a larger order which is the locus of more than human significance; in the modern case, it is an order of nature which is meant to be understood free of any significance at all, merely naturalistically. And this is by no means a minor difference. That is not my claim. Rather it is that beyond this difference, something of the same aspiration is evident in both. And this is linked with my belief that the aspiration to spiritual freedom, to something more than the merely human, is much too fundamental a part of human life ever to be simply set aside. It goes on, only under different forms – and even in forms where it is essential that it does not appear as such; this is the paradox of modernity.

But whatever the motive, this first conception of the person grounds a certain view about moral deliberation. Our ends are seen as set by nature, and thus discoverable by objective scrutiny, or else as autonomously chosen; but in either case, as beyond the ambiguous field of interpretation of the peculiarly human significances. In the light of these ends, reason is and ought to be instrumental. Utilitarianism is a product of this modern conception, with its stress on instrumental reasoning, on calculation, and on a naturalistically identified end, happiness (or on a neutral, interpretation-free account of human choice, in terms of preferences). The stress on freedom emerges in its rejection of paternalism. And in rationality it has a stern and austere ideal of disengaged, disciplined choice. This is by no means the only fruit of this modern conception, but it has been one of the most widespread and influential.

The alternative perspective, which I have called the significance view, has arisen in the last centuries as a reaction to the first. It objects to the first as a flight from the human, and sets up a completely different model of practical deliberation. Rather than side-stepping the peculiarly human emotions, and turning to instrumental reason, the main form this deliberation takes is a search for the true form of these emotions. Typical questions of this kind of thinking are of the form: what is really, that is, properly, shameful? What ought we to feel guilty about? In what does dignity consist? And so on.

This deliberation, of course, takes place in a modern context, one in which no larger order of more than human significance can be just assumed as an unargued context. And this gives it its tentative, exploratory nature. Those who hunger for certainty will only find it in the first perspective, where the ends of man are thought to be defined by a naturalistic science.

I believe that both these models of the person are current in modern Western culture, and that most people operate with a (perhaps inconsistent) combination of the two. It is on the level of theory that they are sorted out, and become exclusive alternatives. But this does not make them unimportant. Theoretical models with their inner coherence have a great impact on our thinking even where – perhaps especially where – they are not fully conscious or explicit. I have tried to demonstrate elsewhere something of the baleful effects of the natural science model in social science. Here I have been trying to dig deeper, into some of the sources of that model. I have been looking for these in a conception of the person, which is also the background of modern views about practical deliberation. I have tried to contrast this with an alternative conception, which I believe is its chief rival in modern Western culture.

Some of my reasoning here has been perhaps too tenuous to be fully convincing. But I believe that a deeper examination must show that the struggle between rival approaches in the science of man, that we have been looking at here, is no mere question of the relative efficacy of different methodologies, but is rather one facet of a clash of moral and spiritual outlooks. And I believe that we can only make even the first halting steps towards resolving it if we can give explicit recognition to this fact.

PART II

PHILOSOPHY OF PSYCHOLOGY
AND MIND

CHAPTER FIVE

PEACEFUL COEXISTENCE
IN PSYCHOLOGY

I

Psychology is a vast and ramified discipline. It contains many mansions. But this does not prevent it from being intellectually divided against itself. I would like to discuss in particular one major division in psychology, and in so doing suggest a way of reconciling the two sides. Out of such reconciliation, there might come a new perspective on the discipline.

The deep division in the discipline which I would like to examine concerns basic notions about science and the methods of science. At bottom it is a difference of epistemology. The epistemology which is dominant among experimental psychologists in America is the one which emerged with the scientific revolution in the seventeenth century. There are many ways of characterizing this view of science, but for the purposes of this discussion we can single out two features, because they are the principal sticking points in any confrontation between the two epistemologies.

The first is the principle that science must be grounded in data that are intersubjectively univocal. This point is often put by saying that experiments must be replicable by anyone, and any results must be such that others can check them. Science achieves its impressive show of objectivity through intersubjective agreement. Now this puts a restriction on what can be counted as data of a science. There are many ranges of judgements we make in ordinary life which cannot come close to meeting this requirement of intersubjective univocity. For instance, the judgement I might make about a painting that it reflects a powerful harmony between certain elements, or the judgements we make every day about people's characters and motives – these and others notoriously do not lend themselves to intersubjective agreement, and, what is more important, they do not often lend themselves even to univocal consensus on the meaning of the key terms involved in them. Judgements of this kind cannot be the data statements of a science according to the model we are characterizing here. The phenomena they relate to would have to be identified in a quite different vocabulary in order to be studied scientifically.

This requirement, then, is for what one might call 'brute data' – to coin a term for it, that is, data which are available without any personal discernment or interpretation on the part of the observer.[1] For as long as such an element of discernment is present, there will be unarbitrable differences of judgement between observers. And this should on no account be allowed, according to our model of scientific procedure. Differences of theory will inevitably exist in any domain where the established data allow for more than one, and allegiance to different theories will repose on differences of judgement about plausibility, the importance of certain factors, and so on. But this theoretical Babel which any science may fall prey to must be held within certain bounds by the univocity of its data.

The companion requirement to the need for brute data is that the operations which are carried out on the input data must be similarly interpretation-free. Any science which is more than a list of correlations obtained by enumerative induction must contain a component which is not simply a record of data, but which purports to map in some way the processes or transformations which underlie regularities in observable data. Hypotheses in this domain are ultimately verified by observable data. But if this is to be so, then their links with these data must also be univocal. A proposition about underlying processes can only be intersubjectively verified if its implications for observable data are univocal. If these implications cannot be unambiguously settled, agreement is impossible.

This second requirement – let us call it 'univocal operations' – is what

---

[1] Of course, this characterization still needs a lot of refinement. Paradigmatic as brute data are states which are recognized by clear criteria and where the recourse to criteria can continue through indefinitely many stages. Certain physical states meet this condition; e.g., an object's being x metres long: there is no limit to the procedures we can go through to check the measurement, check our yardsticks, apparatus, etc., in order to meet any doubt and objections. Intuitive judgements can always be checked.

But we may also be led to admit as brute data statements certain judgements for which we can give no clear criteria but on which there is in fact no disagreement – e.g., judgements in chicken-sexing, or the data of certain experiments in cognitive psychology where subjects attribute a certain degree of density to sounds. (I owe this latter point to Susan Carey.) This shows the importance that intersubjective agreement plays in our notion of scientific objectivity.

For a further discussion of 'brute data' see my 'Interpretation and the sciences of man', *Review of Metaphysics*, 25:1 (Sept. 1971), pp. 3–51.

underlay a number of ill-starred formulations of the high days of positivism, such as 'operational definition'. But this requirement is not implicated in the confusions of extreme positivism. It does not call for any kind of reduction of 'theoretical entities' to 'observational' terms, but simply asks that the calculations and transformations carried out on the input data used to map the underlying processes be univocal. For instance, in a paradigm case for this model of science – say, mathematical physics – the operations are expressed in mathematics and hence are thought to be beyond dispute arising out of personal discernment or intuition.[2]

Now these two requirements have been viewed by many psychologists as entailing a third – that of 'physicalism'. This was not always the case; earlier attempts at a rigorous scientific psychology on this model were prepared to include mental states, and the deliverances of introspection among their data. But in American psychology, this approach was swept aside a half century ago by the behaviourist revolution. One may well ask whether introspection was really done away with, or whether it is not still with us in another guise – in, say, sensory threshold experiments and other experiments in cognitive psychology – but there is no doubt that the intent was to do away with it.

The attraction to physicalism on the part of those who accept the two prior requirements stems from more than the obvious consideration that a subject's introspective data are available only to him. Indeed, this is not in itself a very serious obstacle, since replication in introspective experiments can be interpreted to mean that others obtain similar introspective data under the same conditions, and this is how it was interpreted by those who carried on introspective psychology. The more important connection with physicalism lies in the fact that physical parameters can be more reliably identified as brute data. A dispute about a physical parameter can often be settled by observing the object's interactions with other things. Thus we can devise machines, like scales, thermometers, and so on, to increase the accuracy/certainty of our observations.

And so the mainstream of academic psychology in America, which took up the two requirements of the classical model of science, also took up physicalism – first in a behaviourist form; but when the star of behaviourism began to pale, other approaches with a richer theoretical component took over the allegiance to physicalism. Take, for example, the family of

---

[2] Of course, it is very much a debatable question whether mathematics is really interpretation-free in this sense. My point here is just that there is an influential tradition from the seventeenth century that regards it as a paradigm domain in which disputes are intersubjectively arbitrable, and hence as a central guarantee of scientific objectivity.

computer-inspired theories of mental function. These are based on the two classical requirements: brute input data, and a set of subsequent operations which are specified univocally enough so that they can be run as a program on a machine. Indeed, their expressibility in a machine program is the criterion of their univocity (as Minsky makes clear in his definition of an 'effective procedure').[3] The computer model thus also infers from the two classical requirements the necessity of physicalism.

II

This package of the two classical requirements plus physicalism runs up against an obvious objection in psychology – or indeed any science dealing with human emotion or action – which is that the phenomena of this domain, that is, acts and feelings, are partly characterized in terms of the thoughts, images, intentions, and ways of seeing of the people concerned. How do we identify an action as being of a given kind? By the purpose it aims to achieve. In many cases, of course, we read this purpose easily from the overt action, aided by our knowledge of the context. We see that someone is 'turning off the light' when we see him flip the switch, or 'reaching for a chocolate' when someone proffers the box. But even in these relatively unproblematic cases we can be led to change our mind if the agent tells us credibly that he had some quite different intention – that he wanted to align the switch with others on the wall because it looked better that way, or that he reached out to stop the box from falling. If we believe these explanations of purpose, we re-describe the actions. The purpose is therefore crucial here. And beyond these relatively transparent cases, there are all those where we have to understand the agent's vision of things in order to know what he is doing: is he trying to save face, or is he really expressing indignation? The answer to this takes us deep into the meanings that things have for him, deeper perhaps than he can consciously go or at least admit.

The same point can be made about feeling. What makes a feeling one of shame? That it is occasioned by a sense that something I am or have done or that belongs to me is dishonourable, demeaning, and something that I very much want to hide from others. The emotion is defined by the thoughts and perceptions of the subject individual, by the meanings things have for him.

But if this is so, then the data of psychology are of a peculiar kind, one

---

[3] Marvin Minsky, *Computation* (Englewood Cliffs, NJ, 1967), p. 105.

to which the first requirement of the classical model may not be applicable. This first requirement called for 'brute data', that is, data which were beyond dispute arising from personal interpretation or discernment. But if action and feeling are characterized partly by the way agent or subject sees the situation, then his personal interpretation can enter into the definition of the phenomenon under study. So, far from these being obstacles to the science of psychology, they are essential to the constitution of its objectives.

Thus to return to the example of shame above, we saw that the feeling is identified as such by its object being dishonourable in the eyes of the subject. But what is dishonourable to a man is very much a function of his personal interpretations. Of course, he is using a generally available concept, that of dishonour, or perhaps a more particular characterization of the dishonourable action, such as – let us say – 'cowardly'. And there may be widespread or even general agreement on the appropriateness of this description. But still this kind of judgement is similar to the judgement about the painting given above, in that if there is disagreement there are no criteria we can use to settle the dispute which are themselves beyond interpretive dispute. Agreement about dishonour, as about harmony in paintings, reposes on common discernment; once this is lost the only way to regain agreement is to recover the community of insight. There is no way we can reach agreement by finessing insight, as it were, through an appeal to brute data as criteria.

This is far from saying that there are no criteria in this area. If we disagree about harmony in a painting or about the dishonourable nature of an action, there is a lot we can still say to each other. We can point to the balance of strength and weakness in the painting, or depth and movement; we can point to the pusillanimity, or cowardice or pettiness, and so on, of an action. But in both these cases, the concepts we have recourse to – 'strength' or 'depth' in the painting, 'pusillanimity' or 'pettiness' in the action – themselves require the same discernment in their application. It is not that dishonour and harmony are without criteria; but rather that the criterial terms demand the same degree of insight. We cannot step outside the circle of interpretations. Thus an argument about harmony or dishonour is not won by pointing to irrecusable data; rather it comes to an end when one side communicates insight to the other, and hence they both come to use the terms in the same way, to 'speak the same language'. But one comes to grasp the language of the other the way we pick up our first language, not through unambiguous explanations, but through hearing it. Hearing the language brings to light what the language is about.

Action and feeling are thus partly defined by judgements and perceptions which are not brute data and cannot be reduced to judgements about brute data. If one takes one's cue from this, then the classical model of science will be seen as inapplicable to the sciences of man. Rather one will opt for a type of science which is partly founded on interpretation – what has been called a 'hermeneutical' approach. This means that instead of trying to build a science grounded on brute data which can be seen as linked together through some underlying processes (or optionally, where these underlying processes can be set aside altogether, as in the extreme, caricatural behaviourism of B. F. Skinner), we strive to define correctly the interpretations of the agent, even those of which he is not aware, and relate these in terms of underlying mechanisms of a quite different sort.

A number of examples could be given of this kind of science of man. In fact, the dispute between the two epistemologies, the classical scientific and the hermeneutical, seems to crop up in all the disciplines which study human behaviour. So in political science, for instance, we have 'behaviouralism' versus an approach founded on political theory;[4] in sociology we have a theory like that of Max Weber versus an empiricist approach (although attempts have been made in American sociology to reduce the *verstehen* dimension of Weber's thought and thus recruit him for the opposite school). But in psychology, the most obvious case of a hermeneutical science is that of psychoanalysis and the various approaches which have descended from it, for example, the psycho-history of Erikson, certain personality theories, like that of Rogers, and so on.

This is not universally appreciated, since Freud himself was very much under the spell of the classical scientific epistemology. But in fact psychoanalysis is a science grounded on interpretation. It involves reading, from the patients' symptoms, lapses, associations and the like, what the meaning of his situation is for him, a meaning which he cannot himself disclose – rather, against whose disclosure he fights vigorously. Ricoeur has presented this understanding of psychoanalysis very convincingly in his *De l'Interprétation*.[5]

But it is easy to make a symmetrical mistake about psychoanalysis to that which aligns it with the classical model. This is the view which sees it as purely a science of interpretation, as only concerned with understanding, and not with the causal forces which shape behaviour and feeling. And this

4 For a discussion of the debate in this field, as well as further treatment of the characteristics of a hermeneutical science, see my 'Interpretation and the sciences of man'.
5 Paul Ricoeur, *De l'Interprétation* (Paris, 1965).

is wrong; the metaphors of force and distortion in Freud's vocabulary – 'repression', 'condensation', 'displacement', and so on – are to be taken seriously. The meanings which Freud is interested in reading are meanings which have suffered distortion, through having undergone great pressures, as it were. Psychoanalysis is not simply a hermeneutics, but one which is also bound up with a causal theory, as Ricoeur shows.

The fact that it is a causal theory which appeals to underlying forces does not mean that it can be aligned with the classical model. For the operation of these forces is traced not through brute data, but rather through the data of interpretation. The verbal slip reveals the repression and displacement not *qua* physical event, but in terms of its meaning. There is no way of finessing this level of interpretation and observing the forces outside its medium. That is why Freud's underlying force terms are not quantifiable.[6]

Epistemologically, this means that psychoanalysis cannot meet the requirements of the classical model because disputes within it cannot be settled by pointing to brute data. Instead disputes turn on the plausibility of rival interpretations, and the plausibility of an interpretation cannot be reduced to cut and dried criteria. On the contrary, it requires a certain discernment to appreciate it. Hence the grave dissatisfaction, not to say frustration, with psychoanalysis on the part of those who are wedded to the classical model – and there are many of these in academic psychology, to whom psychoanalysis seems almost scandalous when viewed as a putative science.

Let us take the oft-repeated complaint that concepts like 'resistance' enable Freudians to have it both ways: if one admits to an interpretation, this helps confirm it; but if one rejects it, this also may be viewed as confirmation, since the repressed interpretation is one that the patient resists, and indignant rejection is predictable in these circumstances; indeed, the more definite the rejection, the more likely the hypothesis. This seeming 'heads-I-win, tails-you-lose' predicament is thought to make psychoanalytical hypotheses irrefutable; and, by a well-known principle of classical science, what is irrefutable is also devoid of explanatory content.

But this objection appears strong only to those who have assumed beforehand the exclusive validity of the classical model. To start with, it cannot be the intention of those who hold this objection to claim that a

---

[6] Cf. a discussion of 'affective charge' by Judith Winter, 'The concept of energy in psycho-analytic theory', *Inquiry*, 14: 12 (1971), pp. 138–47.

phenomenon like resistance is impossible. This would be a bit of wholly gratuitous *a priori* legislation. But if resistance is a feature of human psychology, then there will be cases where rejection of an interpretation does not weaken it, but rather may help to confirm it. What one can legitimately ask of the analyst is that he be able to distinguish the case where an interpretation is rejected because it is false from that case where it is rejected because it is true and inadmissible to consciousness. Analysts claim to be able to do this (sometimes – but what more can you ask?) from other interpretations made in the analysis and from the manner of the rejection itself. For instance, is the rejection expressed with more than necessary vehemence, and/or with anxiety? So his judgement is not without criteria, nor his hypothesis irrefutable. Of course, the question then arises of how one determines what amount of vehemence is 'more than necessary', or whether there is anxiety. And here the answer is that although these judgements do not lack criteria, they do repose on discernment and cannot be reduced to brute data. Here we get to the nub of the problem. The psychoanalyst cannot avoid interpretation, nor can he ground his interpretations on brute data. He claims to be able to distinguish the two kinds of rejection, but not by brute criteria. But if one accepts no distinctions as scientifically valid except those founded on brute data, then this claim must appear bogus. Hence it appears perfectly arbitrary that some rejections are taken as confirmations, and the analyst appears to be playing a game he cannot lose. But all this is based on the epistemological premise that science requires brute data, that the classical model is the only one allowable. As an attempt to prove the non-scientific nature of psychoanalysis, it therefore fails because it assumes what it intends to prove.

My intention in citing this objection was not to enter this polemic, but just to show that here, too, the key issue comes down to that between two epistemologies, two models of science, one of brute data versus one which admits of interpretation. The same basic issue crops up in other disputes related to psychoanalysis, such as the attempts that have been made to establish a cure rate for psychoanalytic treatment. This raises the necessity of establishing what will count as a cure, and there are no interpretation-free criteria for a psychological 'cure'.

III

So two rival epistemologies confront each other in psychology, as in other sciences of man, in a sort of dialogue of the deaf. The protagonists of one view – let us call them the correlators – argue that the classical model alone offers the kind of intersubjective certainty that deserves the name of science. It does not rely on a form of intuition which can lead to unarbitrable disputes, and all results are fully replicable. To which their adversaries – let us call them the interpreters – reply: Don't blame us, we didn't make the world, and it's not our fault if it contains phenomena which are arguable and thus require interpretation. The point about science is to strive for the degree of certainty of which the domain under study is capable, not to apply an inappropriate model just because such a model would give more satisfactory results *if* it applied. (At this point the interpreters will tell you the anecdote about the drunk looking for his keys under the lamp-post – which is too familiar to bear repetition here.)

But the correlators are not satisfied with this. They stick to their view that only sciences after the classical model deserve the name. They generally believe that human behaviour characterized as action and feeling cannot be treated according to this model, and their response is to seek other levels of description on which to treat human behaviour. The levels chosen have usually been physicalistic in one way or another. The best known such attempt was classical behaviourism, which strove to account for behaviour by correlating stimulus input and movement. With the decline of faith in behaviourism, various theories have been developed which make appeal to central processes linking input and output, including theories modelled on computer programs. But input and output are still identified physicalistically, and the central processes are thought to be ultimately identifiable with operations in the brain and central nervous system. These 'centralist' theories ultimately converge with a third approach which is trying to develop a thoroughgoing neuro-physiological account of behaviour.

Now all these approaches have run into trouble. This form of behaviourism could not cope with the purposeful, intelligent behaviour even of rats, let alone men. When I say 'could not cope', I mean this: that it could not match the regularities of behaviour characterized in terms of purpose and cognition with descriptions of environment and behaviour characterized as stimulus and response. Faced with some of the insightful and innovative behaviour of some mammals in learning situations, behaviourists turned more and more to *ad hoc* hypotheses (such as Hull's 'fractional anticipatory goal responses', or the various 'secondary drives'), which became increasingly difficult to give a clear empirical meaning to, and this indeterminacy of empirical meaning began to invade the key terms of the theory as well. Ritchie makes this point in connection with 'reinforcement' in the S-R treatment of latent learning.[7] Chomsky makes a similar case in his review of Skinner's *Verbal Behaviour*,[8] pointing out the circularity involved in Skinner's use of 'response'.

The key concepts of behaviourism were thus stretched and enlarged to a point of near-vacuity in the attempt to cope with refractory phenomena. And, inevitably, these terms began to incorporate surreptitiously the dimensions of purpose and cognition they were meant to exclude. Thus the 'response' which was meant to be identified *qua* 'colourless movement' – and there would be little point in launching on the behaviourist enterprise if it were not – in fact was almost invariably classified in terms of the end-goal of the action concerned. The unit studied was, for example, 'pressing the bar', where this could be accomplished with left paw, right paw, or teeth. If this discrepancy was noticed at all, it was dismissed with the breezy assurance that any correlation linking such an action category could be further reduced to correlations linking the component movement classes – a not terribly plausible assumption, and a surprising thing to leave as an *assumption* when the whole question at issue between behaviourism and its opponents is whether or not one can do without the dimensions of purpose and cognition. Similarly, on the input side, all sorts of fancy additions were allowed, such as 'relative stimuli' and 'comparative stimuli', which in fact reintroduced the perception of relationship and significance which was meant to be excluded.[9]

Now this is exactly what one would expect if behaviourism were on the wrong track. To be on the wrong track in science, not just in the sense of having a faulty hypothesis, but in the more fundamental sense of trying a wrong approach, is to be incapable of finding explanatory correlations on the level of description one has chosen. After fifty years of life, behaviourism has clearly come up against this barrier. When plausibility can only be attained by stretching categories to near vacuity, and surreptitiously incorporating some key categories of the rival view, we have a pretty clear indication of bankruptcy. Appearances can be kept up only by ignoring the difference between a vacuous general description form and a set of categories with some ontological bite. If 'behaviourism' means merely that behaviour alters with experience, and this in a way related to the

---

[7] B. F. Ritchie, 'Concerning an incurable vagueness in psychological theories', in B. Wollmann and E. Nagel (eds), *Scientific Psychology* (New York, 1965).

[8] Noam Chomsky, Review of Skinner's 'Verbal Behaviour', *Language*, 35:1 (1959), pp. 26–58.

[9] Cf. Charles Taylor, *Explanation of Behaviour* (London and New York, 1964).

positive and negative valence of this experience, it will be hard to find anyone to disagree. If, on the other hand, the claim is made that we can trace this alteration of behaviour by characterizing both environment and behaviour in concepts which make no reference to meaning or purpose, and also employ a similarly physicalistic, interpretation-free notion of reinforcement, then 'behaviourism' has real content, but appears unsustainable. The theory can only survive through paralogistic argument, where the sense given to the theory shifts between the loose and the tight interpretations. B. F. Skinner, for instance, excels in this. Old theories, like old soldiers, never die, they just fade into a self-absorbed vacuity.

Behaviourism's inadequacies are now evident to the majority of practising psychologists. And this is part of the reason for the boom in centralist theories, notably those which are inspired by the progress of the digital computer and which try to model human intelligent functions on the Turing machine. But these theories have run into what is at bottom the same difficulty as behaviourism. I say 'at bottom' because on a superficial level the experience of artificial intelligence, seen as a model of human function, and computer simulation run into quite different problems. To start with, the kind of fudging and extending of concepts which behaviourism indulged in is impossible on the level of a computer program. It has precisely to be made entirely explicit in order to be run on a machine. This is why many workers in the field constantly stress the value of computer programming as a test of the coherence of a hypothesis about internal processes. At the same time, Artificial Intelligence and Computer Science also started with human functions, and some difficult ones at that, instead of making things easy by putting rats into the restricted environment of a maze, not to speak of pigeons in a Skinner box.

The result is that this approach has run into evident difficulty a lot faster, and this is all to its credit. The difficulty in matching such behaviour as reaching for an object in space, playing chess, making simple inferences, storing and using vocabulary, and so on, is that approximation to these activities is only possible in a relatively schematic and rigid way, and the task of going beyond this to a fuller matching of the flexible adaption of human performance becomes increasingly difficult. It requires an exponential growth in information storage and program routines which not only exceeds the capacity of existing machines (in itself not a difficulty in principle), but poses seemingly intractable search and selection problems.[10]

[10] Cf. discussion in H. L. Dreyfus, *What Computers Can't Do* (New York, 1979).

But this is exactly what one would expect on the assumption that these computer-modelled theories are on the wrong track. The issue between them and the hermeneutical approach to psychology is whether human functions that on a phenomenological level seem to involve a flexible know-how and perception of things which is not reducible to brute data and an exactly specified procedure can be matched by a machine which does operate on particulate input by just such an exact procedure. If the match were impossible, then one would expect that the programs would be rigid and narrow gauge relative to the live performance, and that they could only meet the full flexibility of the latter by a multiplication of special programs. This is in fact what seems to be occurring. Exponential growth of the *ad hoc* is in general the symptom of a mistaken theory, as can be seen from a classical illustration: the multiplication of epicycles to which the Ptolemaic theory was forced in order to save the phenomena.

As for the development of physiological explanations of human behaviour, this seems an even less likely bet for the moment. Some years ago when our notions of the function of brain and central nervous system were modelled on the reflex arc – or at worst, the telephone exchange – hope seemed possible. But already with Lashley's work, a quarter of a century ago, this perspective began to recede into the middle distance, and everything we have learned about neurophysiological function since has only served to complicate the picture further. Whatever the hope of ultimately achieving a link-up between the explanation of behaviour and neurophysiology, we cannot start with a neurophysiological explanation of mental function and action unless we understand the former better than the latter. But the reverse is the case. A reduction of this kind would be in the cards, if one is possible at all, only after we have achieved further progress on the psychological level. And, in fact, if such a link-up ever comes to pass, it is likely that it will require a great enrichment of our neurophysiological concepts in order to match the rich variety of self-interpretations which human beings are capable of, only a part of which probably has been manifested so far in the transformations of human cultural history.[11]

IV

The attempt by the correlators to finesse the level of interpretation has not been successful. The indications are rather that they have been barking up the wrong tree. But instead of drawing from this the opposite conclusion –

[11] Cf. chapter 7 below.

that the interpreters are globally right and the correlators globally wrong – I would like to explore another possibility: that there is a place for both models in the very diversified field which is psychology; that the trouble comes mostly from the limitless imperialism of the correlators. Once they accept their limits, they can coexist with the other school – hence the title of this paper. But this coexistence can be something more than just an arm's length toleration; it could also be very fruitful for psychology, and therein lies the interest in the proposal.

To speak of psychology as a diversified field is an understatement. A field which contains the different standard interests of experimental psychology, learning, motivation, and discrimination experiments, cognitive psychology, personality theory, social psychology, clinical psychology, developmental psychology, psychoanalysis, psycholinguistics, and lots more, obviously cannot be reduced to a single formula. But for the sake of simplification, I would like to single out three kinds of study within the field, a typology which is probably far from exhaustive, but which will enable me to draw some kind of rough dividing line between the two models of science.

When we talk of psychology in general we sometimes think of the science which attempts to explain why people act the way they do – that is, the explanation of motivated behaviour and the exercise of our capacities. But a tremendously important part of experimental psychology is taken up with the study of the necessary or infrastructural conditions for the exercise of these capacities. These are studies on the psycho-physical boundary – for instance, the study of physiological psychology, or studies in perception of the conditions in the stimulus array necessary for a certain level of discrimination or a certain perception.

Now the relevant point about such a psycho-physical domain is that here the classical model of science is the appropriate one. The aim of these studies is to discover correlations between physically defined dimensions and certain psychic states or capacities which are unambiguously present or absent, for example between a certain state of body chemistry and feeling hungry, a certain stimulus array and discriminating distance. Of course, it can be said that for one of the terms in these correlations we rely on 'introspection', but we have seen above that this is no real problem. If we have qualms about introspection we can say that the second term is the subject's claim, an overt act of speech.

Secondly, aside from the infrastructure of our capacities, we can study the structure of these capacities, our competences. The most-quoted example these days is the transformational grammar pioneered by

Chomsky, but we should also mention Piaget's study of the stages of child development. Here, too, the aim is to discover the structure of competence, the kinds of operations children are capable of at different ages. In both these cases, we have rather sophisticated theories which make appeal to developed formal structures, but the study of competence can be carried out at a more empirical level, such as the correlations involved in intelligence testing.

Both infrastructure studies and competence studies can be distinguished from the study of what is sometimes called performance, that is, actual motivated behaviour, particular exercises of competence toward a given end. What is involved here is the explanation of action and feeling, what we do and the emotions we experience, and this requires more than the understanding of the structure of the competence involved and the identification of the physical infrastructural conditions.

It is in this third domain that the hermeneutic model is appropriate, whereas the classical model invades the domain to its peril. Thus the attempts to develop learning theory – not the identification of physical conditions but the attempt to explain how rats learn to get around an environment or human beings learn a language – carried out according to the classical model have been depressingly sterile. Behaviourism was never anything but an unmitigated disaster in this area, first because it had no place for the notion of the structure of a capacity, the rat's 'map' of space or the speaker's linguistic competence. It was wedded to a unidimensional account, in which there was no possibility of distinguishing between a competence and its multiple uses.

Furthermore, the failure to distinguish competence from performance not only deprived the behaviourists of structural concepts, it also meant that what they were committed to explain was fully motivated behaviour, what the rat does or the man says after the learning period. And its theoretical resources were much too meagre for this, for as we saw above, explaining what we do involves an appeal to what we desire and feel and how we see our situation, all of which cannot be identified within the narrow purview of the classical requirements, particularly if these are interpreted as entailing physicalism.

Take the second example above, that of verbal behaviour. On reflection, it must appear very implausible that what I am actually saying on a given occasion in a real-life situation can be explained by operant conditioning, as Skinner's theory would have it; that is, that the sounds I utter are linked to certain stimulus conditions. For as Chomsky and others have shown, the elements of our speech acts cannot be paired with stimulus conditions of the appropriate, physicalistic kind. I may say 'dog' in the presence of a dog (the first obvious candidate for the 'stimulus condition'), but I may utter it also in the course of a philosophical argument, as here, or on the stage, or when thinking of presents for someone's birthday, or in a whole host of cases. The whole conditioning model prescinds from the fact that there are many different kinds of activities that we carry on in speech, and that our words relate differently to reality as a function of this. Behaviourism cannot distinguish between the capacity and its many uses and hence cannot explore the structure of the former. And even if we could analyse verbal behaviour in terms of the meanings of individual words and expressions, these would not always be linked to genuine stimulus classes – what could be the 'stimulus meaning' (to use Quine's term) for 'charismatic', 'romantic' or 'serene'?

Hence it is not surprising that experiments on the verbal conditioning model generally avoid tackling something analogous to real-life speech acts, but rather focus on marginal ones which can be artificially restricted to meet the needs of this approach, for example learning nonsense syllables, or saying individual unrelated words, or speech within a 'declutched' game-like context created by the experiment. Where conditions of normal interchange are approached, the results become more random and contradictory.[12]

As a step towards an account of human linguistic behaviour, verbal conditioning experiments are doomed to frustration. But this is not to say that they cannot give us information about something else. For instance, studying the learning of nonsense syllables contributed, I believe, to certain discoveries about short-term memory. Experiments which thus contribute to enlarging our knowledge of the psycho-physical infrastructure of certain of our standing capacities have an unquestionable value. But experiments whose only *raison d'être* is to provide building blocks in a chimeric prospective global explanation of verbal behaviour illuminate nothing at all. In a similar way, the behaviourist treatment of motivation as 'drive' has also proved quite unilluminating, moving from a simple base in a few organic drives to an elaborate superstructure of secondary drives which rapidly showed all the vices of vacuity without beginning to match the richness of motivational phenomena.

Thus the conclusion which most naturally flows from the successes and

---

12 Cf. Kenneth Heller and G. A. Marlatt, 'Verbal conditioning, behavior therapy, and behavior change', in C. M. Franks (ed.), *Behavior Therapy, Appraisal and Status* (New York, 1969), pp. 576–9.

failures of the classical model is a division of spheres between the two epistemologies: the classical one in its natural place in the first domain, that of psycho-physical or infrastructural studies; the hermeneutic model as the natural approach to the explanation of fully motivated performance. The third domain, that of competences, is intermediate between the two others. It can admit of a high degree of formalization (e.g., Chomsky and Piaget), but the application of these structural concepts may require an interpretation which cannot be reduced to brute criteria.

The point of this typology of domains is not to establish a boundary between the spheres of influence of the two epistemologies, but rather to account for both the powerful attraction of the classical model and the disastrous results that occur when it is used as a universal key to psychology. Correlators cannot believe that the classical model is all wrong because they are well aware of its successes in the first domain. Where they go wrong is in assuming that the whole of psychology is homogeneous with this first domain, that it is simply a matter of proceeding further and adding more correlations of the same sort in order to account for fully motivated behaviour – that what one discovers in this way about the conditions for recall of a list of nonsense syllables is a step on the road to learning about language acquisition. To see the distinction between infrastructure and fully motivated behaviour is to see why the success of the model at one level is no warrant for its appropriateness at the other. If once this point is allowed, coexistence is possible in psychology.

V

But what use is coexistence, beyond the obvious gain in tolerance and harmonious relations? The answer is that this kind of recognition of the limits of the classical model is necessary not only to create a climate of tolerance in which theories of the interpretive kind can develop; it is also necessary to liberate our imagination, without which these theories are sterile. For the myth of the omnicompetence of the classical model not only prevents us from posing the kinds of questions that only interpretive psychologies can answer; it also severely restricts the answers we can come up with when we do pose them.

To see this, let us turn to a range of questions which are of pressing importance nowadays, questions whose urgency makes the issue I am trying to get at here of more than academic interest. It cannot escape anyone, least of all academics, that a large-scale cultural mutation is taking place in our civilization, and one of the major loci of this change is the young, particularly students. It is hard to characterize this change, and the attempt to do so is one of those creative theoretical tasks to which psychology should contribute. But if I may provisionally use some psychological terminology to identify the phenomenon, I would say that certain of the fundamental reference points for the formation of identity in our civilization are being challenged.

The model of maturity under challenge is that of a self-defining subject, that is, one whose defining aspirations, values and loyalties are determined out of himself, and not in reference to anything outside. This idea was so central to American society that even patriotism was seen as owing to a 'way of life', which was defined in terms of individual freedom. Corresponding to this model of the subject is a view of the world surrounding him not as the locus of reference points for his identity, as earlier cultures had viewed it, but rather as raw material for his productive purposes. Thirdly, connected with this purposive transformation of things is an orientation to the future, a negative relation to the past as something to be constantly surpassed, matching the relation to the world as something to be constantly made over to suit even more fully human purposes.

There is a massive crisis in allegiance to this model among the rising generations. Partly this is due to the disastrous consequences, ecological and social, which can be plausibly laid at its door. But the revulsion is not inspired only by these concrete consequences. There is also a sense that the reigning model of maturity is inhuman, that it cuts us off from the sources of community, creativity, and human feeling. In this respect, the present identity crisis resembles the Romantic revolt against the Enlightenment – but there are radically new elements in it and it is incomparably more widespread. There should be a way for the sciences of man to come to grips with this mutation. Not only should there be, there *must* be, if we are to use our best resources of intelligence and reason to face this transition. Without any understanding on our part, this crisis is not in any sense guaranteed a happy outcome. In revulsion against the models of their own civilization, many young people are reaching back to those of earlier unrecoverable cultures or weaving sentimental images of the cultures of the East. And none of this adds up to a viable alternative. What we need above all is an insightful understanding of what is happening to us.

Psychology should, *must*, contribute to this. It is evident that a very important contribution will be made by those disciplines which have been concerned with cultural change, and with the rise of the modern identity, for example anthropology and history. But phenomena of the kind we are concerned with here cannot be tackled by respecting existing disciplinary lines of demarcation. We need to bring all the relevant theoretical resources to bear together on the problem, regardless of their provenance. In this respect, I believe that the work of Erik Erikson has made a very valuable contribution. Unfortunately, the belief in the omnicompetence of the classical model of science helps hold psychology back from contributing in this domain. Not just because it discourages interpretive psychology in general – this is bad enough, since any science which comes to grips with the problems of cultural change must be interpretive, having to deal as it does with differences in self-interpretation – but also because this belief is an integral part of the culture which is under attack, and therefore cannot offer a perspective from which this attack can be understood.

In all the disciplines where the classical model has been dominant, for instance psychology, political science, and sociology, student rebellion against 'the system' has also been directed against this paradigm of science. The rebellion has frequently been confused and sometimes very destructive, an attempted assassination of treason. (This provides another example of how little we can count on a guaranteed happy outcome to the current crisis.) But there is a correct perception underlying this challenge to the reigning 'methodology'.

In the eyes of its protagonists, the correlators, the classical model is a neutral procedure by which any reality can be approached 'scientifically'. It never occurs to them that this procedure weights the dice in favour of certain solutions, certain theories over others. But this is cannot fail to do. For a normative model of science cannot but involve a notion of the subject, and this in two ways: first, the thesis that all reality can be understood in terms of brute data and univocal operations says something by inclusion about man as an object of science, in that he is not to be understood as a self-interpreting being. But in addition, a model of scientific procedure must say something about the subject of this science. And this is the relevant connection here.

The classical model prescribes a certain stance on the part of the subject towards the world he is to understand. He is to look on this world not as a locus of meanings by reference to which he can understand himself and his world, but as a neutral domain of facts, of contingently correlated elements, the tracing of whose correlations will enable greater and greater manipulation and control of the world. This stance, let us call it the objectification of the world, was what the seventeenth-century revolution in science, the revolution of Bacon, Descartes, Newton, won through to, in an epoch-making polemic against the world-view of the Middle Ages and the high Renaissance, with its reliance on final causes and its vision of the universe as a hierarchy of meaning. This vision was among the 'Idols of the Mind' which Bacon castigated. As against this illusory, interpretive view of things, true knowledge brought power.

This is the stance involved in the classical model, and few contemporaries would want to question its validity for natural science. But the ideology of scientism, the belief that this model is omnicompetent, and that man reaches his greatest perfection and his most appropriate relation to things in the scientific stance, claims far more. It claims that human reality as well, our social institutions, the men in relation with whom we live, even our own lives, must be objectified to be understood. It claims that men reach their highest development in achieving the objectification of everything. Scientism is a transposition of the foundational Western tradition that man's vocation is reason, but reason has been drastically reduced from vision to objectification.

Scientism, the belief in the omnicompetence of the classical model, is closely bound up with the norm of maturity against which many young people are rebelling today. It is both one of its expressions and one of its props. For scientism, too, defends the norm of a self-defining subject, relating to his world not as a locus of meaning but as neutral matter, to be shaped according to his purposes. And since this objectification touches the human world as well as that of nature, this subject tends to define himself as an individual. In effect, the ideal subject of scientism is an extreme version of the modern norm of the conscious, autonomous individual: for he would experience none of his possible objects of awareness – not the human world or even his own body – as necessary reference points for his definition of himself or as indispensable interlocutors, but only as the phenomena of a neutral science of nature, some of which might be of use in the furtherance of his purposes.

In other words, scientism is ultimately bound up with the atomist, utilitarian bent in our civilization, whose orientation towards nature is manipulative, and which, where it is not also manipulative towards men, cannot get beyond the ideal of an arm's-length coexistence of independent individuals to any vision of community. Hence it is that an extreme protagonist of scientism, like B. F. Skinner, comes up with the *ne plus ultra* of manipulative nightmares – although in less spectacular form we can see the connection in the work of, say, D. C. McClelland on the achievement motive. Here the individualistic, productive orientation of our civilization is not only affirmed, but it is prescribed universally for developing nations and groups as the specific which will open the road to progress.

For in spite of the fact that McClelland's legend, folk-tale and story content analyses turn up high achievement motivation in cultures at all stages and ages of development, the 'need to achieve' itself is defined in terms which are specific to the modern identity. People with high need to achieve 'behave like successful, rationalizing business entrepreneurs'.[13] As the term 'rationalizing' implies, such people not only set themselves goals which offer some challenge, but are able and willing to look on the world around them as a task zone, a set of obstacles and potential means to these personally chosen goals. The self is the source of autonomously chosen aims, the world is to be scrutinized to discern the means to bring them to fruition. Increasing a man's achievement motivation, as we see in McClelland's 'missionary' work in India, involves increasing 'his sense of personal efficacy – his feeling that he could rely on himself, take initiative, become activity-oriented rather than just "goal-state" oriented, solve problems rather than avoid them'.[14]

It is plain that McClelland strongly believes in the value of this identity. He thinks it is one of the key factors in economic growth, and his research projects in other countries (such as those in India) in fact double up as exercises in proselytization. The trainees are converted to the new gospel by a combination of techniques ranging from the 'prestige suggestion' of the modern world[15] to more traditional methods outlined by Ignatius Loyola, such as the retreat setting and the foundation of a new reference group. All this will find its defenders, those who believe that what the Third World needs is headlong modernization after our model. But it casts no light on the change in identity itself, nor on possible alternatives. For one thing, 'need to achieve' is understood sometimes in an extremely general sense, as when 'scoring' material from ancient Greek literature, where stress on doing well in some competitive activity is a sufficient criterion; whereas for purposes of contemporary study and 'missionary' work, it also contains extremely important modern elements, for example, self-definition (measuring excellence against some *chosen standard*), a modern sense of time, and a faith in the power of science to shape our destiny.[16]

Moreover, this oscillation between a general and a specific category adds no new insight to the important historic question of the rise of the

---

[13] D. C. McClelland and D. G. Winter, *Motivating Economic Achievement* (New York, 1969), p. 11.   [14] *Ibid.*, p. 334.   [15] *Ibid.*, pp. 66f.   [16] *Ibid.*, p. 378.

modern identity. Here McClelland only offers a simplifying rewrite of Weber: 'So it seems reasonable enough to interpret Weber's argument for the connection between Protestantism and the rise of capitalism in terms of a revolution in the family, leading to more sons with strong internalized achievement drives.'[17] Weber's historically specific account of Calvinism, of the particular goals and cravings which spurred men to make themselves over into the life-form of rationalizing achievement – all this is washed away; what we are left with is merely the drive to achieve for its own sake, weakly generalized across ages and societies. Such a blunt tool provides little explanatory edge.

And finally, there is no sense of cost or of alternatives. On very superficial evidence (questionnaire answers to questions about beliefs and practices), McClelland seems partly convinced that traditional Hindu beliefs and practices are not undermined by the modern identity. But apart from all other considerations, we have good reason to distinguish the effects of a new identity on a few individuals in a largely unchanged society from its impact once the whole society has been made over. Advanced societies are beginning to show some of the latter, which is why many thoughtful people in developing countries are asking themselves whether it is possible to increase production and yields without acquiring a globally manipulative stance toward nature and eventually toward men as well. Perhaps Tanzania, perhaps China, will help the human race answer this. But they will not be helped by Dr McClelland and his exaltation of the need to achieve for its own sake; rather they seek an identity in which the desire for achievement is subordinated to humanly significant purpose.

Just because it is so rooted in one temporally and culturally bound self-interpretation of man, which had its origins in the past and may now be facing its demise, the belief in the omnicompetence of the classical model in science cannot help us understand this transition. It can only serve to entrench us narrowly in one of its terms, precisely that one whose inadequacy is at the origin of the crisis. The only excuse for holding fast to this position would be if it were effectively what it claimed to be, the only viable model of science. But we have seen reason to doubt this. That it is *a* valid model cannot be questioned; that it has a major role in psychology is also beyond doubt. But only if its imperialist pretensions to englobe the whole field are resisted can psychology make its contribution to under-

---

[17] Cf. D. C. McClelland, *The Achieving Society* (New York, 1967), p. 49.

standing the crisis of our civilization. This contribution would then not just be the act of a few inventive outsiders who are out of contact with the mainstream of empirical research, and looked at askance by academic psychology's best researchers. Rather it would be one toward which the many branches of study in this diversified field can converge.

CHAPTER SIX

WHAT IS INVOLVED IN A GENETIC PSYCHOLOGY?

Genetic psychology is dominated by the figure of Piaget, and a philosopher cannot begin to give his comments on the subject without a certain diffidence, as the great man's scathing and uncomplementary remarks about philosophers ring in his ears. So I would like to say something in expiation or extenuation for the lines which follow. The kind of reflection which can be called philosophical cannot simply precede empirical discovery and lay out the field of the possible and the impossible. It can only be a reflection on empirical findings, raising questions about their interpretation, about the connections between them, about the problems they raise or help to solve. In this sense, 'philosophy' shades into the kind of reflection and discussion which any innovative empirical scientist must engage in. It can only be distinguished, if at all, in that we like to reserve the term for questions about the more fundamental issues. But wherever one draws the line, I believe that there is a perfectly defensible sense in which one can speak of the philosophical views and ideas of Piaget. And it is in this sense, I believe, that a philosophical reflection on genetic psychology might be useful, even if it loses greatly in value in not being based on the degree and scope of empirical knowledge which searchers in the field have at their disposal.

I

What is genetic psychology? The term might be reserved for a certain field within psychology, that containing all questions to do with ontogenesis. But it is much more useful if we take the term to designate an approach or a family of approaches to this subject matter, rather than just a neutral specification of the field. And, indeed, the field of ontogenesis only becomes of salient interest if we do adopt a certain approach to it.

Genetic psychology is then the view that there is a special complex of problems of ontogenesis. This contrasts with a view which has been dominant in Anglo-Saxon psychology for some time; this sees growth in general, and growth of cognitive function in particular, as explicable by very non-specific mechanisms at work everywhere that 'learning', or indeed, behaviour change, takes place. Thus, modern behaviourism, the heir to classical empiricism, undertook to attempt to discover an account of all learning by some associative mechanism, in some cases paired with reward, which was thought to operate over the whole field, without discrimination between adult learning and infant development, and without discrimination even between different species. (These two distinctions tend to stand or fall together, as I shall try to outline below.)

The major antagonist to a genetic psychology is thus an incremental view of learning, in which all development is seen as the addition (or sometimes subtraction) of homogeneous units, such as Hull's sHr's (or 'habits' linking stimuli and responses). It was this belief in the ubiquity of simple mechanisms which underlay the *démarche* of behaviourism in approaching a theory of human intelligence by studying rats in a maze or pigeons in a Skinner box. And it was this belief which confined the study of these animals to highly artificial environments, so that really interesting and enlightening discoveries about animal behaviour had to come from what was organizationally a separate discipline, ethology. It may be that subsequent generations will stand aghast at these errors (as I believe them to be), but they do not appear so strange or obtuse from within the premises of traditional learning theory. If the same mechanisms underlie all learning, then one can winkle them out anywhere; there is no privileged locus, so why not try the contexts which are easiest to operate with in practical terms, that is, non-human organisms in an artificially simplified environment.

In other words, the shape, or structure, of the intelligence or learning capacity of a given species, or at a given maturational stage, does not need to be examined at the outset because it will ultimately be accounted for by a specific differential concatenation of the same fundamental building blocks which underlie the behaviour of all other species or stages. On this atomistic view, species and stage differences are *explicanda* which we will ultimately get around to dealing with; they are not the crucial objects of research themselves.

This contrasts sharply with a genetic psychology for which the pattern of intelligence, of learning, of emotional life, and so on is different at each stage in a way which cannot be accounted for by the addition or subtraction of elements. For genetic psychology, these are differences of structure or global organization, and where behaviourism is atomistic, genetic psychology is holistic.

But the difference between these two approaches goes beyond that between atomism and holism. Genetic psychology cannot be satisfied with a simple cataloguing of stages; it also wants to go on and account for the differences and hence for growth. But if we are dealing with atomistically irreducible structures, then growth can only be seen as structural transformation; that is, the onset of a new, more developed structure must be explained in terms of the mesh of experience with an earlier structure, when it is not accounted for by the maturation of an innate structure itself. The theory must therefore have among its basic explanatory notions some features of innate structure, hereditary ways of dealing with the world evident at birth, or arising later through maturation.

Hence, beyond holism versus atomism, genetic psychology tends to differ from traditional learning theory on the issue of innate structures. Behaviourism, faithful to its empiricist ancestry, was generally quite fiercely environmentalistic. Of course, there had to be some spontaneous unlearned activity for there to be association and hence learning, and there were, of course, innate behavioural patterns which we generally call 'instincts' (for example, sucking in the human neonate, nest building in certain kinds of birds); but the first offered merely facilitating conditions for learning, whereas the second was thought just to coexist with learning, a set of unlearned sHr's alongside those which are 'stamped in' by experience. In either case, there is no question of accounting for the present structure of intelligence or learning by reference, among other things, to innate structure. Innate patterns of behaviour were thought, in other words, to play a small role in behaviour, and where they were present they were seen merely as elements alongside learned segments of behaviour.

Quite different is the place of innate structures in genetic psychology. If higher structures arise through transformation of innate ones, then the instinctive pattern is not interesting just as an original concatenation of elements. More important is the underlying structure which will reappear in the transform. A crucial concept of genetic psychology is therefore that of transformation. This requires some distinction analogous to that between 'surface' and 'deep' structure, which I borrow here from the transformational syntactics which Chomsky and his associates have developed; deep structure provides the identical element underlying what on the surface are two very different structures, and hence allows us to delineate the differential factors which account for the transformation of one into the other. (In Chomsky's theory, of course, the transformations are between deep and surface structures rather than between two surface structures, but the distinction between the two is necessary in either case.)

The notion of transformation comes out in Piaget's theory of adaptation. This has two dimensions, assimilation and accommodation; the former preserves some kind of identity through the changes accorded by the latter. It is this which allows us to see identity, or at least filiation, between schemas at very different levels which are superficially very dissimilar, such as the play behaviour of the young infant and his later ability to make deductions as an adolescent. The role of assimilation is what makes the earlier structure essential in the explanation of the later; one is a transform of the other. Because of transformation, the innate is not only interesting as a particular pattern, but even more as a deep structure in which form it combines with experience rather than existing alongside it. In its stark traditional form the nature–nurture controversy is made irrelevant.

The essential role of transformations provides the basis for Piaget's attack on the other three positions, which, along with associationism, he sees as alternatives to his own. Rightly or wrongly, he reproaches Gestalt psychology with a static non-developmental notion of form which allows no role for growth in experience; and vitalism opens itself to a related reproach; while 'trial-and-error' theory sins in the opposite way – it sees no method in the groping which occurs before a correct solution and hence the acquisition of a new behaviour, whereas the notion of ,transformation implies that these intermediate phases are structured in a way that we can understand from the deep structure involved (that is, the groping behaviour is controlled by the schemas which are in the process of undergoing transformation).

For Piaget, transformations ultimately are to be understood in terms of equilibrium theory. There are a number of objections one can make to this as it occurs in Piaget's work, including the familiar one of vacuity: that specification in terms of equilibrium states adds nothing to our understanding of the process which is not already present in our descriptions in terms of contradiction, coherence, etc., for we can only apply the former descriptions via the latter. But the validity of the general approach which we can call transformational does not stand or fall with equilibrium theory.

We thus can single out three important characteristics of genetic psychology, in the sense we are using here: (a) it is holistic as against atomistic, (b) it is transformational as against incremental, and (c) it makes reference to innate structures which determine the relevance of experience rather than deriving development in a linear way from the environment.

This third point reminds us of the controversy which rages between the heirs of 'Cartesianism' and 'empiricism' in linguistics and the philosophy of language; and the use of the word 'transformational' seems to point out the connection.

The idea underlying transformational grammar is that a grasp of deep structures and their relation to surface structures is part of a human being's cognitive repertoire, in this case his linguistic competence. Lenneberg suggests that this capacity to operate with deep and surface structures goes far beyond the linguistic domain and is at work also in our recognition of object.[1] But in the above we were talking about transformations between different stages of the repertoire, rather than those which are part of this repertoire at a given stage. These two levels of discourse have to be distinguished, but in fact they are closely related – so much so that it is often easy to confuse them.

The only way we can characterize a given repertoire, that is, a structure of intelligence and learning, is in terms of the characterizations and discriminations which a subject with this repertoire can make, and the inferences and connections he can establish from them. The picture of a given stage of cognitive development is simply a picture of things as characterized and discriminated and linked together, or inferred to, in a certain way. This poses a number of problems for genetic psychology which I shall try to touch on later, notably the difficulty of constructing this picture of competence from performance, and that of describing a stage of the repertoire which for us is 'illogical' in some way.

For the moment, the point I would like to bring out is this: the repertoire at a given stage is characterized in terms of a number of related skills and capacities to manipulate, describe, make inferences about the world; the repertoire thus is defined by the picture of the world which the subject of this repertoire generates. Transformations between stages of the repertoire are thus transformations from one such complex of interlocking skills to another, and hence from one picture of the world (that is, the world characterized and inferred about in certain ways) to another. But then it is not surprising if the repertoire beyond a certain stage includes the capacity to manipulate, describe, and infer about the world in more than one way, and further the capacity to relate one picture to another and hence to make transformations. Thus, the concept of structures of competence, which include the capacity to grasp things intellectually by means of transformations, goes well with a theory which posits transformational relations between these structures.

---

[1] See E. H. Lenneberg, *Biological Foundations of Language* (New York, 1967), pp. 296–9.

But is there a connection between the debate in linguistics and that concerning genetic psychology in relation to the issue of innateness? I have already tried to show how I believe that genetic psychology must make reference to innate structures, and hence that it must, unlike traditional learning theory, focus study not only on stage differences, but also on species differences. In addition, the difference between the notion of innateness that Chomsky and his associates defend, and that which has been the traditional target of empiricists, is reminiscent of the gap in outlook between genetic and traditional learning psychology. Empiricists have always focussed their attack on 'innate ideas' as specific contents existing in the mind in abstraction from experience (the analogue in behaviour would be rigid patterns of instinct which owe nothing to learning). But what Chomsky defends, along with most defenders of innateness in history, is rather the existence of innate schemas which not only require external stimulation to be activated, but whose content must, in an important sense, be determined by experience. What is innate is not contents, but ways of dealing with contents. One has a strong impression, reviewing this debate in history, that the fundamental issue is not so much nature versus nurture, but rather an atomistic incremental notion of intelligence versus a structural cluster-of-skills conception. If one accepts the first view, then innateness must be a matter of specific contents, and if one takes the second line, the issue is about structures. Thus, the two sides can never really join issue in this debate because of their different notions of the mind. But these rival notions also divide genetic psychology from traditional learning theory.

There is thus a close relation between the two debates, but not necessarily a perfect overlap between the corresponding positions. The reason is that the exact role of innate structures can be an important issue in genetic psychology. For instance, without being able to be entirely sure, I would tend to believe that Chomsky and Piaget would be in disagreement on this matter. A genetic psychology requires some innate structures at the start; but there are a wide number of options concerning the role which later maturing innate structures play in the subsesquent transformations. Piaget, on the whole, seems not to give these much importance, whereas Chomsky postulates a highly selective innate structure underlying language learning. Because of their different concerns, the two positions do not meet head-on, but there is an important difference of emphasis here, or so it seems to me. It might, perhaps, be put better by saying that Piaget seems relatively uninterested in the role of innate structures, other than those which provide starting points for development in babyhood. Maturation certainly makes certain transformations possible, but the further development of schemas is understood almost entirely in terms of earlier schemas and experience. Piaget seems to offer little room for late-developing innate schemas of a highly elaborate kind. Maturation is a necessary condition for development, but it does nothing to determine its direction.

Genetic psychology thus can be characterized as holistic, transformational, and (to a greater or lesser degree) innatist. But there are two other, very non-Cartesian, properties which follow from this. In showing the development of intelligence, from its most primitive forms to its most advanced, (d) genetic psychology leads almost inexorably into an attempt to show the link between intelligence and biological function in general. No comment is needed on the importance of this theme in Piaget's work. And related with this is (e) a view of mature consciousness as evolved out of lower forms and out of the other processes of life. I do not mean here simply a view about its origin, as against one which touches its present nature in the mature adult; for on the principles outlined above, these two cannot be separated. The mature form is the product of a series of transformations on more primitive forms, and cannot be fully understood without a grasp of these primitive forms.

We can see this in relation to one of the major issues of traditional epistemology. The theory of 'ideas' of both traditional Cartesianism and empiricism, which has survived into our century in the form of the sense-datum theory, provides us with an example of a theory of consciousness which is not compatible with the notions about its genesis that we have been describing. From the point of view of genetic psychology, this theory takes our awareness of the world, which can only be seen as the functioning of schemas of perception, and construes it falsely as a set of quasi-objects, tableaux which are assembled out of smaller elements. If we see our perception of objects, space, causality, and so on, as skills which we have to acquire, and which we acquire in part through our commerce with objects, as being capable of manipulating things and being affected by them, then the very idea of a basic building block of perception makes no sense. Perception is transferred from the category of something that happens to us to that of action; it is the exercise of a skill, and the pathologies from which it can suffer are to be understood accordingly. What is immediately seen can no longer be distinguished as something separable from the interpretation a subject brings with him because of his knowledge, understanding, and culture; and hence the idea of a percept identical through changes of interpretation has no application outside of its ordinary everyday one.[2]

We can see from this example how, on a very general level, our concept of consciousness is inextricably bound up with our idea of how it develops. But this connection is of relevance within the bounds of genetic psychology as well. If we describe mature consciousness in terms of certain capacities to describe and make inferences about things, it is impossible to define these capacities without reference to the less adequate clusters which they replace; for the capacities of maturity are defined partly in terms of the ability to go beyond the less adequate ways of generating a picture of things which precede it. In other words, if the description of the mature mind is that of a pattern of achieved skill, we cannot characterize it without reference to that, the surmounting of which represents the achievement.

In this sense a genetic psychology can be said to deserve its name, in the strong sense that the mature present can only be understood in terms of the ontogenetic past. In this broad sense, of course, psychoanalysis must be considered a genetic psychology, and the ultimately adequate genetic psychology would englobe what is valid in the theories both of Piaget and of Freud. In the meantime, we live with the risk that any partial theory – one that deals only with cognition, or emotional development, or whatever – may be incapacitated by its terms of reference, as it were, from discovering the really fruitful connections.

If we define genetic psychology by the three basic properties above and the two corollaries just discussed, then it seems to me to be plainly preferable to the traditional learning theory which is its principal rival. Indeed, the attempt to find a simple universal mechanism at work in learning, which would allow us to abstract from structure, seems to me not far short of a dismal failure. At every turn, we come across undeniable

---

[2] This notion of perception as a cluster of skills, which have themselves developed in relation to the motor skills by which we deal with the objects around us, makes comprehensible a conception of our knowledge of the world which is not entirely explicit. This is the view which has been explored in modern phenomenology (for example, by Heidegger and Merleau-Ponty) and by M. Polanyi, *Personal Knowledge* (Chicago, 1958) and *The Tacit Dimension* (Garden City, NY, 1966). A motor skill has no sharp boundary; rather it is a capacity for dealing with a relatively indefinite range of objects in a relatively indefinite range of ways. An awareness of things grounded in such skills is thus one in which the explicit focus can be surrounded and influenced by an implicit grasp of the situation, which resists reduction to a definite catalogue. This conception of knowledge, of course, also flies in the face of the philosophical tradition – at this point common to both Cartesianism and empiricism – which underlines most modern attempts to develop a science of psychology.

evidence of heterogeneity in intelligence and learning repertoire, for which no coherent explanation in associative terms has been given. The ones that have turn on appalling equivocations on such crucial notions as 'stimulus' and 'response'. This case has been relatively well documented.[3]

Indeed, one might be tempted to believe that the argument is over and that the associationist position has been finally abandoned. Certainly in its original simple form it seems to be on the wane (although the growing production of Skinner-inspired teaching machines may make one nervous). But, even though most psychologists of a behavioural persuasion seem to be turning to some version of 'centralist' theory and looking for models in automata demonstrating artificial intelligence, the gap between the two positions is far from closed. The search for a digital computer model of the mind is certainly compatible with a non-incrementalist learning theory in that it allows us to conceive of qualitative shifts in intelligence and learning mediated by changes in the underlying computing 'machine'. But the actual practice of much contemporary academic psychology remains in the intellectual grip of traditional theory.

Let us accept for the sake of argument that our ultimate aim is to find a mechanical model of the human organism. Then the approach of genetic psychology would still be to discover the shape of the structures of given stages and species, in order to discover what we want a machine analogue, and ultimately a mechanistic explanation, for. It really should not concern us that this first stage of theory will inevitably be in 'mentalistic' terms and will refer to innate schemas, even if we are convinced mechanists. In short, genetic psychology as such has nothing to say on the issue of the possibility or conceivability of mechanistic explanations. What it does deny is the possibility of a mechanistic shortcut via an atomistic incremental approach which could bypass cognitive structures in the explanation it offered. The issue of whether these cognitive structures can be 'reduced' in terms of an underlying mechanistic theory is not prejudged.

The research strategy that follows from this is clear: first find the structures underlying intelligence, and then develop from this end whatever language is adequate, no matter how 'mentalistic'. But the deep-lying and widespread prejudices abroad in academic psychology rule out this approach for many. Any dalliance with mentalism or innate ideas seems like sacrilege. But if one must, at all costs, produce nothing but mechanistic explanations, then one cannot engage properly in the attempt to map

---

[3] N. Chomsky, Review of Skinner's 'Verbal Behaviour', *Language*, 35:1 (1959), pp. 26–58.

competence. All one can do is return to the piecemeal approach, and try to devise good mechanical analogues for particular intelligent behaviours, like pattern recognition, for instance, without any assurance that this particular behaviour, as we have circumscribed it, is relevant to the question of mechanical models of human intelligence – whether, for instance, it is not part of a more general skill which might require a quite different mechanism to explain it, if it can be explained mechanistically at all.

This kind of approach is in danger, to use the image of Dreyfus, of falling into the error of the man who climbed a tree and congratulated himself on having taken the first step to the moon.[4] The belief that a model adequate to reproduce a partial behaviour is a step towards the explanation of human behaviour only makes sense if we accept atomist and incrementalist premises. A machine that will translate for an artificially restricted and simplified vocabulary may have no relevance to the problems of translation of natural languages; we cannot tell until we know something about the kind of structure that language competence is. To plunge on, regardless, in the certain faith of relevance is to say, in effect, that knowledge of the structure has no relevance for research, which is equivalent to an incrementalist position.

The issue is, thus, far from resolved in psychology today; and the approach which I would like to call the more fruitful one is far from being generally allowed. The reasons for this reluctance may have much to do with prejudice, but in fact the path of a genetic psychology is far from being without difficulty and uncertainty, and it is these which I would now like to look at more closely.

II

Once we have accepted the approach of genetic psychology, a number of questions remain unresolved and difficult to resolve. The first concerns the

[4] H. L. Dreyfus, *What Computers Can't Do* (New York, 1979). Dreyfus also shows the powerful hold on workers in the field of artificial intelligence of the assumption that all knowledge is ultimately explicit – an assumption, as I mentioned above (note 2), which is common to both the empiricist and rationalist traditions. Indeed, Dreyfus' argument goes further, and tends to show that a model of the mind drawn from the digital computer cannot free itself from this assumption – cannot cope, in other words, with our implicit grasp of our situation. And this raises severe doubts about the capacity of this model to cope with our basic motor skills and the development from them of our mature consciousness of things; about whether, in short, this model can really come to grips with the subject matter of genetic psychology. Linked with this fixation on the explicit, the digital computer model also involves its own kind of atomism, that of discrete 'bits' of information.

innate schemas which are at work. Among these are obviously certain infantile reflexes and reactions, like sucking, grasping, looking at certain objects, smiling, cooing and later babbling, and so on. These, unlike the fixed patterns of some lower species, undergo transformations and develop into coordinated motor skills, while at the same time, the child learns to perceive and deal with a world of people and objects in three-dimensional space. This development has been studied in (what to this layman is) an admirable way by Piaget.[5]

It is the role of innate schemas in later transformations which is difficult to determine. The growth of language is a case in point. Obviously, the infant's innate tendency to babble plays a role here, as does the tendency to imitate. But it is clearly inadequate to try to account for language by these two tendencies; human language learning is not like superior, more flexible parroting. We have to try to determine what the skills are which underlie this achievement, which is in a way definitive of human intelligence.

For Piaget, the important thing seems to be the development of a symbolic function, that is, the ability to use signifiers (*significants*) to refer to significates (*signifiés*). Being able to produce or respond to signifiers is quite different from recognizing signals or cues (*indices*), whereby we recognize a whole through one of its parts or recognize a motor schema through some concomitant. This kind of achievement is entirely within the reach of higher animals, as is also an understanding of their environment which is largely 'interiorized' (that is, higher mammals can often grasp solutions to problems by 'insight').

Signifiers, on the other hand, refer to their significates not in virtue of a part–whole relation or of some close relationship of schemas, but are in a sense artificial. The symbolic function is thus in a real sense representational: one thing stands for another from which it is clearly separate. This is the case even though for the child (and also primitive peoples) things and their names inextricably belong together: the name *is* in a sense the nature of the thing. For, however unconscious the symbolic function is, the putting together of name and thing occurs here entirely out of the activity of naming, referring to, talking about, or representing things, whereas the relation of a signal to what it points to arises for the subject in, and is sustained by, any of a whole host of other activities in which animals also can engage; and the same goes for cues. Thus, animals can

[5] J. Piaget, *The Origins of Intelligence in Children* (New York, 1952) and *The Construction of Reality in the Child* (New York, 1954).

learn to operate with signals and cues, as when a dog gets ready to go out when he sees his master put on his hat; they can learn to make use of a large range of concomitances in their environment in so far as these are relevant to their activity. In these cases, in other words, the putting together of sign and thing (to use the term 'sign' as a genus term for signals, cues, and symbols) comes from the shape of things as relevant to some motor activity; whereas the relation of signifier to significate can only be accounted for in terms of an activity which we can call (rather vaguely and inadequately) representational.

This holds even when we take account of the distinction which Piaget marks between symbols and signs in a narrow sense: whereas the latter can be thought of as 'arbitrary', in that there is nothing in the signifier which evokes the significate, the true symbol is *motivé*; it resembles or in some way recalls what it signifies. Apart from certain elements of onomatopoeia, most of our vocabulary is sign in this sense, although we can certainly build powerful 'images', hence symbols, with words. But even the symbol in the latter, secondary sense is a signifier; it arises out of the activity of representation and in no other way, however much its resemblance to the significate may add to its power.

For Piaget, the symbolic function arises out of the activities of imitation and play jointly; but it is hard to evaluate this theory without some greater understanding of the symbolic function itself, and we are still far from having a clearly articulated idea of this at the moment. It is not an easy matter to define what kind of activities are involved in the use of language. We have just seen that to think of language just as a relation set up for the subject between signs (in some general sense) and things is no use at all. This gives us no way of distinguishing language from other ways of operating with signs, for example, signals and cues in Piaget's sense. This kind of oversimplification is what underlies the facile but quite unilluminating comparisons of human and animal 'language'. It is a matter of looking at the result without looking at the activity which underlies it; and this leads to the same kind of distortion which we saw above in the sense-datum theory. Somehow in the course of developing or learning language, 'chair' becomes linked to chairs and 'walk' is linked to walking, but this is utterly different from the way the slap of a beaver's tail on the water is linked to flight behaviour on the part of his companions. In order to understand language, we have to come to grips more closely with the complex of activities vaguely subsumed under the cover term 'representational' above.

For the same reason we cannot think of language just as a classification system, for animals also 'classify' in the sense of reacting differentially to different types of things – even though man's classification is obviously infinitely more developed.

Perhaps one way of approaching this question of the nature of representational activity might be this: to be able to talk about things is to be potentially aware of them outside of any particular transaction with them; it is to be potentially aware of them not just in their behaviour relevance to some activity we are now engaged in, but also in a 'disengaged' way. Language is the major vehicle of this capacity to grasp things in a disengaged way, but language users are also capable of using a number of other vehicles with the same effect: mime, acting out, depiction by drawing, probably non-verbal mental images.

To approach representational activity by seeing it as disengaged awareness is not, of course, to say that language users are always engaged in pure contemplation when they talk, though something like contemplation seems to become possible quite early. Obviously, language is used throughout the gamut of 'engaged' human activity. The child who says 'up, up' wanting to be picked up by his mother is deploying this linguistic expression very much as his younger brother deploys the gesture of holding up his arms and/or crying. Indeed, very little may have changed at the stage where the child has only a few words, of which 'up' would be one in the case of the child above. What is crucial is that linguistic capacity, once it attains a certain level, permits an awareness of something like being picked up outside of the sole context of wanting to be picked up, that this 'disengaged' awareness then becomes available in general to figure in new operations which require it, such as telling and hearing stories about being picked up, play acting the whole drama of being (or not being) picked up with a doll; and, much later on, in explicit verbal grasp of geometric and topological relations, and so on. Of course, all these activities are in a very real sense 'engaged' in their own way – the term 'disengaged' is in this sense unfortunate, even though it is hard to find another one which would create no misunderstanding. But, however passionate – and we know how deep the tensions can be which are discharged in children's play acting – these activities are all founded on an awareness of the object concerned which is extricated from its original setting in some behavioural transaction.

But language permits us to do more than achieve disengaged awareness of a particular set of contents; it is a general capacity which makes us capable of describing (and hence disengaging our awareness of) new things, of describing and hence evoking awareness of things that are not present or that may not exist. Language is a capacity which permits us to put finite means to infinite ends, to paraphrase Humboldt.

This open-endedness of language can be seen in two dimensions. Within a given language and way of talking about things, which a child picks up from his surroundings, he can make or understand an indefinite number of descriptions, either in talking about things around him or in telling or hearing stories. But this particular way of talking about things will have particular limitations; certain ways of grasping things will be facilitated, others will be difficult, still others inaccessible. The disengagement of awareness which comes from learning the language will thus be unlimited in one sense – it does not apply to a particular set of contents only – but limited in another, for it allows only certain kinds of descriptions.

The thing about linguistic capacity, however, is that it is not only unlimited in this sense, but also in the stronger one that a language user can in principle transcend the bounds of a particular language and conceptual structure; either by invention of new concepts, or by learning a new language, either a new natural language or a new terminology. I say 'in principle', because not every innovation is accessible to everyone, or we would all be geniuses; there are important differences in intelligence and flexibility of mind which determine the limits of each one of us. But the potentiality for this kind of transcendence is implicit in linguistic capacity in this sense; it is the fundamental ability to disengage our awareness of things which, whatever the concepts which mediate this disengagement in the first case, allows us to examine these things in such a way that we discover new more adequate modes of description. In other words, it is our language, however impoverished in the first place, through which things become objects of disengaged awareness, and thus susceptible of being examined, compared, or related in such a way that new more powerful descriptions can come to light in proportion to our inclination and capacity. This 'discovery', of course, may be entirely our own, or more usually we will be led to it by others, in school, university, or whatever; but in either case, it is the same 'disengaging' feature of linguistic capacity which makes the achievement possible, whatever other conditions it may require (and plainly there are others, as is evident from interpersonal differences in intelligence). This type of transcendence is not achieved only in those comparatively rare cases where we shift cultures or study in some taxing discipline. Something of the same relation that holds between languages, or between ordinary and specialist terminology, also holds between different stages of a child's vocabulary and conceptual and reasoning capacities as he grows up. Transcendence is, in this sense, a commonplace.

Linguistic capacity is thus doubly unlimited. It is a general capacity for disengaged awareness which is not restricted as to level; that is, it can operate on what it has already generated, as we scrutinize more closely what we have already learned to conceptualize and find how to talk about it differently; and it can operate on itself, as we come, at a higher level of sophistication, to examine our conceptual nets themselves. But this general capacity, spiritual and disembodied as it appears to us, is mediated by our ability to deploy and hear articulated sound in a certain way. This statement is, of course, not quite true as it stands; we can transpose sounds into marks on paper, from aural into visual signs, or else into hand movements, as in sign language, or into tactile signs, as with braille. And people who lack sight and/or hearing can learn language in the first place in these other media. But the learning and exercise of linguistic capacity requires some medium of this kind. It involves a certain kind of deployment of the signs of the medium, and hence our linguistic awareness, however unlimited in principle, is always in fact limited in certain ways.

If we think of the 'symbolic function' as a capacity for disengaged awareness, unrestricted as to level, which we exercise by the deployment of signs, in the normal case articulated sounds, what do we have to postulate as innate background to the acquisition of language? Clearly, the tendency to make sounds and to imitate are not enough, although in some descriptions these are necessary. Clearly, the signs themselves are not innately determined, as one can see from the diversity of languages, nor are the types of descriptions (though certain divisions of semantic 'space' may be easier and hence more 'natural' for men than others, for example certain shape and colour distinctions). The innate tendency specific to man is just that to deploy signs in such a way as to achieve this disengagement of awareness. Of course, if this is all that we can say about it, talking about the innate background of language acquisition will not help us much; all we have here is a vague delineation of the area of search there must be.

We are easily led to overlook the need to search for the innate background to language learning because the most obvious fact about language is its diversity; the language a child will speak is a function of his social surroundings. But once we have discovered that the child surrounded by anglophones will speak English, we have still not begun to penetrate the mystery of language learning; and we have no reason to think so unless we believe that the mechanism of language acquisition is some very simple one (for example, of the associationist type) which we already fully understand. But this is far from being the case. We still do not understand why the child will learn English and the baby chimpanzee will not. We have ultimately to understand how the child grasps our articulated sound as being *about* something, and can thus take it up himself as a vehicle of his disengaged awareness of these things, and then go on to make new descriptions of his own.

Perhaps what we are looking for here is the implicit attunedness to the categories of universal grammar which Chomsky holds the child must have to learn language;[6] and we can then express the innate background in terms of certain fundamental grammatical structures and certain sets of rules governing transformations on these. But these structures would have to be seen in a genetic perspective as well. The child does not learn the whole language and its correct grammar at once; he passes through a number of stages, and at the most primitive ones, the vocabulary is very restricted, and the deployment of words follows a few simple patterns (that is, the syntax is rudimentary); and this regardless of how well and grammatically the parents talk to him. The structures which underlie his grasp and reproduction of speech are still relatively simple. They then undergo successive transformations until, in late childhood, he speaks pretty well like an adult.

If we could delineate the successive structures, then perhaps we could come closer to seeing what is required for the transformations which link them. Is it just a matter of slowly maturing capacity, so that the same speech surrounding produces more and more adequate grammar in the child's talk as he grows? Or are certain achievements in understanding necessary to pass from one stage to the next? Or certain developments of the ego? And what does this genesis show about the relation between these basic grammatical structures and the fact that the deployments of language they govern are the vehicles of disengaged awareness of things?

Alongside these general grammatical structures and transformations the innate background of language acquisition also includes man's particular type of gregariousness. The child learns language from within a relationship of communication with others, and this in turn puts the relationship on a new footing. At first the child not only speaks with the words, accent, mannerisms, and so on borrowed from his surroundings, he also does not have a very articulated idea of himself as a subject of thought, in relation to the others. This is what Piaget calls 'egocentrism',

---

[6] N. Chomsky, *Aspects of the Theory of Syntax* (Cambridge, Mass., 1965).

constantly stressing himself that the word may mislead, because what is meant here is rather relative lack of dissociation between points of view, that of self and others, and thus 'egocentrisms' can come out as much in over-compliancy as in self-centred behaviour. It may be that the ability to learn language as a child does, that is, learn a first language (and even learn several languages as 'first' ones), which seems to be restricted to the period before puberty, may be connected with the susceptibility to this type of relation of communication where the subject is as yet relatively undissociated. The child 'resonates', to use Lenneberg's term, to the speech of his surroundings, and in this way the very general structures referred to earlier are embodied in the grasp of a particular language; whereas later we are incapable of resonating in this way; our linguistic style is fixed, and we have, alas, to work hard to acquire a new language.

III

The discussion of language in section II shows the difficulty of defining the innate structures which underlie ontogenesis. But an even more difficult set of questions arises concerning the direction of the transformations they undergo. It is possible to test the child's capabilities at different ages in terms of the problems he can or cannot solve and the inferences he can or cannot make, as Piaget and his associates have done. Piaget has also attempted to abstract from these experiments certain general structures of reasoning. Some of these abstractions seem very well founded. Thus it seems that it is only in his early teens that a child can generate hypotheses by a systematic combination of elements;[7] and it is around the same time that he begins to coordinate movements in different reference systems, and grasp the idea of compensating movements in equilibrium systems.

The step from these to the postulation of a general group-lattice structure, which Piaget characterizes by the initials INRC, is much more problematical. Similar questions arise in connection with some of the 'group' structures which Piaget holds underlie the child's thinking in the period of 'concrete operations'. The difficulty is one of interpretation. In the case of some supposed structures and procedures, there is little problem, because the subject himself is explicitly aware of them, or can easily recognize them as his when they are described. This is the case with the generation of all possible hypotheses through combination when the problem is, for

---

[7] See B. Inhelder and J. Piaget, *The Growth of Logical Thinking from Childhood to Adolescence* (New York, 1958).

instance, to assess the effect of several different factors on a single result. But the case is very different with the INRC structure. As physically embodied in a system in equilibrium, we can perhaps accept it as a general description of the subject's understanding; but here it means no more than that he understands the relation between countering a movement by reversing it and countering it by compensation. As a general structure accounting for a whole range of achievements in problem solution and reasoning, INRC is much more open to question.

What we require here is an interpretation which goes well beyond what the subject is able to avow. In a way, we are in a similar position to that of psychoanalysis: we take a number of protocols, and reconstruct a chain of reasoning which we claim was that of the subject. In the nature of things, the plausibility of this interpretation is bound to repose in part on general hypotheses about how this subject, or subjects of this kind, usually reason; and these in turn will be strengthened or undermined by the plausibility of other interpretations that we make following these hypotheses.

Genetic psychology in this way is 'hermeneutical', that is, it reposes on interpretations, as does psychoanalysis and – I believe – the sciences of man in general; and it suffers the corresponding limitations in exactitude and certainty. But this is a long and complex story, and the point I wanted to pursue here is rather this: since our interpretations repose on general propositions about reasoning at a given stage, we cannot separate them from our general notions of the direction of development, that is, of what is involved in the transformations that take us from one stage to the next.

But our notion of the direction of development is itself bound up with our idea of what mature human life and intelligence are, so that, distressing as this may be to many, we are operating implicitly with a concept of the *terminus ad quem* of human development, a concept of successful maturity. In Piaget's case, for instance, there seem to be two very important directing ideas concerning the path of development: the subject moves away from egocentricity, and his thinking about things becomes more and more reversible. Egocentricity, as mentioned above, is understood by Piaget as relative undissociation of points of view. Although it is not easy to be sure of the exact meaning of this term (and a concept whose exact meaning cannot be finally pinned down is not surprising in a science which makes use of interpretation), it would seem that overcoming egocentrism is a matter of gradually distinguishing oneself as a subject and coordinating one's point of view with others, and consequently being able to 'decentre' one's grasp of things; being able, in other words, to grasp things not just in relation to oneself, or in the aspects that most strike one, but in terms of the inner articulations of the object itself.

This, in turn, is closely related to the growth of reversibility. This term is even harder to characterize in general; but it seems to involve something like this: thought is 'reversible' when it can operate transformations and still recover its point of departure. Now, properly to understand something is to be able to follow the changes it undergoes or could undergo, and to grasp well enough what is involved in these changes so that one can say what would be required to return the object to its initial state; and this either by simple reversal, or by compensating operations of some kind whose relation to the original one understands. Irreversible thought is thus thought which is unconscious of its implications, which cannot operate with the transformations that things undergo, and grasp what they involve and how they are related to each other. It is a form of thinking which is focussed on static conditions of things without being able to understand their relations.

Reversibility is thus a certain concept of objectivity; it is a concept of objectivity which naturally goes with a picture of the real as a system which can undergo a coherent set of transformations. The growth away from egocentrism and towards reversibility thus can be seen as a growth in objectivity, from a view of the world as it impinges on me to a grasp of it as it is 'in itself'. And to see the world objectively is to see it as a coherent set of transformations, as something which would ideally be manipulable in a coherent way.

These are among the ideas which underlie Piaget's particular formulae for intellectual development and performance at given stages. But it is not the only view compatible with his voluminous findings or with certain of his general ideas which no one would challenge.

It might appear that this picture of development dovetails perfectly with the theory of language developed above. Language as the capacity for disengaged awareness must surely set us on a path by which we overcome egocentrism and attain greater objectivity. But when we examine the matter more closely, we can see that this is not necessarily the case.

Play acting, or pretending, is an important activity that children start engaging in about the time that they start to talk. Piaget, as we saw, assigns this a role in the development of the symbolic function. Play represents the supremacy of assimilation over accommodation; it is 'la pensée égocentrique à l'état pur'.[8] It arises because the subject cannot yet

---

[8] J. Piaget, *La Formation du symbole chez l'enfant* (Neuchâtel, 1968), p. 175.

make a balanced adaptation to reality, where accommodation and assimilation are in equilibrium, and hence his grasp on things is an objective one. It is destined to merge more and more into constructive activity, on the one hand, and socialized competitive games with rules, on the other, as the child matures. But it has its importance in preparing the assimilative side of the eventual mature intelligence, that deductive reasoning power which can place the real in a matrix of possibles and which is an essential complement to empirical examination of things.

It is possible to take another view of the nature and function of this kind of symbolic play. Piaget sees it in the context of a growth towards objectivity which is itself defined in terms of reversibility. But we can see it in another light. Make-believe can be seen as a function which is complementary to language. If speech is the vehicle of a disengaged awareness of what surrounds us, pretending or make-believe is a way of disengaging in another sense, by lifting oneself out of one's situation. It is a way of transcending one's predicament, which can also alter this predicament; either because we may come to see and feel it in a different way, or because play acting and its adult derivatives may allow us to work through the predicament and come to terms with it.

This latter is very clearly a frequent function which play acting has for children. A child may act out with her doll a dramatic scene she has just had with her mother. In this context, pretending can be seen as a necessary concomitant to speech. For language, in facilitating disengaged awareness, is also at the root of human feeling. Not only is there a great range of human emotions like indignation or admiration which are 'thought-dependent' in the sense that they can only be attributed to language users; but it also seems plausible to say that even the common core which animals also feel, like fear and anger, are qualitatively different with man in that they are linked with an awareness of their objects which is open only to beings with language. That is why we can feel some reluctance to admit that animals have emotions in the human sense – an animal's fear or anger is confined to the context of provocation, we only use these terms to speak about a quality of his response in this context – and why we can think of human feeling as a mode of effective awareness of an object (even though this awareness may sometimes be repressed).[9]

The experience of a strong emotion is thus the experience of a situation which moves us, which rouses strong affect in us, affect which can be

[9] For a further discussion and defence of this view of emotion, see C. Taylor, 'Explaining action', *Inquiry*, 13 (1970), pp. 1–2.

unbearable. It is tremendously valuable to be able to step out of the situation, not in the sense of escapism (though this, too, may be a relief) but in order to be able to live it from another vantage point; not, in other words, to remain inextricably trapped in the primary experience. And this stepping out of our situation may help us to come to terms with it, to see it as something different, and hence to live it in a different way. This is how I would interpret the behaviour of the child who reenacts the emotional scene with her mother with her doll. The powerful emotion is worked through again in the make-believe situation in which the little girl even takes the other role, and in this way the child can come to terms with it.

The general notion of play acting that I am putting forward here is that it is a kind of complement to language, in that it is a way of stepping out of our situation which allows us to live it in a different way. It allows us to see our predicament from a different vantage point, and it builds up a capacity to live on several levels, which the adult normally has. The adult acts, in fact, in reference to a situation which has many levels beyond that of his immediate spatial or interpersonal predicament; he also lives in relation to social, political, professional, religious, or ideological realities. The life of the imagination is thus in part the successor activity in adult life of the play acting of the child; it continues to feed the ability to extend the situation in which we live.

Now, this view of play acting may or may not be right. It certainly is not without rivals; plenty of theories of play have been put forward in our intellectual tradition; in connection with the above example we have only to think of Freud's analysis of the child's game of 'Fort! da!'. But my purpose in putting it forward was not just to add another view (if indeed this one is new), but rather to show how a different and no less defensible view of play can alter our view of Piaget's conception of development.

In this view, play acting is not an early inadequate substitute for objectivity in Piaget's sense; it is not a deforming assimilation destined to be replaced by a properly balanced one. On the contrary, it may help us to come nearer to an objective understanding of our emotions and our relations with others. But this kind of objectivity is not to be understood in terms of reversibility. Our consciousness of what moves us, of our feelings in relation to it, and of our relations with others is always likely to be clouded over with self-induced illusion. In this sense, our consciousness tends to be 'egocentric', and one of the achievements of maturity can be that we are able to overcome this. Now, pretending and symbolic play, as a way of stepping out of our predicament, can help this process along (but there is no necessity in this; it can also feed our egocentric fantasies). It can also help the child to achieve the articulated understanding of distinct points of view on a common world, that is, to overcome egocentrism in Piaget's sense.

But the objectivity in question here is not Piaget's. Reversibility implies a grasp of things as systems which can undergo a coherent set of transformations as ideally manipulable entities; and connected with this it implies that we abstract from their significance for us in so coming to grips with them. But an objective understanding of our feelings or our relations with others can have neither of these features. Properly to understand one's own motivation, for instance, is not to grasp oneself as the locus of a set of coherent transformations; it is to be able to see one's feelings, desires, and situation in a certain perspective. Our understanding of potential transformations may be very uncertain and fragmentary, and may be far from the coherent systematic interrelatedness which is the essence of reversibility. It may be, indeed, that the findings of a science whose aim is objective understanding of man as a system of reversible transformations will help us to understand ourselves in this way; but the two enterprises are distinct.

If the first feature of reversibility is not appropriate here, the second feature is not either; there is no question of abstracting from the significance for us of what we are examining when we are trying to understand our own feelings. Rather, we are trying to get a balanced view of this significance. The same point can be made even more strongly about understanding our relations with others. It is, after all, intimately bound up with understanding our feelings. As we come to see the hidden sources of tension in a relationship, for instance, we can put it in perspective; and with this we alter the relationship in some degree, so that its past form can become unrecoverable in its entirety; and by this I mean not just that we cannot return to it in fact, but that we cannot even get a clear grasp intellectually of a return path; in other words, our thought here is 'irreversible'. Here, of course, the significance of what we are trying to put in perspective is a shared significance. To attempt to treat it as an object, which can be examined in abstraction from our involvement in it, is itself to stand back from this sharing, and hence alter the relationship.

We are dealing here with situations of involvement, to give them a general name, in which the strategy of seeking objectivity in the sense defined by reversibility is not available to us. We cannot abstract from their significance to us without shifting our object of study, and hence very possibly failing to come to grips with the original problem; and any substantial gain in our understanding of them changes them in ways which are often irreversible both factually and intellectually. We cannot become disintricated enough from them to dominate them as manipulable objects, and hence objectivity here has to mean something else; it can only mean that we come to put them in perspective.

By contrast, the type of objectivity appropriate in other contexts, such as when we are examining a physical system, is very much the kind which Piaget seems to designate by the term 'reversibility', the two aspects of which are closely connected. We attain reversibility when we grasp our object as a system of coherent potential transformations, and hence as an ideally manipulable object whose operations we therefore dominate, intellectually if not in act. And in order to attain this dominance, we have to abstract from our involvement with the object in order to grasp it 'as it is in itself'. Disinvolvement is thus the condition of a gain in intellectual dominance.

The hypothesis I am developing here is that mature intelligence involves the achievement of two different though related types of objectivity; one entails disinvolvement, and leads to reversibility and greater manipulative power; the other cannot achieve disinvolvement, and strives rather to achieve a truer perspective on the predicament concerned. The first can be seen as an advanced development of the basic capacity for disengaged awareness which is implicit in linguistic competence; whereas the second is built up more through our capacity to step out of our situation and 'play it back' from a different vantage point, which in the child takes the form of symbolic play. In other words, where we cannot loosen the affective link with our situation, we can still live it through play in another perspective.

This hypothesis may or may not have validity. I introduce it only to show the scope of potential theories here, among which the choice is not yet foreclosed. Piaget's concept of development is, thus, far from being the only possible one compatible with his data and consonant with some of his basic ideas, such as that growth is away from egocentrism and towards objectivity in some sense. Rather, in contrast to the hypothesis developed here, Piaget would be said to give a privileged position to one form of objectivity, and to have neglected the other. Thus, he sees symbolic play only in the context of the growth towards disinvolved objectivity, and hence simply as a one-sided assimilation unbalanced by accommodation, and not also as a stepping out of our predicament which develops our capacity to alter our perspective and hence achieve the other type of objectivity. (Of course, symbolic play and its successor activities facilitate objectivity without necessarily engendering it; they can just as well serve to entrench egocentric fantasy.)

There is thus a gamut of theories here which have to be weighed and tested. Each determines research paths which diverge at some point from the others. Thus, the hypothesis introduced above would examine childhood play from a different perspective, would try to chart the development in patterns of imaginative stepping out of the predicament as the child grows, would attempt to correlate these with the successive stages of the child's dissociation and articulation of his point of view with that of others, and the consequent development of his ego. Research of this kind would also show the extent to which different theories were compatible. For instance, the form in which our above hypothesis might be eventually validated would have a great deal of overlap with Piaget's theory. Divergences would come in the notions of play, in the gamut of skills which constitute a given stage, and at other points, but there would be a substantial common area.

But these different theories each determine a view of what I have called above the *terminus ad quem* of human development, a concept of successful maturity. In this way, genetic psychology cannot avoid entering one of the domains traditionally written off by academic psychology as 'philosophical', and cannot be thought of in the traditional sense as a 'value-free' science. Concepts of successful maturity are the basis of arguments concerning how we should live. For instance, the opposition between different concepts of objectivity adumbrated above is obviously related to potential differences about the value of 'objective' behaviour in one or the other sense in certain circumstances, about objectivity as an ideal, and so on.

But this need not lead us to write off genetic psychology as 'unscientific'. The fact that it impinges on the domain of concepts of maturity, and hence value, does not mean that it must proceed with any less regard for empirical fact or care in formulation and testing of theories. Genetic psychology is in fact the area where notions of maturity can be brought to empirical confrontation with each other. While the important place of interpretation in this science may make a final definitive and universally accepted selection difficult if not impossible, this does not make the enterprise any the less rational or subject to scientific canons. The fact that a science is not value-free does not mean that dispassionate and (largely in Piaget's sense) objective research is not required.

IV

The upshot of the discussion in sections II and III seems thus to be that genetic psychology operates with two major ranges of basic theoretical notions, those which touch on the nature of maturity – the *terminus ad quem* of development – and those which define innate structures – the *terminus a quo*. The study is, as it were, suspended between these two ranges which determine both its strategy of research and the interpretations it makes of the transformations which the child's intelligence, behaviour, and feelings undergo, including, of course, the definition of the stages of growth. Now, theory of this high level may make many dizzy; and if so, it is always possible to remain on the lower slopes and collect facts about the solution or non-solution of problems and the avowed reasoning of the subject. But only at a certain price: first, of parasitism, since the experiments which have now been made fashionable were themselves designed out of a theoretical approach which they have helped to define further – indeed, in Piaget's case a very far-reaching one which sees intelligence in its biological context. Second, one would be unable to generalize beyond the performance record for different types of problems, and the avowed reasoning of different stages; one would be debarred from seeking the underlying structures. This would mean, third, that one would be condemned to a kind of sterility in which no new frontiers of experimentation would be opened, and the field of study itself would stagnate.

In order to map effectively the transformations of ontogenesis, genetic psychology has to operate with notions of these two ranges, to devise research strategies from them, and to confirm, refute, or refine them in the light of the resultant findings. It is this rich theoretical component, perhaps as much as its rejection of incremental and environmental approaches, which makes genetic psychology appear still foreign and slightly discreditable among many academic psychologists in the Anglo-Saxon world. It is still too often the case in this world that theory seems to be the more valued, the less conscious it is. But this moratorium on basic theory seems now to be coming to a close, and genetic psychology will in the future arouse the interest it merits.

CHAPTER SEVEN

HOW IS MECHANISM CONCEIVABLE?

Must a neurophysiological account of human behaviour be a mechanist one? This is the question I would like to address myself to in this paper.

The common sense of our age, informed to some degree by the scientific tradition, seems to fall naturally into a Kantian antinomy on this question (as Marjorie Grene has pointed out),[1] that is, both the thesis and the antithesis seem to be grounded in solid argument. On one hand, it appears natural to proceed on the assumption that there is no upper limit to our ability to account for the functioning of ourselves and other animate organisms in terms of body chemistry and neurophysiology, and it is equally natural to assume that such accounts will be mechanistic – particularly in view of the sterility of rival approaches, such as vitalism. It even seems plausible to argue that 'mechanistic explanation' is a pleonasm, for any other kind of account appears rather to sidestep the problems of explanation; it does not, in other words, increase our ability to predict and control the phenomena as explanations should.

On the other hand, common sense is alarmed by the prospect of a complete mechanistic account of behaviour; not just alarmed practically, because of the unscrupulous use to which this knowledge might be put, but alarmed metaphysically, if I may use this term, because of what such an explanation would show about us. One of the commonest expressions of this concern centres in the issue of determinism, and the sense that somehow a complete mechanistic explanation would radically undermine our whole complex of notions which centre around freedom and moral responsibility.

But before going on to look at the arguments here it would be well to try to define more closely what distinguishes a mechanistic explanation and makes it both so plausible and threatening.

The features we are looking for are best brought out by contrast with

---

[1] Cf. M. Grene, 'Reducibility – another side issue?', in Grene (ed.), *Interpretations of Life and Mind* (London, 1971), pp. 14–37.

our ordinary way of talking about and explaining our behaviour at the everyday level. This talk has two features which mechanistic explanation does away with: first, it is teleological, that is, it describes our behaviour in terms of purpose, bent, desire, and other such concepts; second, it is 'intentional', that is, it constantly takes account of the meaning of things, environment and self, for the agent. A further word about these two features might help here. In saying that our talk is teleological, I am pointing to the fact, for instance, that our characterization of action in ordinary speech is usually in terms of the purpose sought in the action, so that we tend to withdraw or at least modify action ascriptions if we find that we were mistaken about the purpose. But this is not all: crucially, our explanations in ordinary language terminate with the invocation of a purpose, desire, or feeling, itself partly defined by what it disposes us to do – in short, our explanations terminate with a view of the agent as disposed to behave in a certain way, or as inclined to react in a certain way. We explain what someone does typically by sentences like these: 'he aims to become President', 'he loves her very much', 'he was terrified of meeting her again', 'that was a very provoking remark' (*sc.* a remark which tends to anger the person addressed), and so on. Hence the background to explanation in ordinary life is a picture of the agent as the subject of goals, desires, inclinations, susceptibilities of certain kinds. We are usually satisfied with an explanation when it relates the behaviour to be explained to one of the pictures of an agent which we accept as 'normal' in our civilization – for instance, in our case, when we explain someone's following some training by his aim to get ahead. Of course, these pictures of the normal agent vary from civilization to civilization, and sometimes from milieu to milieu within a society, which makes them very unsatisfactory in a scientific context.

The implications of our talk being intentional are not just that we distinguish between the situation and agent as they are *simpliciter* and as they are for the agent, but also that mediating propositions concerning what can loosely be called relations of meaning enter into our explanations. Suppose we are puzzled by why my interlocutor suddenly left the room, slamming the door behind him. It seems that he was angry at what I said; but why? The answer will come by filling in something of the background of his life and/or how he sees and feels about things (and in this context these two cannot be separated). We feel we understand when, for instance, we see that granted this background, and hence this way of seeing/feeling about things, what I said was insulting, or could be mistaken for an insult. Perhaps it sounded as though I was mimicking the accent of his region, or perhaps I showed insensitivity to a form of suffering which he has massively undergone.

In filling in this background we show how what I said could have the meaning of an insult, or an expression of contempt for him. What is crucial here is a relation of meaning: saying 'P' here in this way and at this time is insulting because it is (taken for) an expression of contempt; and as always, its having this meaning is contingent on its being embedded in a complex of other relations of meaning – on that regional accent's betokening for some an obtuseness or lack of sophistication, on that suffering's being for my interlocutor constitutive of his own identity and sense of worth, and so on.

Now these two features allow us to see more clearly both sides of the antinomy. On one hand, the model of explanation in natural science which has been applied in physiology has no place for ascriptions of bent or inclination; at the same time, it shies away from meaning relations as from the plague. For these can only be made clear, as we saw, against the background of a whole web of meaning, and this kind of thing is notoriously difficult to make clear in an unambiguous way and intersubjectively. Thus it would appear that the neurophysiological explanation to which we can ascribe no upper limit must continue to eschew these features and, hence, be mechanistic in the way I would like to define it here.

But on the other hand, these features are an essential part of our notion of ourselves. If we can give a complete mechanistic explanation of our behaviour and feeling, then, we feel obscurely, this will amount to saying that these features are not essential after all. But surely, our having goals is essentially involved in our being creatures capable of freedom and responsibility, and our very existence as talking animals seems inconceivable unless our behaviour is partly determined by relations of meaning.

We are thus torn apart by the warring tendencies of our intellect. It is at this point that philosophy often enters as a peacemaker and tries to convince us that there is really no question of incompatibility here. It is perhaps always unfair to plant the straw men one wants to attack in someone else's garden, but it seems to me that among recent Anglo-Saxon philosophers, Ryle[2] and Melden[3] have presented variants of this position. The argument seems to be something like this: our ordinary account of behaviour and the scientific explanation of it in neurophysiological terms

[2] G. Ryle, *Dilemmas* (Cambridge, 1954).   [3] A. I. Melden, *Free Action* (London, 1961).

cannot clash because they are talking about different things, and more-over serve quite different purposes. Our ordinary account characterizes our behaviour as action, while a mechanistic account is interested in explaining it *qua* movement. The latter account aims to lay bare the causes of this movement, while our explanation of action in ordinary terms is not causal at all: it explains in the sense of filling in the back-ground, of giving further information about what kind of behaviour it is.

I think all such attempts to make peace by keeping the combatants in separate rooms are doomed to failure. The basic problem is that our ordinary accounts of action are causal in a perfectly straightforward sense, even if they are not mechanistic. When I know that someone is doing what he is doing because he has goal G, I am able to predict and also in certain circumstances affect the course of his behaviour in a way I could not before. To know the purposes, desires, feelings or whatever, that condition people's behaviour is to know the causal background of their actions, and hence to know better what would alter it, or deflect it, what is likely to happen in future under what circumstances, etc. In short, our ordinary accounts license subjunctive and counter-factual conditionals just as mechanistic causal accounts do. Moreover, the fact that the two accounts use different descriptive languages, that of action and movement respectively, does not allow us to conclude that they are talking about different things in any relevant sense, for identity-relations can easily be mapped between the two ranges of things described.

But two such causal accounts, that is accounts which generate condi-tionals, are automatically potential rivals. Let us say that we explain a given stretch of behaviour in the ordinary way as action and also by some mechanistic physiological explanation as movement. *Ex hypothesi*, the *explicanda* in these two accounts are compatible, since these represent two descriptions of the same behaviour which has in fact occurred. But this does not mean that the two accounts are compatible; for both generate conditionals, and these have to be compatible at every point if the two explanations are to be judged so. Thus to explain the behaviour by neurophysiological state P_1 is to say, in terms of the mechanistic theory, that it would not have occurred, or would have occurred in modified form, if the state had been P_2. But this state P_2 may correspond to a motivational state which would be described in ordinary terms as G_b. Assuming that we originally explained the behaviour as action in terms of G_a, then the substitution of G_b for G_a would have to have the same consequences in cancelling and modifying the behaviour as the shift from P_1 to P_2. But supposing our explanation in terms of G_a were such that it would lead us to predict that the shift to G_b would intensify the behaviour, or alter it in some other way (while the shift from P_1 to P_2 would entail no parallel prediction)? In this case the two explanations could not both be true; typically we would decide between them by bringing about P_2-G_b and seeing what happened.

Two such accounts of the same events are thus potential rivals in the sense that they each trail a cluster of conditionals that may clash at some point. It is because of already recognized clashes of this kind that we accept that certain physiological explanations rule out certain motivational ones. To class some behaviour as reflex is to take it right out of the realm of purposive explanations, so that we cease to count it as action at all. This is so because a reflex in this sense is behaviour which can be produced by certain conditions in complete independence of the purposes of the agent. We know therefore in advance for any and every purposive explanation that some of its conditionals will be false, i.e. those which delineate the circumstances in which the action will not come about.

But this is not to say that causal accounts of the same phenomena are always rivals. On the contrary, they can be compatible, but this is only so when they are systematically related in some way. For each account generates an indefinite number of conditionals. It is not just enough that there is no clash for a given list of such conditionals; conflict must be absent over the whole non-infinitely delimitable range. In other words, it must be impossible to generate a conditional from one which will put it into conflict with the other. But this can be so only if there is some systematic relationship between the two.

Of course, there could be two unrelated laws stating necessary conditions, where both had to be met to provide a sufficient condition, and there could be two unrelated laws stating sufficient conditions where neither is necessary. But one could not state a sufficient and the other a necessary condition without there being some relation between the two. Now to focus on our problem, it is clear that our hypothetical complete mechanistic explanation in neurophysiological terms would provide us with both necessary and sufficient conditions for all our behaviour. ('Sufficient' here means 'sufficient within the system'; we take for granted that a whole host of external conditions for the normal functioning of the organism – enough air, absence of cosmic catastrophe, temperatures between certain limits, and so on – is met.) And with our ordinary explanations too, we frequently offer – in a quite unsystematic way, it is true – necessary and/or sufficient conditions (where 'sufficient' has the same restrictions as above).

Hence it would follow that these two accounts are potential rivals and that we cannot see them as coexisting happily in two unrelated universes of discourse. But then the threat of an antinomy returns. On one hand, the bent of our scientific culture seems to point us toward an eventual complete mechanistic account of behaviour; on the other hand, as a potential rival, this account could clash with and hence brand as erroneous the whole range of our ordinary explanations which we give and accept in everyday life. But this, quite apart from being disquieting, is unthinkable.

This last point requires, perhaps, further comment. Why should a clash of this kind be unthinkable? If it should arise, why couldn't we just reject our ordinary view in favour of the 'scientifically' better-grounded one? Is this not what has happened in all other spheres where scientific enquiry has taken us beyond common sense? After all, we have not privileged the ordinary teleological view of inanimate object behaviour which earlier attempts at physics enshrined. Why should we be more tender with animate behaviour?

The answer to this is an argument which seems to have no parallel elsewhere in philosophy. It is just that this supposition is too preposterous to be believed. For we are not talking here about the rejection of this or that old-wives' tale about behaviour, such as that rhino horn increases sexual desire. If all efficient-causal physiological explanation had the same logical relation to our ordinary account by motive as has the explanation in terms of reflexes, we would have to say that no part of our behaviour deserved the name 'action', that our entire vocabulary with the distinctions it marks had been systematically inapplicable, that the connections we experience between Xing and the desire to X were without foundation, and so on. And this is just too preposterous to swallow.

The difficulty here springs from the fact that our descriptive language for behaviour and feeling is closely tied to a certain sort of explanation. In other words, it is a peculiarity of the language with which we describe our behaviour and feelings that it characterizes these as susceptible of explanation of a certain sort. To characterize something as action in a certain context is to say that it is explicable by goals or inclinations, and to give a particular action-description is to narrow the range of acceptable goals or inclinations which can be invoked. To characterize a feeling by a certain emotion term is to say that it is linked to a certain situation which is seen as being of a certain type, viz. the appropriate object of this emotion. If I am feeling guilt, then it is over some wrong of which I am guilty; if I cannot see an adequate object in the putative cause, then I search further in my unconscious feelings to see what (perhaps highly irrational) sense of wrong is at the root of this.

Now I may be mistaken, this may not be guilt that I feel. But it is not possible to accept the proposition that we are always mistaken, that a concept of this kind has no application at all. Similarly we are often wrong in our action-descriptions, but we cannot claim that all our action-descriptions are misplaced on the grounds that all behaviour is explicable by the type of physiological efficient-causal explanation, which like that by reflexes rules action out. This 'cannot' does not repose on any argument, but simply on the impossibility of believing that we have been talking nonsense all these millennia.

We can thus imagine hypothetical mechanistic explanations which we would be led to reject out of hand because they clashed with our ordinary account in such a way as to make nonsense of all our current vocabulary. In order to avoid this consequence, we must conceive any mechanistic explanation as systematically related to our ordinary account, and hence as *grosso modo* avoiding rivalry with it.

And in fact the model of this coordination is readily available: it is that of the reduction of one theory or set of laws to another in the sciences. An example of this is offered by the reduction of the Boyle-Charles law, and also various phenomena of thermodynamics, to a more basic explanation in terms of the kinetic theory of gases. In this case, two explanations are coordinated in that once we can establish connections between descriptions of states in the languages of both theories (meeting Nagel's 'conditions of connectability') we can derive the laws of the less basic system from those of the more basic together with those connecting correlations (hence meeting Nagel's 'conditions of derivability').[4]

We can call one system more basic than another when the two are coordinated in this way: when one has a broader application than the other, or itself stems from the specification of laws which are broader in application, so that the conditions of the less basic laws' holding can be stated in the more basic theory. In this sense the more basic can be said to offer us an explanation of the regularities holding in the less. It is clear that the kinetic theory has this status *vis-à-vis* the Boyle-Charles law.

In our case, the mechanistic theory would be the more basic, since it would supposedly be founded on the principles of physics and chemistry, which have an application to a much wider range of phenomena than just living beings; and it is expected that it would allow for a much finer

---

[4] E. Nagel, *The Structure of Science* (New York, 1961), pp. 353–4, 433–5.

prediction and control of human behaviour, and hence would fill in the many gaps and uncertainties in our ordinary explanations-by-motive and in those theories which have developed with these as a starting point. In other words it would prove its broader scope by allowing us to derive new, unsuspected explanations on the ordinary level of motive. This kind of performance is, of course, another of the prerogatives of a more basic theory (and has analogues with the kinetic theory above).

Thus our mechanistic theory would have to be coordinated in such a way that we could connect many of the state-descriptions in everyday language with state-descriptions cast in the language of the theory: such and such a pattern of excitation corresponds to the state of desiring peanuts, such and such another to that of feeling guilty over failing one's exams, and so on. And these connections would allow us to derive plausible motive explanations from those of the theory in a large number of cases (of course, not in all: the advantage of such a mechanistic theory would presumably be that it would give us the first foolproof counter to self-deception, repression, etc., and, hence, allow for new discovery in human psychology).

Now the fact that the mechanistic theory would be a potential rival to our ordinary account has been the ground for arguments to the effect that mechanism is in some sense inconceivable. These repose on the preposterousness of the claim that our ordinary talk is radically mistaken. Malcolm's recent article seems to take a variant of this line, although here the preposterousness comes out in a kind of pragmatic paradox involved in the statement of the mechanist position.[5] But in order to make his argument stick, Malcolm is forced to show that the mechanistic account cannot be related to our ordinary one as more to less basic explanation. And it would follow from the above that any argument to the effect that mechanism is inconceivable must do the same; for if both accounts are systematically related, then there is no clash, and mechanism is freed of the embarrassing claim that our everyday consciousness of action is radically in error.

Now I believe that all arguments against the conceivability of mechanism fail because they cannot rule out this possibility of systematic coordination. Let us look at Malcolm's argument. This runs roughly as follows: if we want to set up the two kinds of explanation in canonical form, where a general proposition and a particular proposition of fact allow us

[5] N. Malcolm, 'The conceivability of mechanism', *Philosophical Review*, 77 (1968), pp. 45–72.

to derive the *explicandum*, then there is a significant difference in logic between the two general propositions. For ordinary explanation is in terms of an inclination of the agent, as we have seen; but this means that to set it up like other explanations is to produce a major which is non-contingent. Thus supposing we explain A's doing B by saying that A saw that B leads to G. In ordinary life, we understand as given that A has goal G, and this is then a satisfactory explanation. But supposing we are asked to spell out the explanation? If we follow the model of explanation of inanimate things, we might look again at the following example. Why was there an explosion? Because A lit a match near the leaking main. In order to fill this out we need to add: and lighting matches near leaking mains produces explosions (or some general proposition from which this could be deduced with a few simple statements of fact). Now if we return to our action example, we find that what corresponds to the particular circumstances related in 'A lit a match near the leaking main' is 'A has G as a goal' and 'A sees that B leads to G'. What then takes the place of the general law about fire, gas and explosions is 'when A has goal G and sees that B leads to G, he does B'.

But translated out of this gobbledy-gook, and joined with a *ceteris paribus* clause, this is not a contingent proposition; for if A wants G and sees that he can get it by B, then if there are no deterrents or obstacles (this latter protasis being the burden of the *ceteris paribus* clause), he does B of necessity: that is, this is what we mean by 'want', for it ascribes a bent of the agent toward a certain consummation, and if with no obstacles or deterrents he fails to move in this direction, we cannot go on ascribing it to him.

But no comparable *ceteris paribus* clause will transform the major about fire, gas and explosions into a non-contingent proposition. And the difference is once more this pervasive one noted above: that our ordinary explanations are teleological, that they operate with the notion of incli-nation. But since the antecedent circumstances which one marshals to explain action include inclinations, the sum of these circumstances is already non-contingently likened to the *explicandum*; or to put it another way, the sum of them must show the disposition to the *explicandum*. But this means that it is not a contingent matter that *ceteris paribus* these circumstances lead to the action to be explained. The addition of a general truth proposition is therefore unnecessary, and any we do add will not be contingent.

Now Malcolm argues that since the general 'laws' of ordinary explana-tion are not contingent they cannot be seen as related to mechanistic laws on a more basic level; for this would mean, as we have seen, that they would be 'explained' by the latter in the sense that we would be able to express in the terms of the mechanistic theory the conditions of their holding. But, Malcolm argues, 'the a priori connection between intention or purpose and behaviour cannot fail to hold', and thus 'it cannot be contingently dependent on any contingent regularity'.[6]

But this argument is invalid; and Malcolm gives the wherewithal to answer it on the very next page. And so he must; for he wants to go on to argue that 'the verification of a comprehensible neurophysiological theory of behaviour' would refute our purposive explanations,[7] which is of course essential to his argument about the conceivability of mechanism. But if we construe these explanations as reposing on *a priori* principles, how can they be refuted? Malcolm is thus forced to introduce the following distinction: what cannot be shown false to all eternity is the truth that if A wants G and sees that B leads to G, then *ceteris paribus* he will do B.[8] For this depends on the meaning of 'want'. But what can be established empirically is whether or not this set of concepts, and the accompanying 'laws', really apply to human behaviour. This is enough for Malcolm's purposes, for the claim that they do not, while logically sound, is preposterous.

But if we take this distinction back to the preceding page, then the argument against more basic mechanistic explanations disappears. For we would not be claiming to show in neurophysiology the conditions of the truth of these *a priori* propositions about 'want', but only the conditions of their application to the animate organisms to which we apply them. And this seems a just statement of what such a mechanistic theory could claim to show. The logic of the two languages is very different. But this by itself is never an obstacle to the reduction of one theory to another; indeed, there is always such a non-congruence of the conceptual mesh. There would thus be nothing in the neurophysiological theory like the concept 'want', but this would not prevent us from using connecting propositions such as 'the state P_x is the state of the CNS which corresponds to what we call "wanting peanuts"'. We could indeed never show why wanting peanuts is followed by trying to get peanuts, but we could show why this behaviour follows P_x; and this contingent nomological regularity would be what underlies (all unknown to us at present) our present use of the concept 'wanting peanuts'. The regularity makes a concept with this logic applicable, and included in the logic are 'laws' of the type Malcolm cites.

Hence, if the above reasoning is right, there is no blanket argument to the

---

[6] *Ibid.*, p. 50.   [7] *Ibid.*, p. 51.   [8] *Ibid.*

inconceivability of mechanism; we cannot argue, that is, from the fact that mechanistic explanations are irreducibly different in logic to the (teleological and intentional) explanations of ordinary life to the conclusion that a mechanistic account is untenable. But there does emerge from the above an important restriction on mechanistic explanations of behaviour: any acceptable such account must in fact be coordinated with our everyday account so as to 'save the phenomena'.

I would like now to look more closely at what this restriction involves. It does not mean, as I said above, that all the explanations which we accept in everyday life as valid or even obvious must be upheld by being shown to be derivable from true statements of the mechanistic theory. On the contrary, we would expect that many of the ideas of our present conventional wisdom would be upset. But it does mean that the type of explanation which is shown to be so derivable must be such that it upholds in the general case the logic of our ordinary language of feeling, action and desire.

An example may make clearer what is meant here. Let us say that I am racked with guilt because I have slain my brother. Now the logic of this notion of guilt over fratricide is that the feeling is related to the thought (in this case, memory) of my killing my brother and also to a complex of other thoughts and feelings whose upshot is to present this act as a heinous offence. Now to say that the feeling according to its concept is related to these thoughts is to say something about its aetiology. Had I not killed my brother, or could I suppress the (even unconscious) memory of this act, or could I really come (in the depths of emotion and not just by a superficial judgement) to feel that it was not a terrible wrong, my guilt would be assuaged. If this aetiology is not true, that is, if one of these conditions is met and the feeling remains, then the original ascription was wrong: perhaps I am feeling guilty over something else; perhaps what I feel is not guilt at all.

Now imagine that we are accounting for this in our mechanistic theory. Then the requirement of compatibility means that our mechanistic account must back up the aetiology which is implicit in the logic of the concept used. Now the corresponding state-descriptions of the mechanistic theory will, of course, have nothing of the logic of our everyday feeling language. Corresponding to the guilt-feeling will be, say, a neurochemical state of the organism G; this in turn will be explained by, let us say, various patterns of excitation in the brain, $P_1, P_2, P_3, \ldots P_n$. The links between these will then be purely contingent.

But the question is whether the mechanistic account supports the aetiology, and this is a question of the counterfactual and subjunctive conditionals it contains. For in general, as we have seen, two causal theories which seem to apply equally well to a given case will still be judged incompatible if the conditionals they support diverge. To say that they are coordinated is to say that they are linked in such a way that their conditionals cannot diverge.

Granted, then, that we can link the necessary conditions above, that I have killed my brother, that I remember this act, etc., with some members of the series of P-states, $P_1 \ldots P_n$, or with the causes of P-states, the question is whether we can derive the same conditionals from the mechanistic theory together with those connecting propositions. If not, and if we accept the mechanistic theory as true, then we will have shown that the ascription of guilt over fratricide was untrue. If, for instance, we could show that the P-states linked with the memory (even unconsciously) of my killing my brother, or those linked with my seeing fratricide as wrong, had nothing to do with the feeling, and that their suppression would leave the feeling intact, then we could not go on describing this feeling as guilt about the act.

Now it is conceivable in this case that we might discover that I was self-deceived, that I was not really guilty over fratricide, but over something else; it is even conceivable that we might discover that my psychic pain was to be understood in the light of quite another feeling than guilt. We might thus find in this case that the appropriate aetiology was not backed up.

But the general requirement of compatibility is that this must be the exceptional case, rather than the rule. For if it happened in every case, this would mean that the concept 'guilt' would never be correctly applied. And that is just too much to swallow. And even if we could open our dialectical throats wide enough to swallow this, we certainly could not cope with the whole range of similar concepts which describe our feelings and aspirations: gratitude, indignation, compassion, shame, pride, remorse, awe, contempt, regret, ambition, and so on, and with the whole range of action concepts, which would have to go down if we allowed for general incompatibility between the mechanistic explanation and our ordinary language.

This problem of compatibility would arise not only where we already feel we know the explanation, as in the case above (for nothing could be clearer according to our accepted background than feeling guilt because one has killed one's brother). It is just as germane where we are still looking for an explanation. Let us suppose that an immigrant who has become very rich in the new world feels guilt about having left his native land and family. Let us say that in terms of his values, there is something irrational about this. So we look for an explanation.

Now this explanation will involve our tracing irrational leaps in unconscious thought. Perhaps an infantile sense of wrong for having acted in a certain way toward his brother extends to the thought that here he is rich today while the same brother moulders away in the native village. Perhaps even this guilt does not come out until some other development, only irrationally linked with it, brings it out: let us say that the immigrant feels quite happy until the beginning of financial adversity triggers a sense that he deserves this 'punishment' which he is now receiving.

Or perhaps, rather, this guilt object is a screen; he is really guilty because he has become rich by exploiting his workers, but finds it easier to admit to himself the sense of 'wrong' over leaving his family, a feeling which he and his friends will after all go on castigating as irrational but honourable, rather than acknowledging the real object.

These and many other explanations are possible, as explanations of guilt (in both cases) or as explanations of guilt over this object (in the case of the first explanation). Compatibility means, in this example, not that our mechanistic account backs up an already known explanation, for there is none, but that it backs up an explanation which is in keeping with the logic of 'guilt over leaving family' or at least 'guilt'. There must, that is, be some account of it as guilt whose counterfactual or subjunctive conditionals are derivable from the mechanistic account and the connecting propositions.

This example is of interest because it shows, first, that while giving an account of a feeling as guilt does not mean that one accounts for it as rational guilt, this nevertheless does not abolish the distinction. If we are to be able to defend the use of the concept, the explanation must make the feeling understandable as one of guilt, and this involves reference to wrong or sin for which we are responsible; in short it involves reference to the 'guilty'. This may take the form of a childish sense of wrong-doing earlier experienced, which we have long ceased to judge as wrong, and hence may be irrational; and even further irrationality may enter in, such as in the case above when the guilt is triggered by the financial adversity perceived as 'punishment'. But we remain within the same circle of ideas, and must, if we are to speak of 'guilt'.

The requirement of compatibility is thus that there be some explanation based on these ideas which is supported by the mechanistic account, in the sense that its conditionals are derivable from those of the mechanistic account in the way mentioned in the previous paragraph.

And this case shows, second, that once more the principle of compatibility which we demand that mechanistic explanations fulfil has nothing necessarily to do with supporting the explanations of behaviour which we currently may accept, that it applies even where we have the wrong explanation or confess ourselves to have none at all. The principle does claim, however, to put a limit on possible types of mechanistic theory, namely, that they must provide accounts which, via the connecting propositions linking theoretical states with action and feeling descriptions, support explanations of our actions and feelings which do not violate the logic of the terms we use to describe them – if indeed not invariably, then at least generally and for the most part. And this on pain of saddling us with the preposterous conclusion that we have been talking nonsense all these millennia, that the criteria for the application of our ordinary terms for feeling and behaviour are never or hardly ever met.

What are the consequences for the pursuit of the sciences of behaviour which flow from this principle of compatibility? Well, first, that *a priori* arguments against a more basic mechanistic explanation, such as that cited from Malcolm above, are invalid.

But second, the idea of a science of behaviour which could link 'receptor impulse' and 'colourless movement' via some theory of the brain and CNS, and which might have no relation at all to our ordinary vocabulary and the distinctions it marks, which would give us no basis for distinctions, for example like that between shame and guilt, or anger and indignation, and so on, treating these in the way that post-Galilean physics treats, for instance, the Aristotelian distinction between supra- and sublunar – this idea is an epistemological monstrosity.

It follows, thirdly, that any mechanistic theory which can claim to account for behaviour will have to be rich enough to incorporate the basis of a very wide range of distinctions which, at present, mark the intentional world of human agents and which are essential to understand their behaviour. I have mentioned above just a few important feeling-terms which are general to men. But incorporated into the description of much of human behaviour is some reference to the set of institutions in which men live and are formed (as seen by them, either in terms of their own descriptions, or in terms of their real meaning for them), to the set of social meanings on the basis of which they operate to understand themselves and each other, and so on. And these, of course, vary greatly with the culture, or even in some cases the circle to which people belong.

Imagine that we are accounting for the following event: a vassal remains covered in the presence of the king, and this he does deliberately as an incitement to revolt, or even perhaps as a signal to his confederates to rise. Now any explanation of this event must support counterfactuals which involve reference to kingship, revolt, the symbolism of uncovering oneself before majesty, and so on. For it must be true that our hero would not have remained covered had he not perceived this man entering the room as the king, rather than as the new pretender whom he supports. And that he would not have remained covered either if this act had not had this significance of refusing allegiance, or if his forces had not been ready (in the case where this is a signal to rise), and so on. Unless these counterfactuals or others like them are true, our original description is in jeopardy.

Central to any understanding of human behaviour which starts from explanation by motive is the fact that man is a cultural animal, that his behaviour can vary very widely, and that these variations must be understood in the light of the differences in human culture. This is not to say that explanation must always be couched in the language of the given culture, but a people's self-understanding must be among the things which any adequate theory can explain. We must therefore be able to express in our theory the major distinctions by which men understand the differences in their behaviour from person to person and time to time. And this means that a neurophysiological mechanist theory must have this property as well.

It follows from this that the idea of such a mechanistic science as representing a simpler road than a science of behaviour which comes to grips with human culture is an illusion. Our neurophysiological theory will have to be rich enough to mark the major distinctions of all the varied human cultures. We can only explain behaviour in terms of what goes on 'under-the-skin' if we incorporate 'under-the-skin' state-descriptions corresponding to all the wide range of furniture of the human agent's intentional environment, the inventory of which requires that one explore the entire range of his culture. For a neurophysiological short-cut which by-passed cultural differences would make nonsense of a great part of the descriptions men use to speak of themselves.

Hence the requirement to 'save the phenomena' defines a criterion that any neurophysiological theory must meet to be worth considering. Of course, this criterion can and should be developed in greater detail, and in some dimensions with considerable exactness. Recent developments in psycho-linguistics provide a good example. Unless we want to by-pass altogether the distinction between understanding and not understanding a sentence, or finding it well- or ill-formed, which would once more be preposterous, our explanation of verbal behaviour has to be able to account for the full complexity of the operations by which we form and recognize these sentences. Any approach which does not address itself to this requirement is not worth pursuing.

In the foregoing we have considered some arguments which could serve as the antithesis to mechanism in our antinomy. As blanket arguments against the conceivability of mechanism, they cannot be sustained; but something interesting does necessarily come out of all this, viz. a restriction on any mechanistic theory, that it must 'save the phenomena' by generating the distinctions which underlie our vocabulary of action and feeling and those implicit in our culture. Now this may suggest to us that after all the sharp opposition between neurophysiological explanation and our ordinary account might be misguided.

What if, in order to generate the rich variety of distinctions which must be saved, future neurophysiological theory found it necessary to enrich its vocabulary and hence its conceptual armoury? And supposing that the new ranges of concepts incorporated some of the purposive and intentional force of our current ordinary vocabulary? This would be the case, for instance, if certain global patterns of excitation in the brain and nervous system could be adequately understood in their functioning, conditions and consequences only if we identified them partly in terms of or in relation to the psychological processes or states they mediate.

It is very difficult to say anything very sensible about this prospective conceptual enrichment at this stage, just because any conceptual innovation cannot be mapped until it has occurred. All I can claim at this stage is that we have no reason to look on our present categories as so fixed that a conceptual convergence of this form is ruled out. It is therefore perfectly conceivable that we may move toward a neurophysiological theory which will not be reductive, in the sense that it will not show teleological and intentional concepts to be eliminable at a more basic level. If this were to be the case, then the problems connected with the above antinomy would disappear.

This statement of possibility is all that can be argued at this stage, as I said above. But it is evident that even this will not be accepted without argument; and so I must turn now to the other side of the antinomy, the arguments in favour of the thesis of mechanism. It seems to me that these fall basically into two categories, the methodological and the ontological.

The crux of the methodological argument is the belief mentioned above that any explanation other than a mechanistic one leaves some questions unanswered. If we introduce purposive concepts, like the famous 'entelechies' of vitalism, then we simply close off certain questions, viz. those dealing with the mechanisms which underlie the functions specified by our entelechies. This would only be justifiable if there were nothing here to discover, but the history of biology rather leads us to believe the opposite. Great progress has been made by attempting to discover the mechanisms underlying certain holistic functions; we have only to think of the recent breakthrough by Crick and others which has opened the mechanisms of cell-replication.

Now this is less an argument from logical necessity than it is a persuasive use of historical analogy.[9] Even if in the past the introduction of non-mechanist concepts has closed avenues which turned out to be worth exploring, this does nothing to show that such consequences necessarily follow on the use of such concepts. But the case for the possibility of convergence can be presented in a more positive light. The kind of conceptual enrichment alluded to above would not necessarily have the effect of closing off further enquiry concerning the phenomena characterized, as has been widely claimed for Driesch's entelechies; on the contrary, we can imagine a whole range of questions which would open on the border of psychology and neurophysiology. Others, including some avenues of enquiry of a strictly mechanist kind, would be closed. But it is true of any range of explanatory concepts that in characterizing a given range of reality by means of them we open some avenues of enquiry and close others. Nothing can be concluded from this in general about the validity of any given range; it all depends how fruitful are the avenues opened and closed. And this we can only find out by looking; no *a priori* arguments are valid.

Hence arguments from striking historical parallels, like vitalism, cannot be conclusive *a priori*. For they all depend on clinching the case that the parallel really holds, and this may depend on our showing that in practice the new range of concepts has the same drawbacks as others putatively similar have had. Thus a fault of vitalism is that it seemed to allow no place at all for further enquiry, but this cannot be claimed about future conceptual enrichment of the type I am suggesting until we have a chance to examine actual cases of suggested conceptual revisions and additions.

The fact is that many of the great paradigms of scientific progress can be used to teach more than one lesson. Does the revolution in physics in the seventeenth century tell in favour of mechanism because it was mechanist, or does it show rather how the hold of a powerful traditional conceptual scheme (Aristotelian in the seventeenth century; mechanist, in ours) on the

---

[9] Grene, 'Reducibility – another side issue?'

scientific community can impede progress? We shall have to await the outcome of present disputes to see who has been cast in the role of Galileo and who in that of his obtuse Aristotelian critics.

The ontological objection is deeper and harder to state and, hence, naturally, to criticize. But it goes something like this: human beings are after all physical objects; they must therefore obey the laws of physics and chemistry, those which have been found true for all physical objects. It follows that some form of reductivism must hold, that is, that higher level explanations, like the psychological or the sociological, must be ultimately explicable on a more basic level, in terms of physics and chemistry; on the way down this reductivist road, we would obviously pass a neurophysiological stage.

In order to see the necessity of reductionism here, the argument runs, we have to examine the alternatives. If there were true explanations of behaviour on the psychological level which were not reducible to a neurophysiological account (as a first step, of course, but all the questions of principle can be posed about this first step) and hence were not coordinated with this more basic explanation, then it follows (as we saw above) either that one or other of these accounts must be inadequate in some respect, or else that they hold of different things. Since by hypothesis the psychological account is valid, we have to conclude either that the neurophysiological account is inadequate, that is, that on its own it goes astray at certain points (the points of conflict), or else that the psychological account applies to something which the neurophysiological account cannot encompass. But the latter conclusion amounts to some form or other of mind–body dualism, for it entails that there is a level of reality accessible to psychological description and explanation, description of which cannot be formulated in neurophysiological terms. Or else this level of reality would provide a set of events susceptible of neurophysiological explanation, and this would land us back in the first alternative.

Now this first alternative is unacceptable, because it amounts to saying that the laws of neurophysiology (and hence at lower stages those of physics and chemistry) have exceptions at those points where there is conflict with our psychological explanations. But a doctrine of exceptionalism seems hard to justify intellectually. We are thus forced back on to dualism, but this scarcely seems plausible to the contemporary mind, even if *sub specie aeternitatis* it may be as tenable as any other hypothesis. We have trouble believing that there are functions of the mind which are not in some sense embodied in neural activity of some kind or other (though this is not the same thing as holding what is called among con-temporary philosophers the 'identity theory', for this involves a prior acceptance *holus bolus* of mechanism). But quite apart from this, the form of dualism entailed by this horn of the dilemma is a particularly implausible one, since it involves non-interference between the two realms of mind and matter. For if what goes on on the psychological level were to have an effect on the neurophysiological level, then there would be some interruption in the smooth operation of neurophysiological function according to neurophysiological laws; and once more these laws would have exceptions.

But how could we even exist as rational life if the realms of mind and matter functioned independently of each other? Hence they must be coor-dinated. But how coordinated if not by systematic relation between the causal laws? The only alternative model of coordination would seem to be some rather fantastic hypothesis like Malebranchian occasionalism.

The weirdness of such occasionalist hypotheses may force the dualist back into the notion that mind and body after all interact; but then by this he only succeeds in impaling himself on both horns of the dilemma at once, for he holds both dualism and exceptionalism and seems to have involved himself in a set of insuperable epistemological problems.

Now since this whole dilemma arises from denying that there is a systematic relation between valid psychological explanations and those on a lower level, we seem bound to accept this premise. But if we accept systematic relation, then there can be little doubt that the neuro-physiological (and later the physico-chemical) is the more basic level; for these laws apply to a wider range of phenomena, and the 'higher' explanations must represent special cases of these. Lower must mean more basic here, and everything must be reducible to physics and chemistry.

Something like this underlies the current faith in mechanism. The argu-ment is powerful as long as we remain with the old fixed alternatives; but once we examine a hypothesis like that of conceptual convergence above, its weaknesses come to light. In fact, there are two related places where key questions are begged. One is hidden in expressions like 'the laws of physics and chemistry' or 'the laws of neurophysiology'; the other is hidden in the terms 'governed by' or 'apply' when used in connection with these laws.

To take the first one: on the convergence hypothesis I adumbrated above, it will be true that all behaviour will be accounted for in neurophysiological terms, only the neurophysiological theory adequate to this purpose will be an enriched one relative to what we know at present. When we put it in this way, the mechanistic argument founders; for it amounts to a denial *a priori* that such an enrichment will prove necessary or possible; and who can justify this? It would have been as absurd for nineteenth-century mechanist physics to have denied that any conceptual enrichment would be necessary in order to account for physical phenomena. Some physicists were tempted then, but no one would make such a denial on behalf of contemporary physics.

The mechanist argument rests here on an equivocation on 'the laws of neurophysiology'. If one wishes to avoid dualism and all its consequences, one will hold that in some sense we can give a neurophysiological account of all behaviour, for all behaviour has a neurophysiological embodiment and so falls *ipso facto* into its domain. But the sense of 'neurophysiological account' which figures in this denial of dualism is not restricted as to the explanatory concepts deployed; the term here means only an explanation which accounts for neurophysiological phenomena. The equivocation lies between this quite general sense and one which is closer to 'account in terms of the presently accepted concepts of neurophysiology and extensions of them'. By moving from one to the other unconsciously, we can believe that we have ruled out the kind of conceptual convergence I mentioned above by the argument against dualism. Indeed, one *can believe* that the only alternatives are dualism and the present assumptions of the science. And this is really the crucial belief; if one accepts this, then it is easy to identify all neurophysiological explanation with explanations according to present canons. But this premise is far from necessary.

This equivocation on 'the laws of ...' (neurophysiology or physics or chemistry) also underpins the view that our hypothesis of convergence is exceptionalist or interactionist. For it lies behind the whole dilemma which forces us into some such position to avoid dualism, by defining any novel explanatory principles as outside 'the laws of neurophysiology' (or physics or chemistry). But the accusation of interactionism is backed up by another equivocation, that on notions like 'governed by' (laws), or (laws) 'applying'. This may still worry us even when we have set aside as an unimportant verbal question how we are going to use expressions like 'the laws of physics' or 'the laws of neurophysiology'.

The worry can perhaps be expressed most clearly in connection with physico-chemical explanation. If the principles of such explanations as we know them now are not adequate to account for the behaviour of animate beings, or of men, while remaining generally appropriate for the rest of nature, then surely there must be something very odd about animate beings. For those laws of physics and chemistry which apply to nature in general will somehow not apply, or will at least admit of exceptions, in the case of animals; and is this idea not a species of exceptionalism – once we admit, that is, that animate beings are also physical beings *à part entière* – that is, once we abandon any form of dualism? It must follow, therefore, that animate behaviour must be explicable in terms of the laws of physics and chemistry and, hence, that all other explanations must be reducible to those in terms of these laws, where 'the laws of physics and chemistry' designates simply those laws which are found to apply to the whole domain of nature, whatever these turn out to be. The argument hence avoids *a priori* legislation concerning these laws.

Now, of course, the argument in these terms does not necessarily rule out non-mechanist explanations of behaviour, if we accept as possible some Teilhardian hypothesis in which we might need enriched concepts to deal adequately with inanimate nature as well. But even leaving aside such long shots, the argument does not hold. There is no reason in general to hold that animate behaviour must be accountable for by the same principles as inanimate – outside of the notion that since animate behaviour is, like everything else in nature, governed by the general laws of physics and chemistry, it cannot also be governed by other principles, without these in some sense breaching these general laws and, hence, creating exceptions.

But this notion is based on a confusion which centres in the notion of 'governed by'.[10] Thus to say that a range of things is governed by a certain set of laws, defining, say, a given force, is not to say that these laws can account for all the behaviour of things of this range; we may have to invoke laws defining some other force to explain what occurs. Moreover, both forces may operate on the same behaviour, so that we have to invoke both together to explain certain events. Such is the case with gravity and electromagnetism, for instance, in physics. To put it crudely, one can lift things with a magnet that otherwise would fall to or remain on the ground.

But in these cases, even if we might speak of one force 'interfering' with the other, in that if one were to cease operating, the course of events determined uniquely by the other would be different from what it in fact is, it would still be absurd, for example, were we to start with a physics which recognized only gravity and then modify it to take account of

---

[10] *Ibid.*

magnetism, for us to say that we had discovered that not all bodies are 'governed by' the law of gravity after all. That is not what we mean by 'governed by'; rather gravity remains essential to our understanding how things behave even when we discover with the operation of other forces that things are more complicated. The fact that things would be different if, in some way rather difficult to imagine, gravity were the only force operating on bodies is neither here nor there, unless anthropomorphically we want to think of gravity as taking umbrage at this.

A similar reasoning applies to our problem. On my convergence hypothesis above, the present principles of neurophysiology, and *a fortiori* those of physics and chemistry, would be supplemented by concepts of quite a different kind, in which, for instance, relations of meaning might become relevant to neurophysiological process. If this turned out be of explanatory value, then, we could conclude that these new principles also govern the phenomena. We can hope that the predictions we make with the aid of these new explanatory concepts differ from those which would be made with an exclusive reliance on the old ones, for otherwise there would have been little point in introducing them. In this sense, the new 'forces' can be said to 'interfere'. But it would be absurd to say that our hypothesis entails that the original principles no longer govern the phenomena, that we have found 'exceptions' to them.

In fact we would only be tempted to say that a given range of laws suffered exceptions if the additional 'forces' could not be understood in terms of *any* principles, but remained quite refractory to scientific explanation of any kind. What underlies this accusation of exceptionalism is, in fact, the deep-seated prejudice that scientific explanation is impossible on other than mechanistic principles. If we accept this premise, then we can reason that any attempt to supplement our existing scientific languages with non-mechanist principles can only introduce gaps in our explanations, and to believe that this is justified one would have to hold to some kind of exceptionalism.

The argument which flows from the confusion around the term 'governed by', like that around the term 'the laws of ...' which we discussed above, thus reposes in the end on the identification of scientific laws and explanation in general with laws and explanations based on principles currently in vogue, viz. mechanistic ones. It is only by accepting this identification that we can show that the only alternatives to reductionism are dualism and exceptionalism. But then the reductive argument against our convergence hypothesis, which aims to prove that non-mechanistic explanation of this kind will not do, assumes what it sets out to prove. It can only get going if we assume mechanism from the start.

In other words, to look on a conceptual enrichment of neurophysiology of the kind I have been discussing as a species of exceptionalism, as a claim that the laws of neurophysiology and a portion of physics and chemistry do not apply, is to have covertly identified the laws of science *tout court* with laws of the type now in vogue. If this were the case, then indeed, the introduction of any other principle of explanation would be tantamount to a claim that these laws do not apply universally, do not govern all the phenomena. And thus we could argue that all higher level explanations must be reducible to physico-chemical ones, else they cannot be considered scientific explanations. ·

But if we define mechanistic explanation as we did at the beginning, as a form of explanation which eschews teleological and intentional concepts, and mechanism as the doctrine that all scientific explanation must be of this type, then we have in this identification a mechanist premise. And this means that the reductive argument against our convergence hypothesis, which is an alternative to mechanism, is based on a *petitio principii*; it can only get going if we assume that mechanism is right from the start.

The arguments for this side of the antinomy, the thesis of mechanism, have not fared any better than those for the other side. In fact, mechanism is neither a certainty, as the sole metaphysic compatible with science, as its protagonists claim, nor is it inconceivable, and necessarily doomed to deny the undeniable, as some philosophers have argued. But in examining these invalid arguments, some clarity has been gained. What this examination seems to point toward is a dissolution of the alternative mechanism–dualism; it invites us to examine a non-dualistic conception of man which is nevertheless not linked with a reductivist notion of the sciences of man. This would, of course, involve an ontology with more than one level; in other words, if would mean that although some principles govern the behaviour of all things, others apply only to some; and yet the latter cannot be shown as special cases of the former.

This hypothesis flies in the face of entrenched dogmas of our scientific tradition. But I believe it has the merit of plausibility when we come to the sciences of man. And it would have the incidental benefit of surmounting the antinomy of mechanism.

CHAPTER EIGHT

COGNITIVE PSYCHOLOGY

I

Is there something wrong in principle with the major direction of cognitive psychology these days? A blindness which comes from a too great confidence in its rationalist and mechanist assumptions?

Take our everyday performance, like catching a ball, or carrying on a conversation. The current mainstream in cognitive psychology sees as its task to explain these by some underlying process which resembles a computation. When we reflect, we are struck by the skill we exhibit in these performances: knowing just where to reach to intercept the ball, knowing just where and how to stand, what tone to adopt, what nuance of phrasing to use, to respond appropriately to what our interlocutor has said. To explain the performance would then be to give an account of how we compute these responses, how we take in the data, process them, and work out what moves to make, given our goals.

To reach an answer by computation is to work it out in a series of explicit steps. The problem is defined, if necessary broken up into sub-problems, and then resolved by applying procedures which are justified by the definition. We resort to computation sometimes when we cannot get the answer we want any other way; and sometimes when we want to show that this is the right answer. Explicit procedures can be crucial to a justification of our result.

But in the case of skilled performances like the above, we are not aware of any computation. That is not what we are *doing*, in the sense of an activity that we are engaged in and could be made to avow and take responsibility for, granted undistorted self-knowledge. The computation would have to be an underlying process, on a par with – or, indeed, identical with – the electrical discharges in brain and nervous system.

The nature of the activity as *we* carry it on is in some respects antithetical to a computation. When we catch the ball, or respond appropriately to our neighbour's conversational opening over the back fence, we make no explicit definition of the problem. Indeed, we would be very hard put to it make one, even if we set ourselves the task, and might find it beyond our powers. There is correspondingly no breakdown into sub-problems, or application of procedures. We operate here, as in most contexts, with the task implicit, that is, not expressly formulated. That is part of what people mean when they say that we are applying know-how here, not explicit knowledge.

Our awareness of our activity shows that computation is something we do sometimes, not all the time. But more, we can see that it is quite beyond our powers to do it all the time. It is not just that there are some performances where an explicit definition of the problem seems beyond our capacity. The fact also is that every activity of computation deploys skilled performances which are themselves not explicitly thematized, and cannot be right now without disrupting the computation in train. As I define my problem in some explicit formulation, I draw on my capacity to use language, build declarative sentences, zero in on salient issues, and others again, which I have to leave tacit for the moment while concentrating on the matter at hand. In different ways, Wittgenstein and Polanyi have made us aware of this inescapable horizon of the implicit surrounding activity, which the latter discusses in terms of 'tacit knowing'.

On the other hand, it is clear that we can only match these performances on a machine by defining the problems explicitly and building the machine to compute. There is nothing comparable to tacit knowledge in a machine. The fact that we have in the last half century developed the theory of such machines, and then made considerable progress in building them, has been of great moment for psychology. It has given rise to a new explanatory paradigm, which seems to offer the hope of a materialist theory of behaviour, which would not be as idiotically reductive as classical behaviourism.

It is the prestige of this paradigm – and the strength of the underlying commitment to a mechanistic materialism – which powers cognitive psychology; that, and the continuing influence of the epistemological tradition of rational reconstruction. We are after all material objects, susceptible like all others to some mechanistic explanation: so runs the reasoning. We are moreover material objects which bring off these extraordinary performances of ball catching and conversation. Where more plausible to look for an explanation than in that other range of things which we design to realize (supposedly) comparable performances, viz., computing machines?

So cognitivists feel justified in ignoring the deliverances of self-understanding of agents, which cannot but draw a distinction between computations and the exercise of tacit skills, and plumping for the machine paradigm.

Is this move justified? This is what I would like to explore in this paper. More generally, I want to ask whether features which are crucial to our self-understanding as agents can be accorded no place in our explanatory theory. Is this extrusion a justified move to a properly scientific theory, or is it rather a way of side-stepping the important explanatory issues? Of 'changing the subject', as Davidson puts it?

The implicit/explicit distinction is one such important feature. Before grappling with the main question, I would like briefly to introduce another. This resides in the fact that human beings are self-interpreting animals. This means among other things that there is no adequate description of how it is with a human being in respect of his existence as a person which does not incorporate his self-understanding, that is, the descriptions which he or she is inclined to give of his emotions, aspirations, desires, aversions, admiration, etc. What we are at any moment is, one might say, partly constituted by our self-understanding.

This is another feature unmatched by machines; or we find in them only the weakest analogies. A computer may indeed be monitoring some of its own operations, and this may seem an analogue to self-understanding. But in this case, there is a clear distinction between description and object. The operations are there independent of the monitoring, even if this may bring about other operations which interact with them.

But in our case, our self-understanding shapes how we feel, for example, in such a way that there is no answer to the question 'What is our state of feeling?' independent of our self-description. The analytical distinction description/object cannot be made.

To look at some examples: I love A, I admire B, I am indignant at the behaviour of C. My love for A is, let us say, not just a momentary élan; it is bound up with the sense that our lives are permanently or definitively linked, that being with her is an essential part of being who I am. Now these last clauses constitute a description of how I feel. They are not just predictions or counterfactuals based on what I feel. I am not just predicting, for example, that were we to separate, I should feel terrible, or be at a loss. What I am doing is describing the quality of my emotion, which is quite different in what it is and how it feels from other kinds of attachment which lack this defining character.

And the quality of the emotion is essentially given by this description; that is, having this emotion is defined in terms of being inclined to give this kind of description. This is not to say that there are not cases where one might love in this way and not be ready to describe one's feelings in this way. One might only later come to recognize that this sense of lives being joined was the essential character of one's feeling. But in attributing the feeling to oneself even before one was ready to speak in this way, one is still saying something about one's self-understanding. When I say that I loved her in this way last year, before I came to understand properly how our lives are bound up together, I am grounding myself on the sense I had then of her importance to me, and I am purporting to give a more adequate characterization of that sense. Presumably, I was even then making plans which involved a life-time together, or committing myself to some long-term path, and it is in virtue of *that* that I can say now: 'I loved her in this way then.'

Put another way, I could not attribute this kind of love to an agent who was incapable of having in any form whatever the sense of being bound to someone for life. That is why we cannot attribute many human emotions to animals. Some animals do in fact mate for life; but they cannot have the kind of love we are talking about, because this requires the sense that it is for life, and therefore the possibility of making a distinction between the passing and the permanent.

Thus even before we are fully conscious of it, this emotion is characterized essentially by our self-understanding, by the sense we have of the meaning of its object to us. Similar points could be made in relation to admiration and indignation. We admire someone whom we think is great, or exceptional, or exhibits some virtue to a high degree. This emotion is defined by this kind of understanding of its object. And once again this does not prevent us ascribing admiration to people who do not recognize their favourable judgements of those they admire. I recognize now that I not only felt well-disposed towards B, but I also admired him. I did not want to admit it at the time, because I have trouble avowing that I grudgingly recognize a virtue in his way of being. But I acknowledge that I have all along, and *therefore* that I admired him then, albeit without recognizing it. I can only attribute the admiration retrospectively because I attribute the virtue-judgement retrospectively as well. I see it there, in the things I thought and said and did, even though I did not allow it its right name. A parallel point could be made about the judgement encapsulated in indignation, that the object of our feeling has done some flagrant wrong.

In this way our feelings are constituted by self-understandings; so that, as I said above, the properly human feelings cannot be attributed to animals; and some feelings are specific to certain cultures. But all this occurs in a way which defeats any attempt to distinguish description and object. If one searches for some core of feeling which might exist independently of the sense of its object which constitutes it, one searches in vain. More, the very nature of human emotion has eluded one. An emotion is essentially constituted by our sense of its object, that is, by what we are inclined to say about its significance for us. That is what is contained in the slogan that human beings are self-interpreting animals: there is no such thing as what they are, independently of how they understand themselves. To use Bert Dreyfus' evocative term, they are interpretation all the way down.

This is a second feature of ourselves, as we understand our activity and feeling, which has no machine analogue. And in fact the two features are linked.

I was arguing above that we can have a certain emotion before we are ready to apply what we can later recognize as the essential description. We can make these later attributions in virtue of what descriptions we *were* ready to make, which we retrospectively understand as expressing the sense of things which is properly encapsulated in the essential description. Our emotions can be better or less well understood by ourselves, can be more or less explicitly formulated. We might want to say: 'Yes, I loved her in this way before, but it wasn't explicitly formulated for me as it is now; it was still something implicit, unsaid, unrecognized.'

But this transposition from the implicit to the explicit is an important one. The emotion itself changes. An emotion clarified is in some way an emotion transformed. This is a corollary of the fact that emotions are constituted by self-understandings. And it will typically play a crucial part in our explaining someone's behaviour that he did not explicitly understand what he was feeling, or perhaps that at the crucial moment he began to understand explicitly.

In other words, because of our nature as self-interpreting animals, the quality of our self-understanding plays an important role, and the distinction implicit/explicit has a crucial explanatory relevance. That is, it has relevance in the understanding we have of ourselves as agents and subjects of feeling.

Now there is no analogue of this in computing machines. The connected features of self-interpretation and a partly implicit sense of things have no place there. Should this worry us in adopting such machines as paradigms for the explanation of human performance?

II

No, say the cognitivists; why should this worry us? It would not be the first time that the way things look to the uninstructed eye, or to ordinary consciousness, or to common sense, turns out to be misleading. The progress of science is littered with such over-rulings of appearance. Right back at the beginning, we had to disregard the fact that the sun seems to go around the earth, that moving objects feel as though they stop when we cease to exert effort. Now we recognize that the four-dimensional space–time continuum of ordinary awareness is crucially different from the one invoked in physics. Closer to home, we learn that the pain in my arm really comes from a malfunction of the heart; that the pain I feel in the area of the heart in my hypochondriac panic really comes from my pectoral muscles. Why should the case be any different with acting, thinking, feeling?

The answer to this (would-be rhetorical) question might be that the supposedly phenomenal features of action and understanding are a crucial part of the explanandum.

An objection that comes to mind right away to the proposal that we explain human skilled performance in terms of underlying processes resembling those of computing machines is this: the two kinds of process differ in what looks like a crucial respect.

We do attribute some of the same terms to both humans and machines. We speak of both as 'calculating', or 'deducing', and so on for a long list of mental performance terms. But the attribution does not carry the same force in the two cases, because we cannot really attribute action to a machine in the full-blooded sense.

Why do we want to say that a machine computes, or for that matter that a machine moves gravel, or stacks bottles? Partly because the machine operates in such a way as to get these tasks done in the proper circumstances. But also, and more strongly, in the case for example of computers, because the way the machine gets these tasks done has a certain structural resemblance to the way we do them. Characteristically, the machine's operation involves breaking down the task into sub-tasks, the fulfilment of which can be seen as logical stages to the completion of the computation; and this breaking down into sub-tasks is essential to what we call computation when *we* compute – you would not say someone was computing, if he gave the answer straight off without any analytical reflection.

More generally, to borrow Fodor's formulation, we can see a physical system as a computational device, if we can map different physical stages of that system on to formulae of some language of computation, in such a way that the causal relations between the physical states match the logical relations among the formulae.[1] 'The idea is that, in the case of organisms as in the case of real computers, if we get the right way of assigning formulae to the states it will be feasible to interpret the sequence of events that *causes* the output as a computational *derivation* of the output.'[2]

Thirdly, we say that a machine 'does' something when we have designed it to accomplish the task. All three factors apply in the case of computers; at least two in the case of bottle-stackers. But there could be objects which we would describe as *phi*-ing just because they were very useful at accomplishing the task of getting something *phi*-ed, even though they were discovered in nature and not manufactured.

But it is clear from this that the attribution of an action-term to such artefacts or useful objects is relative to our interests and projects. A machine *phi*s because we have manufactured it to *phi*, or we use it to *phi*, or we are interested in it in respect of the *phi*-ing it gets done. If we ask why we want to say that it is *phi*-ing and not *psi*-ing, where 'things being *psi*-ed' is a description of some other outcome of the machine's operation (our computer also hums, heats up the room, keeps George awake, increases our electricity bill), the answer is that *psi*-ing is not what we use it for, or what we built it for.

Of course we normally would say quite unproblematically that the machine hums, heats the room, and so on; but where we want to make a distinction between what it is really engaged in, as against just incidentally bringing about (it is a computer, dammit, not a room-heater), we do so by reference to our interests, projects, or designs. A changed economic picture, or the demands of a new technology, could make it the case that the *psi*-ing was suddenly a very important function, and then we might think of the same machine as a *psi*-er and as *psi*-ing (provided it also was an efficient device for this end). Indeed, we could imagine two groups, with quite different demands, sharing time on the same device for quite different purposes. The computer also makes clicks in strange patterns, very much valued by some eccentric group of meditation adepts. For them, the machine is a 'mantric clicker', while for us it is computing payrolls, or chi-squares.

But what is it *really* doing? There is no answer to the question for a machine. We tend to think in this case that it is really computing, because

---

[1] J. A. Fodor, *The Language of Thought* (Hassocks, Sussex, 1975), p. 73.   [2] *Ibid.*

we see it as made for this purpose, and only by accident serving the purpose of helping meditation. But this is a contingent, external fact, one external, that is, to the machine's make-up and function. It could have been designed by some mad yogi with a degree in electronic engineering, and just happen to serve as a computer. Or it could just have come into existence by some cosmic accident: a bolt of many-tongued lightning fused all this metal into just the structure needed to fulfil both these functions.

So attributions of action-terms to such devices are relative to our interests and purposes. As Fodor puts it: 'it is *feasible* to think of such a system as a computer just insofar as it is possible to devise some mapping which pairs physical states of the device with formulae in a computing language in such a fashion as to preserve the desired semantic relations among the formulae'.[3] And he adds later: 'Patently, there are indefinitely many ways of pairing states of the machine with formulae in a language which will preserve [the right] sort of relation.'

But the same is not true of ourselves. There is an answer to the question, What is he doing? or What am I doing? – when it is not taken in the bland form such that any true description of an outcome eventuating in the course of my action can provide an answer – which is not simply relative to the interests and purposes of the observer. For action is directed activity. An action is such that a certain outcome is privileged, that which the agent is seeking to encompass in the action.

This purpose may be unconscious, as when my awareness of certain desires is repressed; it may be partly unformulated, as when I walk in such a way as to avoid the holes in the pavement while concentrating on something else; it may be at the margins of attention, as when I doodle while talking on the phone. But in all these cases, our willingness to talk about action depends on our seeing the activity as directed by the agent, on their being such a privileged outcome, which the agent is trying to encompass. This is the basis of the distinction between action and non-action (e.g., events in inanimate objects, or reflex-type events in ourselves, or lapses, breakdowns, etc.).

So in contradistinction to machines, we attribute action to ourselves in a strong sense, a sense in which there is an answer to the question, What is he doing? which is not merely relative to the interests and purposes of an observer. Of course, there are issues between different action-descriptions which may be settled by the interests of the observer. For any action may

[3] *Ibid.*, my emphasis.

bear a number of descriptions. Notoriously, there are further and more immediate purposes, broader and narrower contexts of relevance. So, we can say severely, 'I know you just wanted to do the best by him, but did you physically prevent him leaving the house?', or 'I know you only meant to scare him, but did you shoot the dog?' Here we have classic examples of the distinction between the description which is salient for the agent, and that which is crucial for someone assessing his conduct.

But however great the interest-relative variability in the description of what I do, a distinction can be drawn among the outcomes that eventuate in my action between what I *do* under whatever description, and the things that cannot be attributed to me at all in any full-blooded sense. This distinction is not observer-, or user-, or designer-relative; and that is the difference with machines.

Thus there are descriptions of things which get done when I act which I can repudiate as action-descriptions: for example, that I move molecules of air when I talk, or even give clicks with my teeth which are highly prized by the eccentric meditation circle. We can imagine that they hire me to come and give lectures in philosophy, and I am puzzled why they keep inviting me back, because they do not seem interested in what I say, and indeed, sink into a deep trance when I talk. There is some sense in which 'putting them to sleep' is an action-description applying to me; but we recognize that this applies in a quite different way than, for instance, the description 'lecturing on philosophy'; and hence we have a barrage of reservation terms, like 'unwittingly', 'inadvertently', 'by accident', 'by mistake', and so on.

Now *this* distinction, between what I am full-bloodedly doing, and what is coming about inadvertently, is not relative to observer's or designer's interests and purposes. Unlike the case of the artefact, it remains true of me that what I am doing in the full-blooded sense is lecturing on philosophy, and not mantric clicking; even though I may be much more useful as a device to accomplish the second end than the first, may do it more efficiently, and so on; or even though everyone else becomes interested in mantric clicking, and no one even knows what philosophy is any more besides me.

Nor can we account for this difference by casting me in the role of crucial observer, and saying that the crucial description is the one relative to my interests. For this neglects the crucial difference, that with the artefact the observer's interests are distinguishable from the machine. So that it makes sense to speak of a machine as surviving with its functioning intact even when no one is interested any more in its original purpose, and it serves quite another one, or none at all. But an action is essentially constituted by its purpose. This is a corollary of the point above, that men are self-interpreting animals. The attempt to make a comparable distinction to the one we make with artefacts, between external movement and some separable inner act of will, breaks down, as is now notorious; for the inner act shrinks to vanishing point. Our ordinary conception of an act of will is parasitic on our ordinary understanding of action.

So mental performance terms, like 'calculating', have a different sense when attributed to artefacts than when attributed to humans. In the latter case, we mean to describe actions in the strong sense, in a way which is not merely observer- or user- or designer-relative. Let me say quickly, as a sort of parenthesis, that this represents as yet no decisive objection against cognitivism; it just puts the issue about it in clearer perspective. It is a point about the logic of our action-attributions. It does not show by itself that what goes on when people calculate is something very different than what goes on in computers. For all we can say at this stage, a computer-type, observer-relative 'calculation' may underlie every act of calculating; and it may provide the best explanation for our performance.

The point is only that our language of action attributes something quite different to us agents, viz., action in the strong sense; something for which there is no basis whatever in machines, or in the functioning of the organism understood analogously to that of a machine; and indeed, for which one cannot easily conceive of any basis being found in a machine.

I have made the point in terms of action, but the same point goes for other 'functional' states of machines in contrast to ourselves. We might try to find states of machines which parallel our desires and emotions. A machine might be said to 'want to go' when it is all primed, and started, and only being held back by a brake, say. But it is clear that an analogous distinction applies here to the one in the case of action. What the machine 'desires' is determined by the observer's interest or fiat, or that of the user or designer; while this is not so for the human agent. Actually, the temptation does not even exist here, as it does in the case of action, to apply such terms to machines, except as a kind of anthropomorphic joke.

This is because the crucial difference is even more evident here than in the case of action. For the clear upshot of the above discussion is that human and animal agents are beings for whom the question arises of what significance things have for them. I am using the term 'significance' here as a general term of art to designate what provides our non-observer-relative answers to such questions as: What is he doing? What is she feeling? What do they want?

Ascribing action in the strong sense to some being is treating that being as a subject of significance. The full-blooded action-description gives us the action as purposed by the agent. We define the action by the significance it had for the agent (albeit sometimes unconsciously), and this is not just one of many descriptions from different observers' standpoints, but is intrinsic to the action *qua* action. So we can only attribute action to beings we see as subjects of significance, beings for whom things can have significance in a non-observer-relative way.

We have to add this last rider, because there is, of course, another, weaker sense in which we can speak of things having significance for inanimate beings: something can be dangerous for my car, or good for my typewriter. But these significances are only predicable in the light of extrinsic, observer-relative or user-relative purposes. By contrast, the significances we attribute to agents in our language of action and desire are their own. It is just the principal feature of agents that we can speak about the meanings things have for them in this non-relative way, that, in other words, things *matter* for them.

Let us call this essential feature of agents the 'significance feature'. Then the crucial difference between men and machines is that the former have it while the latter lack it.

This difference is less immediately evident to us in wielding our action-descriptions, or at least some of them. For action-descriptions focus our attention on what gets done; that action is directed by the agent is usually subsidiary to our main point of concern. Thus we have no trouble applying action-terms in a weaker sense to inanimate things. But desire- or feeling-descriptions focus our attention directly on the significance things have for the agent. That is why there is something strained or metaphoric in applying these to machines.

The strain gets even greater when we come to emotion terms. We might speak of our car as 'raring to go', because at least 'going' is something it is capable of, albeit in a weak, user-relative sense. But when we get to an emotion term like 'shame', we could not have even the remotest temptation to apply it to the inanimate.

'Shame' is in fact intrinsically bound up with the significance feature – one might say, doubly bound up. It is not just that to attribute shame is to say that the situation has a certain significance for the agent: it is humiliating, or reflects badly on him, or something of the kind. It is also that the significance or import of the situation is one which only makes sense in relation to beings with the significance feature.

This contrasts with an import like danger. My car can be in danger, if there is a rock about to fall on it, for instance. This is, of course, a user-relative attribution: the danger is only to it in its function as car; *qua* collection of metal and glass bits, the rock represents no danger. But at least the attribution user-relatively makes sense. A car *qua* car can be in danger.

But 'shame' points to a different kind of import. Someone can only experience shame who has a sense of himself as an agent. For I feel ashamed of what I am like/how I appear as an *agent* among other agents, a subject of significance among others. It may seem sometimes that the immediate object of my shame is some physical property that a non-agent could bear. I may be ashamed of my small stature, or outsize hands. But these can only be objects of shame because of their significance: small stature means being overshadowed, failing to have a commanding presence among others; outsize hands embody indelicacy, lack of refinement, are proper to peasants.

The import of danger can be physical destruction, and this can happen to a car *qua* car. But the import of shame touches us essentially as subjects of significance. It makes no sense to apply it to any but agents (and not even to all of them; not to animals, for instance).

The significance feature is crucially bound up in our characterization of ourselves as agents. It underlies our attributing action to ourselves in a strong sense, as well as our attributions of desire and feeling; and reference to it is essentially involved in the definition of our emotions. With these, it is not just a matter of our attributing them to ourselves in a stronger sense than to inanimate objects; these concepts cannot get a grip on non-agents, even in a metaphorical manner. They only make sense in relation to us. In a world without self-aware agents, they could have no senseful application whatever.

The significance feature underlies the two features I singled out in the first section. We have these two, interpretation and the implicit/explicit distinction, because we are agents with a linguistic capacity, a capacity to formulate the significance things have for us.

But to formulate the significance of something, to make it explicit, is to alter it, as we saw above. This is because we are dealing with agents, subjects of non-observer-relative significance. My making explicit the danger my car is in does not alter the import of the situation for it; but my coming to see clearly the import of my situation for me can be *ipso facto* an alteration of its significance for me. Our being agents is a condition of our self-interpretations being constitutive of what we are; and it is because these interpretations can be explicitly formulated that the distinction implicit/explicit plays a crucial role for us.

These three features are closely connected, and are essential to us in our understanding of ourselves as agents.

III

Let us return to the main issue. Should the fact that our ordinary self-understanding attributes to us features which have no place in the computing machine paradigm make us wary of this in explaining human performance? Or can we dismiss these features as misleading surface appearance, on all fours with the sun's apparent movement around the earth?

At least a prima facie objection arises to just dismissing them. Are they not an essential part of what we have to explain? This objection could be spelled out in the following way. We are asked to believe that some behaviour of ours in computing, or some behaviour which involves no computing but involves skilled selection of response, is to be explained on the same principles as those accounting for the operation of a computing machine. This is pressed as an overwhelmingly plausible line of approach, given the similarity in outcome given the (physically defined) input.[4] It appears plausible, in other words, because we seem to be able to apply terms like 'computing', 'figuring out the answer', 'finding the solution', to the machine which we also apply to ourselves. If they do the same things as us, perhaps they can show us how to explain what we do.

But, the objection goes, they do not do the same thing as us, or only within the range of the analogy between weak and strong action-attributions. They do something we can call 'computing' in a weak, observer-relative sense of this term; which relative to another observer might be described as 'mantric-clicking'. We do something we call 'computing' in the strong sense, not observer-relative. How can we be so sure that an underlying process describable by the weak sense explains the overt action described in the strong sense? These are after all, *very different*, distinguished by everything that divides things possessing the significance feature from things without it. 'Computing' engines present some analogies to computing people, but they offer as yet no hint of how one might account for this salient feature of the latter, that they are agents,

---

[4] This claim involves a big promissory note, because there are all sorts of performances by us we have not even begun to match on machines, but I will not take this up here. For cogent objections, see H. L. Dreyfus, *What Computers Can't Do* (New York, 1979).

and act. Indeed, it has been essential to their utility that we can understand and operate these machines without reference to the significance feature.

Those who are nevertheless sure of the machine paradigm must be grounding their confidence on the belief that we can somehow ignore the significance feature. Why? Well, presumably because of the analogy I mentioned above with the misleading appearances which the progress of science has had to ignore. Cognitive psychologists are frequently dismissive of arguments of phenomenologists on the grounds that phenomenology can be very misleading as to underlying structure. The implication is that phenomenology gives us surface appearance, not anything about the nature of the explanandum.

The assumption underlying this dismissive attitude must be that the significance feature is a misleading surface appearance, like the movement of the sun, or perhaps a purely phenomenal one, like phenomenal colour or felt heat, to be set aside in any rigorous characterization of the events to be explained. This gets to seem a plausible view the more we repeat to ourselves that computing machines compute. The difference between computing and 'computing', between real and observer-relative performances, comes to seem a rather secondary matter. The significance feature comes to seem like a pure matter of the inner feel, something to do with the way the whole process is experienced from the inside, or perhaps, at best, a tag of honour we accord to agents, that they bear their predicates non-relatively; but in no case an important defining feature of the explanandum.

But this is, of course, mad. There is all the difference in the world between a creature with and one without the significance feature. It is not just a detachable feature that action has in some medium of internal representation, but is essential to action itself. The supposedly secondary, dispensable character of the significance feature disappears once we cease to dwell on that small range of actions which have plausible machine analogues. Once we look to feelings, emotions, or actions which are defined in terms of them, or of moral categories, aesthetic categories, and so on, like 'saving one's honour' or 'telling the truth', we run out of machine analogues to be bemused by.

Or if we are still bemused, it is because we are in the grip of an old metaphysical view, one embedded in our epistemological tradition, which makes us see our awareness as an inner medium of representation, which monitors (partly and sometimes misleadingly) what goes on in our bodies and the world. This is the ghost of the old dualism, still stalking the battlements of its materialist successor-states.

Consciousness is primarily understood as representation (Foucault has shown – if that is the term – how central this notion of representation is to the modern epistemological tradition). As such it is separable from the processes which it monitors, or of which it is a symptom. If it plays any role in explaining these processes, it must be in interacting with them. Since interaction is ruled out on materialist assumptions, it cannot be allowed any explanatory role at all. It can only serve as a (possibly misleading) way of access to the processes which are the stuff of behavioural science.

On this view, the primary difference between us and machines is that we are clearly conscious and they do not seem to be. Even this latter is not entirely sure, and cognitive theories begin to hedge bets when they are dragged on to this terrain: perhaps after all one day machines will get sufficiently complex to have consciousness? And will we ever know?

The discussion here gets ragged and rather silly; a sign that we are on the wrong track. And so we are. For the crucial difference between men and machines is not consciousness, but rather the significance feature. We also enjoy consciousness, because we are capable of focussing on the significance things have for us, and above all of transforming them through formulation in language. That is not unimportant; but the crucial thing that divides us from machines is what also separates our lesser cousins the dumb brutes from them, that things have significance for us non-relatively. This is the context in which alone something like consciousness is possible for us, since we achieve it by focussing on the significance of things, principally in language, and this is something we *do*.

The crucial distinction to understand the contrast between us and machines is not mental/physical, or inner/outer, but possessing/not possessing the significance feature. Once we understand this, we can see that this feature cannot be marginalized as though it concerned merely the way things *appear* to us, as though it were a feature merely of an inner medium of representation. On the contrary, it plays an absolutely crucial role in explaining what we do, and hence defines the kind of creatures we are.

We can see this best if we look again at our emotions, such as the example of shame above. As beings capable of shame, we experience certain emotions, and we react in certain ways to our situation and to each other. This is not just a fact of how things appear to us inside; this is a crucial fact about how we are and what we do. This is evident in the fact that in order to explain our behaviour, we have to use emotion terms like 'shame' and corresponding situation descriptions like 'humiliating'. In accounting for what we do, there is no substitute for a language which only makes sense applied to beings with the significance feature, the language of shame, humiliation, pride, honour, dignity, love, admiration, and so on. It is as fundamental as that.

In other words, when we say that the significance feature is essential to our self-understanding as agents, we are not saying that it is inseparable from our representations in an inner medium, whose deliverances are as dispensable to an explanation of behaviour as our perceptions of the sun in the sky are to our account of the solar system. We are rather saying that once we understand ourselves as *agents*, rather than, say, as physical objects on all fours with others, including inanimate ones, we understand ourselves as beings of whom the significance feature is an essential character, as beings such that it is essential to what has to be explained, if we want to explain their behaviour.

Once we see this, we have to stop treating it as a matter of surface appearance, and the plausibility begins to dissipate that surrounds the notion that we can explain computing, and much else, by the 'computing' of machines.

But perhaps one more desperate measure is possible. Supposing we challenged our entire self-understanding as agents. Perhaps it is all systematically misleading. Perhaps the only way to explain what we do is to look at ourselves as machines, and explain what we do in the same terms.

This is a radical suggestion, and one which undercuts cognitive psychology from another direction. Its ambition is just to give an account in psychological terms, terms that apply peculiarly to human beings, and perhaps some animals, and that can be seen as developments or more rigorous variants of the terms we understand ourselves with in ordinary life. Cognitive psychology is looking for a relatively autonomous science of human behaviour. It would not be satisfied just with a science that entirely abandoned the psychological, and dealt with us simply in the language of physics, say.

But it is also a suggestion that does nothing to solve our problem. For we cannot abandon our understanding of ourselves as agents. This is bound up with our practice as agents. Self-understanding is constitutive, as we saw, of what we are, what we do, what we feel. Understanding ourselves as agents is not in the first place a theory, it is an essential part of our practice. It is inescapably involved in our functioning as human beings.

The significance feature is at the centre of human life, most palpably in that we come to understandings with people about the significance of things. There is no relationship, from the most external and frosty to the most intimate and defining, which is not based on some understanding about the meanings things have for us. In the most important cases, of course, one of the things whose significance is understood between us is our relationship itself.

That is why the significance perspective is not an arbitrary one among human beings, one way of explaining how these organisms work among other possible ones. It is not even primarily a theoretical perspective on our behaviour. We could not function as human beings, that is as humans among other humans, for five minutes outside this perspective.[5]

In other words, we could have no relations at all if we did not treat ourselves and others as agents. (But by this, I do not mean that we necessarily treat them ethically, or as ends in themselves. Even our exploitive behaviour in the vast majority of cases takes our victims as agents. It can be argued, however, that there is a profound connection between our status as agents and the validity of such moral precepts as those of Kant.)

We can put this another way, and say that this self-understanding as agents is part of the reality it purports to understand. That is why a science of behaviour in terms of physics alone, even should such a thing prove possible, would still not answer the legitimate questions which psychology sets for itself: what is it that underlies and makes possible our functioning as agents, and the self-understanding that goes with it?

But, to sum up the objection announced at the start of this section, it is not at all clear how the machine paradigm is going to help us with these questions either.

IV

But hold on. I do not think one can say flat out that the machine paradigm will not help us. Maybe it can produce some startling goods further down the road. What can be said is that it is not much more plausible than a number of other approaches; and that it only looks strongly plausible as long as you overlook the significance feature. And you only do *that*, I think, if you are still in the grip of the dualist metaphysic (even though

[5] I think this is what emerges from the very interesting analysis in P. F. Strawson, 'Freedom and resentment', *Proceedings of the British Academy*, 1962, reprinted in Strawson (ed.), *Studies in the Philosophy of Thought and Action* (Oxford, 1968).

transposed in a materialist key) which comes to us from the epistemological tradition.

Once you do see the importance of the significance feature, it is evident that computing machines can at best go some of the way to explaining human computation, let alone intelligent, adaptive performance generally. To be told that underlying my ball catching are patterns of firing in the cortex analogous to those in electronic computers gives me as yet no idea of how these can help to account for (non-observer-relative) *action*, producing as they do a quite different kind of operation in the machine. What we have to discover is how processes analogous to machine computations could combine with others to produce real action, if this paradigm is to have a future. And this is no mean task. Indeed, no one has the slightest idea even how to go about pursuing it. In this context, the glaring disanalogies between machine and human performance, for instance the features discussed in the first section, can no longer be dismissed as mere appearances. They are rather major challenges to the very legitimacy of the paradigm.

Machine-modelled explanations of human performance, of the kind cognitive psychology offers, would have to relate to this performance understood as action in the role of an underlying explanation. We have this when phenomena on one level are explained by a theory invoking factors at another level, where this second level offers us the more basic explanation. An explanation in theory T is more basic than one in T′, where the explanatory factors ultimate for T′ are in turn explained in T.

We can clarify the predicament of cognitive psychology if we lay out three types of cases of such underlying explanation.

Case 1. The descriptions made and factors cited at the higher level turn out to be confused or mistaken when we achieve the deeper level explanation. In this case, we have not so much an explanation as an explaining away. An historical example of this is the distinction in Aristotelian cosmology between the supra-lunar and incorruptible, and the infra-lunar and corruptible. This was important to explain a whole host of things, including why the stars above go in perfect circles. The whole thing was just a mistake, and what survives is just *appearances* which can be explained in terms of the new cosmology; but the crucial distinctions of the old one turn out to be unfounded. We can now explain why things *looked* that way, but we know they are not.

The higher level explanation is discredited, because the distinctions it draws do not in fact correspond to any genuine explanatory factors. The higher level operates with concepts and descriptions among which no explanatory factors are to be found. There never was a science here – just as if I tried to explain the movements of the planets in terms of their colours in the telescope. I might note all sorts of patterns, but I should never in a million years be able to explain why they move as they do. For the relevant factors are mass and distance.

Case 2. Here we have a genuine explanation on the higher level, which is the object of a more basic explanation on the lower. As an example: we explain the wood disintegrating into ash by its being put in the fire. But we can give a deeper explanation in terms of the kinetic energy of the molecules. This is more basic, in that it accounts for the regularity by which we explained things at the higher level. With the kinetic theory, we understand the why of heat-transmission in general, and can see now why the same effect could be produced by a laser, for instance; why similar effects do not flow from heating metal, and so on.

The higher level explanation is genuine; in this, the case differs from 1. But it is dispensable. The higher explanation can always be eliminated in favour of the lower without loss. The latter not only gives us more, but covers all the same terrain as the former. There are no factors explanatory of heating/burning phenomena which are available on the higher level in such terms as 'fire' or 'charring', for which there are no correlates on the lower level, which can do the same explanatory job in the context of a more comprehensive theory. So for explaining heat, there is nothing we do with our phenomenal language which we could not do better in the kinetic-theory language. The phenomenal language is indispensable for describing how things are for us in our everyday identification of things; we need them to identify things as they figure in our perceptions, but otherwise, for the purpose of scientific characterization of the domain, not at all.

Case 3. Here there is also a valid higher level explanation. And there is also a theory of underlying structures which helps us explain how things happen as they do, and gives us some of the conditions of the higher level events occurring as they do. But unlike case 2, we cannot dispense with the higher level descriptions for the purpose of explaining the phenomena of the domain concerned. Some of the crucial explanatory factors are only available at this level; or to put it negatively, they cannot all be identified at the lower level. To seek them all there would be as fruitless as seeking the factors explaining planetary orbits in their colours.

I do not have an incontestable example. Let me just offer one which is relative to our explanatory resources at the present time, without pre-judging whether we will take things beyond this in the future or not. A fleet assembles for war. This is a pattern of ship movements. At what corresponds to the more basic level, these can be explained in terms of the operations of engines, pistons, screws, etc. This level is essential if we are to get an explanatory handle on some of the features of this pattern. For instance it is indispensable to explain why, in some cases, ships stopped and began to be tossed by the sea (cases of engine failure), why some ships went faster than others, why some took a circuitous route (e.g., to get more fuel), and so on.

But if you want to understand why they are steaming towards this pattern, you have to be told that war has been declared, and that they are forming the fleet for such and such an offensive action. You need to have recourse here to the 'highest level' language of policy and politico-military goals and intentions. If you remain on the lower, engine-room level, you will never identify the crucial factors, in the same way as the factors behind planetary motion could not be found in colour discourse.

I repeat that this example is relative to our present explanatory resources. It is not meant to *prove* that we could not discover one day some explanation on a neurophysiological level which would render our policy- and intention-descriptions dispensable. I am just trying to give a picture of a third possible case, which *may* turn out to have instances at the end of the day. Because, though no one can say that such a neurophysiological language of explanation is impossible, there is even less ground for assuring us that it must be there to be found. Case 3 may yet turn out to be the model for deeper level explanations of human behaviour. My hunch is that it will.

But forget my hunches. The point of this was to provide a typology in which to understand the possible relations of underlying explanations to our action account.

It is clear that case 1 has no application here. To say that it is analogous to the infra-/supra-lunar distinction amounts to saying that our classifications of events as actions are wholly illusory. But since the self-understanding of ourselves as agents is essential to our acting, this is a claim which must remain meaningless and preposterous to us. Really to see the distinction between action and non-action as like the infra-/supra-lunar one would be to be incapable of acting. This is not an alternative we need consider.

There remain 2 and 3. The assumption of cognitive psychologists seems to me that case 2 offers the appropriate model. The underlying explanation, in a language appropriate to computing machines, gives us all the explanatory factors; the action account presents things as they look to us.

The model here would be the kinetic theory in relation to a phenomenal account of heating and heat transmission.

But I have argued above that this claim is prematurely made. Certainly the machine paradigm at present does not offer any hint of how we could hope to discover all the explanatory factors in its terms. In particular, we do not have the foggiest idea how it might help us to account for the significance feature of agents. If we ever do manage to account for the significance feature in mechanistic terms, then we will indeed have instantiated case 2. But until that day – should it ever come – case 3 has got to figure as a very plausible contestant.

For in fact, that is where we are now. Underlying explanations, especially neurophysiological, can offer us more basic explanations of some important phenomena: of certain features of development, of differential capacities, of breakdowns, and a host of other matters. But to explain fully motivated behaviour, we need an account of what is happening in terms of action, desires, goals, aspirations. We have no metaphysical guarantee that after an immense series of discoveries, refinements, and breakthroughs, the basic structure of our explanations of ourselves will not still be the same: a variant of case 3. What purport to be assurances to the contrary are based on the illusions of traditional dualism.

On one reading of the term, case 2 can be called a case of reduction of the higher to the lower level. (In a more denigrating sense, we sometimes reserve 'reduction' for cases of 1.) On this reading, it looks as though I am classing cognitive psychologists as proponents of reduction, more particularly, reduction of psychology to some underlying explanation. But this they (or many of them) claim not to be.

We have only to look at Fodor's book.[6] In his first chapter, he defends the independence and viability of the psychological enterprise against both behaviourism and physicalistic reductivism. A reductivist relationship holds, Fodor argues, between a special science (like psychology) and a more general one (like physics), when the laws of the former can be linked to laws of the latter via correlation statements which are themselves law-like. The crucial feature of this relationship would be that the natural-kind terms of the special science, those in which its laws could be formulated, would be type-indentical with the natural-kind terms of the general science, that is, physics.

Fodor's characterization of reduction resembles case 2 above, in that the special science is dispensable – although perhaps he makes the

---

[6] Fodor, *The Language of Thought*.

requirement a bit too stringent in demanding that the correlations be all law-like.

Now Fodor thinks that this kind of reductive relation is very unlikely to hold between the sciences of man and physics. He takes an example from economics: Gresham's Law. It is surely extremely unlikely that all cases of monetary exchange of which Gresham's Law holds, that is, where moneys of different quality are in circulation, should all fall under the same physical description; or otherwise put, that the physical description of all such cases should exhibit a natural kind of physics. 'Banal considerations suggest that a physical description which covers all such events must be wildly disjunctive.'[7] Even if one should manage, at the moment when human society was about to go under, to survey all previous cases of monetary exchange, and find some vast baggy disjunction under which all these cases fit in physical terms, this would still fail to be a law; because it would not necessarily help at all in counterfactual cases. We would not be able to conclude that, if the universe had gone on for another year, the physical conformation of the monetary exchanges in it would have been such and so.[8]

But, Fodor argues, we do not need to espouse type-type identities in order to save materialism, science, and so on. It is sufficient to embrace what he calls 'token physicalism': 'the claim that all the events that the sciences talk about are physical events'.[9] This is compatible with the type of event that a special science picks out (like monetary exchange) being realized physically in an indefinite number of ways – so long as it is always realized physically.

Espousing token physicalism, and rejecting type-type identities, allows for the special sciences deploying concepts which are unsubstitutable. The special sciences need these if they are to 'state such true, counterfactual supporting generalizations as there are to state'.[10] For if the natural-kind terms of a special science only correlate with loose, open disjunctions in another science, then we cannot state the laws explanatory of the events that the special science deals with in the other science. For to explain, to give an account of what happens, is to license counterfactuals; and open disjunctions by definition license no counterfactuals. The natural-kind terms of our special science are in this case unsubstitutable.

Another science may cast a great deal of light on the underpinnings of these natural kinds. In particular, it may lay bare important conditions of

---

[7] Ibid., p. 15.   [8] Ibid., p. 16.   [9] Ibid., p. 12.   [10] Ibid., p. 25.

their functioning as they do; so that the other science may give us explanations of exceptions and breakdowns. But it cannot substitute for the special science; and in this sense, we can see the natural kinds this latter science designates as part of the furniture of things.

Fodor's description of the status of a special science like psychology fits my case 3. The special science is indispensable, because the crucial explanatory factors (read, natural kinds) are only discoverable on its level; on the lower level they are not identifiable. Just as, for example, the class of planets of a given mass form an indefinitely open disjunction described in colour terms, so do the cases of monetary exchange in physical terms.

But then surely I am wrong to tax cognitivists with reductionism, with taking case 2 as their model?

No, I am not; first, because we are not talking about the same things. When Fodor talks of the relation of psychology to physics, he is not talking about our account of ourselves as agents. His 'psychology' is an account of what we do in computational terms, and the reductive issue for him arises between an account at this level and one at the physical or neurological level. He is quite oblivious of the difference between an account in computational terms and one which characterizes us as agents with the significance feature.

Indeed, Fodor's thesis of the irreducibility of psychology emerges originally from a reflection on computing machines. It was the recognition that two machines might be the same in the program run on them, and yet be very different in their physical structures and principles, which gave rise to the notion that an account of what they do in computational terms could not correlate with general laws on a physical level.

This was the basis of the thesis known as 'functionalism' in psychology. But this was because it was simply taken for granted that a 'psychological' account of what we do would be a computational one analogous to those we apply to machines. Fodor clearly makes this identification. Part of his argument against reductionism assumes it. Even if there are neurological kinds coextensive with psychological kinds as things stand now, he argues, the correlations cannot be lawful. 'For it seems increasingly likely that there are nomologically possible systems other than organisms (viz. automata) which satisfy the kind predicates of psychology but which satisfy no neurological predicates at all.'[11]

The 'psychology' here is obviously not what I am talking about. What

---

[11] *Ibid.*, pp. 17–18.

we normally understand as the predicates of psychology, those which involve the significance feature, plainly do not apply to machines. Nor have we anything but the vaguest fantasies as to how they might apply to machines we design in the future. The 'kind predicates' of psychology which we might think it 'increasingly likely' that automata will satisfy are computational performance terms applied in their weak, observer-relative sense.

The psychology whose irreducibility Fodor is defending is one which is just as much a science of computing machines as of humans. It has nothing to do with our account of ourselves as agents. The difference between these he just ignores, most likely for some of the reasons discussed above, owing to the baleful influence of traditional dualism. So whatever the relation between the computational and physical levels, Fodor plainly construes that between the computational account and the one in terms of agency in a reductive way, on the model of cases 1 or 2.

Secondly, it is not so clear after all that Fodor really can carry through his account of the psychology–physics relation as a case 3. If a paradigm of this relation is to be found in computing machines, whose program can be matched by machines of different design, then it is not so clear that counterfactuals cannot be found at the more basic level.

For any given (physical) type of machine, there are no counterfactuals on the computational level that cannot be matched, and explained by counterfactuals at the engineering level. Counterfactuals like 'if the program had been changed in such and such a way, then ...', or 'if the problem had been posed in such and such a way, then ...', can be given a deeper level explanation in terms of the way the machine is wired, connected up, or whatever. If this were not the case, we would not be able to build, design, or improve such machines.

Of course, other machines can be constructed on other principles, such that the deeper level explanations would invoke quite different factors. One machine, let us say, operates electronically; the other is run by fuel and has gears. The underlying accounts will be very different. And there may be an indefinite number of such machines which we might design to run the same types of program.

This certainly shows that the level of program design is in some way essential to us, that we could not go about what we do if we were to abandon this level of discourse. But we could not go so far as to say that the crucial explanatory factors are unavailable on the lower level.

Contrast what seems plausible with the Gresham's Law example. It is not just that one case of monetary exchange with media of different quality will involve gold and silver, the next gold and bronze, the next dollars and Deutschmarks, the next old and new currency, and so on. Even in a given case, you cannot match counterfactuals on the economics level with those on the physical level. 'If people come to believe that the king is no longer adulterating the silver coinage, then gold will come back into circulation' corresponds to no counterfactual on the level of bodily movement, say, even if we restrict our attention to this context. People can come to believe this in all sorts of ways; they can be told in French or English, or in sign language; they can come across silver coins newly minted, that seem heavier; they can deduce it from the behaviour of merchants; and so on indefinitely.

We might complain that this comparison is unfair, that we have to draw the boundaries of a context narrower in the Gresham's Law case. But this just makes the difference more palpable. We do not know how to draw such boundaries in the monetary exchange case so as to make for stable relations of deeper level explanation. The ever-present possibility of original speech acts which inaugurate new extensions of meaning makes this impossible.

By contrast, in the domain of computing machines, there are such stable relations of more basic explanation in each context; and the boundaries between the contexts are clearly and unambiguously demarcated by the (physical) type of machine. We are never at a loss for lower-level counterfactuals to explain our higher-level ones. True, there are an indefinite number of such possible contexts of computation. But they are each clearly demarcated, and within each one the relation between levels of explanation conforms to case 2. The absence of match between natural-kind terms at the two levels of discourse can itself be explained in terms of a difference between kinds, viz., the types of machine.

This suggests that we ought to distinguish two questions: (a) Do the laws and licensed counterfactuals have the same scope on the two levels? and (b) Are there laws and licensed counterfactuals at all on the lower level? The answer to (b) may be affirmative, even while that to (a) is negative. In this case, it is not unambiguously true that reductive relations do not hold. This is the kind of case where we want to speak of systems which are analogous but not homologous. For each homologous class of machines, however, the reduction is a perfect case 2, and if this were the only domain we had to consider, it would never occur to us to question a reductivist construal.

But in a genuine case 3, the answer to (b) is a negative, and this is a quite different predicament.

Fodor seems to have elided what I have called case 3 and what I might call a multi-contexted case 2; and this may be connected with his having elided the two issues: the reduction of computational psychology to physics, and the reduction of our action understanding to computational psychology; or rather, his having invisibly subsumed the second question in the first. Because the second does seem to call for a case 3 solution, while the first seems to conform to this special kind of multiplex case 2.

But this is all part of his ignoring the issue around the significance feature, which amounts, I have tried to show, to a reductionism of a very strong kind.

PART III

PHILOSOPHY OF LANGUAGE

CHAPTER NINE

LANGUAGE AND HUMAN NATURE

I

Language is a central area of concern in the twentieth century. This is evident on all sides. First, our century has seen the birth and explosive growth of the science of linguistics. And in a sense 'explosive' is the right word, because like the other sciences of man, linguistics is pursued in a number of mutually irreducible ways, according to mutually contradictory approaches, defended by warring schools. There are structuralists in the Bloomfieldian sense, there are proponents of transformational theories, there are formalists.

These schools and others have made a big impact. They are not just collections of obscure scholars working far from the public gaze. Names like Jakobson and Chomsky are known far outside the bounds of their discipline.

But what is even more striking is the partial hegemony, if one can put it this way, that linguistics has won over other disciplines. From Saussure and the formalists there has developed the whole formidable array of structuralisms, of which Lévi-Strauss is the pathfinder, which seek to explain a whole range of other things: kinship systems, mythologies, fashion (Barthes), the operations of the unconscious (Lacan), with theories drawn in the first place from the study of language. We find terms like 'paradigm', 'syntagm', 'metaphor', 'metonymy', used well beyond their original domain.

And then we have to add that some of the most influential philosophical movements of the century have given language a central place; they have not only been concerned with language as one of the *problems* of philosophy, but have also been *linguistic*, in that philosophical understanding is essentially bound up with the understanding of the medium of language. This is true not only of logical positivism and what is often called 'linguistic analysis' in the Anglo-Saxon world, but also of the philosophy of Heidegger, for instance, in a very different way, as well as of the philosophies which have arisen out of structuralism, for example those of Derrida and Lacan.

The concern for language as a medium links up with the twentieth-century concern with meaning. What is it that makes speech meaningful, or indeed that makes meaningful any of the things that have meaning? For this question has been raised not just in connection with language, which is what philosophical theories of meaning have been concerned with. It has also been raised acutely for the arts, for instance music and painting. It is necessarily posed by the rise of non-representational painting, and of music which stepped outside the seemingly fixed code of the eight-tone scale. The revolutions of the beginning of the century, for instance, of Schönberg and cubism, put these questions on the agenda; and they have been kept on it by all the revolutions we have seen since. They have taught us to ask the question, What is meaning?, in a broader context than simply that of language. They induce us to see language as one segment of that range of meaningful media that men can deploy. And this range comes to seem all the more problematic.

On top of this, the range of the meaningful has been further extended dramatically by Freudian psychoanalysis. Now not just speech and art objects, but also slips of the tongue, symptoms, affinities and tastes, can be 'analysed', that is, interpreted.

And 'interpretation' itself has become a key term. 'Hermeneutical' approaches have a wide audience in a number of fields, most strikingly in history and social science.

What emerges from this, I believe, is that the twentieth-century concern for language is a concern about meaning. And I believe that this concern reflects a largely inarticulate sense of ourselves which is very widespread in our century, and which I shall try to formulate in two related propositions: (1) that the question of language is somehow strategic for the question of human nature, that man is above all the language animal; (2) that language is very puzzling, even enigmatic – and all the more so, if we take it in a wide sense to include the whole range of meaningful media; something we seem bound to do once we see language as the defining character of man, for man is also characterized by the creation of music, art, dance, by the whole range of 'symbolic forms', to use Cassirer's phrase. The paradox involved in this is that in an age of great scientific advance, and after spectacular progress in so many fields, human language appears to us much more enigmatic than it did to the men of the Enlightenment. But I recognize that this is a controversial point, and that my thumbnail sketch of our sense of our situation will be strongly resisted by all those who believe or who want to believe in the competence of the methods of natural science to explain human behaviour. Indeed, the trouble with the above sketch is that it is not neutral in one of the big debates of our civilization; so that some will find it banal and others tendentious.

What I ought to attempt now, therefore, is to make it less sketchy for the first group, and less implausible for the second. But this is something I find hard to encompass by a direct assault. What I want to do instead is trace the origins and hence the growing shape of our intellectual landscape. In doing this, I hope to cast enough light on it to achieve my ends by indirection – to allay at least some doubts, and fill in at least some contour.

This will involve weaving together two themes: first, how did we get here? How did we come to see language as central and meaning as puzzling? This is the historical, diachronic theme. The second theme is problematic: what is the problem of meaning, and why is it puzzling?

A word about each to start.

On the first: our traditional view of man was of a rational animal. That is the definition according to the major philosophical tradition of our civilization, going back to the Greeks. How did we slide to the sense that the secret of human nature was to be found in man as a 'language animal' (to use George Steiner's phrase)?

The answer is that the slide was not all that great. If we go back to the original formula in Aristotle, for instance, that man is a rational animal, we find that it reads 'zôon logon echon', which means 'animal possessing logos'. This 'logos' is a word we are already familiar with because it has entered our language in so many ways. It straddles speech and thought, because it means, inter alia, 'word', 'thought', 'reasoning', 'reasoned account', as well as being used for the words deployed in such an account. It incorporates in its range of meanings a sense of the relation of speech and thought.

If we wanted to translate Aristotle's formula directly from the Greek, instead of via the Latin 'animal rationale', and render it 'animal possessing logos', which means in fact leaving it partly untranslated in all its rich polysemy, then we do not have such a leap to make between the traditional formulation of the nature of man and the one that I want to claim underlies much twentieth-century thought and sensibility. There is a shift, but it is one within the complex thought/language, the displacement of its centre of gravity. A shift of this kind in our understanding of thought/language would explain the change from the old formula to the new. And in fact, I want to claim, there has been such a shift. This is my historical theme.

On the second, problematic theme: what is the problem about meaning? And what is it to find it puzzling – or for that matter, unpuzzling? What questions are we asking, when we are asking about meaning?

We are not asking about meaning in the sense that we may ask about the meaning of life, or in the sense of 'meaning' where we speak of a love or a job being meaningful. This is a related sense, but here we are talking about the significance things have for us in virtue of our goals, aspirations, purposes.

The question I am talking about here is the radical question: how is it that these segments of a medium that we deploy, when we talk, make music, paint, make signals, build symbolic objects, *how is it that these say something*? How is it that we can complete sentences of the form: 'What this means (to say) is ...?' whereas we cannot say this of sticks, stones, stars, mountains, forests – in short, of the things we just find in the world?

Or if we object to this way of putting it, because it seems to rule out one of the great traditional ways of understanding the world, as signs made by God, or embodiments of the Ideas – a view we will look at in a minute – we could equally ask: what is it that we see in things when we understand them as signs which we do not when we fail to apprehend them as such, but just as the furniture of a non-expressive universe?

There are two sides or dimensions of meaningful objects, which can each be taken up as the guiding thread of the answer. The first is what we could call the designative: we could explain a sign or word having meaning by pointing to what it designates, in a broad sense, that is, what it can be used to refer to in the world, and what it can be used to say about that thing. I say 'The book is on the table'; this is meaningful speech, and it is so because 'book' designates a particular kind of object and 'table' another, 'the' can be used to pick out a particular object in some context of reference, and the whole phrase puts together the two referring expressions in such a way as to assert that the designatum of one is placed on the designatum of the other. On this view, we give the meaning of a sign or a word by pointing to the things or relations that they can be used to refer to or talk about.

The second dimension we could call the expressive. The sentence 'The book is on the table' designates a book and a table in a certain relation; but it can be said to express my thought, or my perception, or my belief that the book is on the table. In a wider sense, it might be said to express my anxiety, if there is something particularly fateful about the book's being on table, or perhaps my relief, if the book were lost.

What is meant by 'expression' here? I think it means roughly this: something is expressed, when it is embodied in such a way as to be made manifest. And 'manifest' must be taken here in a strong sense. Something is manifest when it is directly available for all to see. It is not manifest when there are just signs of its presence, from which we can infer that it is there, such as when I 'see' that you are in your office because of your car being parked outside. In this kind of case, there is an implied contrast with another kind of situation, in which I could see you directly.

Now we consider things expressions when they make things manifest in the stronger sense, one which cannot be contrasted with a more direct manner of presentation, one where things would be there before us 'in person', as it were.

Take the example of facial expressions. If you have an expressive face, I can see your joy and sorrow in your face. There is no inference here; I see your moods and feelings, they are manifest, in the only way they can be manifest in public space. Contrast this with your neighbour, who is very good at hiding his feelings; he has a 'poker face'. But I happen to know of him (because his mother told me) that whenever he feels very angry a muscle twitches just beside his ear. I observe the muscle, and I see that he is angry.

But the muscle twitching does not amount to an angry expression. That is because it is like the case above where I see you are in your office from your car's being outside. In these cases, I infer to something that I am *not* seeing directly. Expressions, by contrast, make our feelings manifest; they put us in the presence of people's feelings.

Expression makes something manifest in embodying it. Of course, a given expression may reveal what it conveys in a partial, or enigmatic, or fragmentary fashion. But these are all manifestations in the above sense, that however imperfect we cannot contrast them with another, more direct, but non-expressive mode of presentation. What expression manifests can *only* be manifested in expression.

Now we can see much of what we say in both the designative and the expressive dimension, as we did with the sentence above. In each dimension we relate the sentence to something different: to the objects it is about, in one; and to the thought it expresses, in the other.

Each may seem to offer the more natural approach to the question of meaning in different contexts. In discussing the meaning of a sentence like 'The book is on the table', we are more naturally inclined to give an account in designative terms. When we are thinking about a poem, or a piece of music, on the other hand, we more naturally think of its meaning in the expressive dimension. Indeed, with a symphony or a sonata, it is hard to speak of designating. This dimension seems to disappear altogether.

But although each is more natural in a certain context, there seems no reason to see the expressive and the designative as rival modes of explanation wherever they both apply, as in ordinary speech. Rather they seem to answer different questions.

But there is an important dispute in the history of thought over the issue of which of these dimensions is more fundamental in the order of explanation. If 'The book is on the table' expresses my thought to this effect, is this because the words concerned have the designative meanings that they have? If this is so, then the fundamental phenomenon is that of designative meaning. This is what we need to understand in order to get to the root of things. The expressive function of words will be dependent on this.

Or is there something about the expressive function which cannot be so understood? Is there a dimension of expressive meaning which is not simply determined by designative meaning? Are the tables even to be turned, and is expressive meaning in some way primary, providing the foundation or framework in which words can have designative meaning in the first place? If this is true, then the fundamental thing in language is expressive meaning.

These two approaches define very different ways of understanding the question, What is meaning? A long struggle between the two has led up to our present understanding of language. Before turning to look at this history, I would like to say something about the metaphysical motivations of the two types of theory.

Designative theories, those which make designation fundamental, make meaning something relatively unpuzzling, unmysterious. That is a great part of their appeal. The meaning of words or sentences is explained by their relation to things or states of affairs in the world. There need be nothing more mysterious about meaning than there is about these things or states of affairs themselves. Of course, there is the relation of meaning itself, between word and thing, whereby one signifies or points to the other. But this can be made to seem unmysterious enough. At the limit, if talk about signifying makes us nervous, we can just think of this as a set of correlations which have been set up between noises we utter and certain world events or states. At the end of this road, we have behaviourist theories, like that of Skinner (followed by Quine, who has in turn been influential for Davidson).

But if we are not all that metaphysically fastidious, we can simply take the designating relation as primitive and hope to illuminate meaning by tracing the corrrelations between words and things – or, in more contemporary guise, between sentences and their truth conditions.

By contrast, expressive theories maintain some of the mystery surrounding language. Expressive meaning cannot be fully separated from the medium, because it is only manifest in it. The meaning of an expression cannot be explained by its being related to something else, but only by another expression. Consequently, the method of isolating terms and tracing correlations cannot work for expressive meaning. Moreover, our paradigm-expressive objects function as wholes. Take a face or a work of art. We cannot break either down into parts, and show the whole to be simply a function of the parts, if we want to show how it is expressive.

The sense that expression is mysterious can be formulated more exactly. The point is that expressive theories run counter to what is considered one of the fundamental features of scientific thought in the modern age, where designative theories do not. Scientific thought is meant to be objective; and this means it must give an account of the universe not in terms of what we could call subject-related properties, that is, properties that things have in the experience of subjects, and which would not exist if subjects of experience did not exist. The most notorious example of these in seventeenth-century discussion were the secondary properties, and it was an integral part of the great scientific revolution of that time that these were expelled from physics.

Now an expressive account of meaning cannot avoid subject-related properties. Expression is the power of a subject; and expressions *manifest* things, and hence essentially refer us to subjects for whom these things can be manifest. And as I said above, what expression manifests can only be made manifest in expression, so that expressive meaning cannot be accounted for independently of expression. If we make expression fundamental, it seems impossible to explain it in terms of something else; but it is itself a subject-related phenomenon, and hence does not allow of an objective science.

By contrast, a designative theory accounts for meaning by correlating signs to bits of the world, and these can in principle be identified objectively. It offers the promise of a theory of language which can fit within the canons of modern natural science. It is in this sense that they promise to make language unpuzzling and unmysterious.

On this terrain, expressive theories cannot follow.

II

I turn now to the historical account. If we trace the development of these rival theories of meaning, we can see that the pre-occupation with *language* is a modern one. The actual doctrines about language, about words, were rather unimportant and marginal among the ancients. They were not that concerned about speech, they were concerned about thought.

But then how about the insight implicit in the many-meaninged word *logos*? *Logos* meant 'word'; and the root it came from, *legein*, meant 'to say'. What underpinned this connection between saying, words and reason was what one could call a discourse-modelled notion of thought. Thought was seen as like discourse; it revealed things as discourse can do. When we take something which is puzzling and we give an account of it in speech, we lay it out, articulate its different aspects, identify them and relate them. Because thinking was like discourse, we could use the same word, *logos*, for both. Plato says that you do not really know something unless you can give an account of it. Otherwise you have just opinion (*doxa*) and not real knowledge (*epistêmê*). But 'give an account' translates *logon didonai*.

The striking fact about the preponderant outlook of the ancients, which was bequeathed to the European Middle Ages, was their view about reality. It too was modelled on discourse-thought. In Plato's version, underlying reality, are the Ideas. Of course, it is we moderns who are tempted to put this by saying that reality was modelled on discourse-thought. For Plato this was no false projection, and we should better say that our discourse and thought ought to be modelled on reality. Reality itself, the ultimate reality of which empirical things are in a sense copies, was Idea; it articulated itself in its aspects which necessarily connected together according to its inner logic. It should be the aim of our thought to limp along after this and try to match it.

Now beside this powerful line-up of an ontic *logos*, or discourse-thought, which was followed by a *logos* in the thinking subject, words did not seem very important. They were the mere external clothing of thought. They could not aspire to more, not human words, for clearly they were not necessary to the ontic *logos*. So language plays a small and marginal role in the theories of the ancients.

But a powerful theory of meaning is in embryo here. The ancient view develops through several stages, notably through neo-Platonism, and then through the thought of the early Fathers, which owes so much to neo-Platonism: St Augustine in the West, and the Greek Fathers in the East.

In this amalgam of Christian theology and Greek philosophy, a notion is developed that Plato first adumbrated in the *Timaeus*. God in creating the world gives embodiment to his ideas. The Platonic Ideas are the thoughts of God.

And so we get an obvious analogy, which St Augustine makes explicit. Just as our thought is clothed externally in our words, so is the thought of God, the *Logos* – the *Verbum*, for Augustine – deployed externally in the creation. This is, as it were, God's speech. That is why everything is a sign, if we can see it properly.

So the paradigm and model of our deploying signs is God's creation. But now God's creation is to be understood expressively. His creatures manifest his *logos* in embodying it; and they manifest the *logos* as fully as it can be manifest in the creaturely medium. There can be no more fundamental designative relation, precisely because everything is a sign. This notion is nonsense on a designative view. For words can only have designative meaning if there is something else, other than words or signs, which they designate. The notion that everything is a sign only makes sense on an expressive view.

So what we have in Augustine and his successors is an expressive theory of meaning embedded in their ontology. The originator of meaning, God, is an expressivist. This sets the framework for the theories of the Middle Ages and the early Renaissance, what one could call the semiological ontologies, which pictured the world as a meaningful order, or a text. This kind of view of the world is dominant right up to the seventeenth century, when it was pulverized in the scientific revolution.

It was a view of this kind which understood the universe in terms of a series of correspondences, linking for instance the lion in the kingdom of animals, the eagle among birds, and the king in his realm, or linking the stars in the heavens to the shape of the human frame, or linking certain beasts and plants to certain planets. In all these cases, what is at stake is an expressive relation. These terms are linked because they embody/manifest the same ideas. To view the universe as a meaningful order is to see the world as shaped in each of its domains and levels in order to embody the ideas.

We have here a very powerful expressive theory of meaning, a theory of the divine language. But all this is compatible with the relative unimportance of human words. Indeed, it rather requires their taking marginal status; because the real thought, that of God or the Ideas, is quite independent of human expression. The theory of language is still in its infancy.

It was the rebellion against this semiological view of the universe, in nominalism, which began to make *language* important.

Medieval nominalism rejected the discourse-thought model of the real. It denied that there are real essences of things, or universals. True, we think in general terms. But this is not because the world exists in general terms, as it were; on the contrary, everything that is is a particular. The universal is not a feature of the world, but an effect of our language. We apply words to classes of objects, which we thus gather into units; that is what makes general terms.

Now this theory gives language a crucial role. The word is that whereby we group things into classes. It is the new home of the universal, which has been chased out of the real. But in giving language a role this view propounds a purely designative theory of what this role amounts to. It generates a thoroughly designative theory of meaning.

It does so, first, in rejecting the expressive theory of the cosmos, in refusing to see the things which surround us as embodiments of the Ideas; and secondly, in seeing words as acquiring meaning only in being used as names for things. Words mean because they designate something. So we cease to see everything which exists as a sign. The only signs are those which are recognized as such, and they are signs because they signify something.

This theory of language came into its own in the seventeenth-century scientific revolution, which we associate with such names as Descartes, Bacon and Hobbes. This revolution involved a polemical rejection of the vision of the world as meaningful order, and its replacement by a conception of the world as objective process, in the sense of 'objective' described above. The thoroughly designative theory of meaning was one of its main pillars.

The philosophies of the seventeenth century remade our conceptions of man, thought and knowledge to fit the new dispensation. The very notion of what thought is changes. Once we no longer think of discourse-thought as part of the furniture of the real, then we focus on our subjective thinking as a process in its own right.

It is the process by which we are aware of things. How can this be? Once discourse has lost its ontic status, it is not so much the discursive dimension in thought which seems to account for this, but rather its representative dimension. Once we focus on thought as a process going on only in our minds, and we ask how can we know about things in thought, the obvious answer seems to be that thought in some way mirrors or represents things.

And so we get the new conception of thought as made up of ideas, of little units of representation, rather like inner ghostly snapshots. This is the famous 'way of ideas', inaugurated by Descartes and taken up by his successors both rationalist and empiricist, and which dominates psychology and epistemology for the next two centuries. As the writers of the Port Royal *Logique* put it: 'nous ne pouvons avoir aucune connoissance de ce qui est hors de nous que par l'entremise des idées qui sont en nous'.[1] And they conclude from this that these ideas themselves must be the focus of our study. Thought as a kind of inner incorporeal medium becomes of central interest.

But it is through our ideas that we know what is outside. How do we do this? No longer by grasping the forms of the real, for there are none such. Rather knowing things outside means grasping how things are put together. And this means that we put them together in idea as they are in reality.

So the method of thought becomes the famous resolutive-compositive one. We break things in our ideas down into their component elements, and then we put them together in idea as they are in reality. That is what understanding is, for Galileo, Descartes, Hobbes. As Hobbes puts it in *De Cive* (II.14):

for everything is best understood by its constitutive causes. For as in a watch, or some such small engine, the matter, figure and motion of the wheels cannot be well known, except it be taken insunder and viewed in its parts; so as to make a more curious search into the rights of states and duties of subjects, it is necessary, I say, not to take them insunder, but yet that they be so considered as if they were dissolved ...

This means, of course, that our thought too must be broken down into its component bits. These bits are the ideas of seventeenth- and eighteenth-century epistemology.

So what is thinking? It is assembling ideas, properly the assembling of clear and distinct ideas, and according to the way components of the world are assembled. Thinking is mental discourse, to use Hobbes' term; where this is no longer the articulating and making evident of the ancients, but a kind of inner disassembly and reassembly.

But if thinking is mental discourse, what is the role of language? Sometimes it seems, in reading the writings of seventeenth- and eighteenth-century thinkers, that its role is as much negative as positive, that words can mislead us and take our attention away from the ideas. Language is seen by them as the great seducer, tempting us to be satisfied with mere words, instead of focussing on the ideas they designate.

[1] Antoine Arnaud and Pierre Nicole, *La Logique ou l'art de penser* (Paris, 1970), p. 63.

But no one held the view that we should try to do without language altogether. This was evidently impossible. For any relatively complex or long drawn-out thought we plainly need words; all thinkers concur in this. And indeed, this is not only intuitively evident, it is implicit in their nominalistic starting point. It is through words that we marshal our ideas, that we group them in one way rather than another. Words allow us to deal with things in generalities, and not one by one.

And this is the role which this age assigns to language. It is through words that we marshal our ideas, not painstakingly, one by one, in which case we would not get very far in constructing an understanding of the world, and would lose through forgetfulness as fast as we gained through insight; rather we marshal them in groups and classes. This is Hobbes' doctrine when he likens reasoning to reckoning; where we get our global result by casting up a number of partial sums, and not simply counting one by one. Condillac in the next century has basically the same idea when he says that language gives us 'empire sur notre imagination'.

From this role of language we can see why words are so dangerous. If we use them to marshal ideas, they must be transparent. We must be able to see clearly what the word designates. Otherwise where we think we are assembling our ideas to match the real, we will in fact be building castles of illusion, or composing absurdities. Our instruments will have taken over, and instead of controlling we shall be controlled.

Language for the theory of these centuries is an instrument of *control* in the assemblage of ideas which is thought or mental discourse. It is an instrument of control in gaining knowledge of the world as objective process. And so it must itself be perfectly transparent; it cannot itself be the locus of mystery, that is, of anything which might be irreducible to objectivity. The meanings of words can only consist in the ideas (or things) they designate. The setting up of a designative connection is what gives a word meaning. We set these up in definitions, and that is why thinkers of this period constantly, almost obsessionally, stress the importance of recurring to definitions, of checking always to see that our words are well-defined, that we use them consistently.

The alternative is to lose control, to slip into a kind of slavery; where it is no longer I who make my lexicon, by definitional fiat, but rather it takes shape independently and in doing this shapes my thought. It is an alienation of my freedom as well as the great source of illusion; and that is why the men of this age combated the cosmos of meaningful order with such determination.

As Locke puts it, 'every man has so inviolable a liberty to make words stand for what ideas he pleases'.[2] Even the great Augustus has no power over my lexicon.

III

The seventeenth-century revolution which in a way did so much to establish our modern modes of thought gave us a thoroughly, polemically, designative theory of meaning. This was challenged in the late eighteenth century by a climate of thought and feeling which is loosely called Romanticism. This term is certainly loose, because it is stretched to include many people, Goethe for instance, who did not define themselves as Romantics and who were not Romantics in any exact sense. But it is a handy label, and I want to go on using it here.

One of the founding texts of this expressivist reaction is Herder's *On the Origin of Language* (1772). (Herder himself was not properly speaking a Romantic; but one of the originators of the *Sturm und Drang*.) In an important passage of this work, Herder turns to consider one of the typical origin stories of eighteenth-century designative theory, that of Condillac in his *Essai sur l'origine des connaissances humaines*.[3] It is a fable of two children in the desert, who come to invent language. We assume certain cries and gestures as natural expressions of feeling. Condillac argues that each, seeing the other, say, cry out in distress, would come to see the cry as a sign of something (e.g., what causes distress), and would come to use it to refer. The children would thus have their first word. Their lexicon would then increase slowly, item by item.

Herder rebels against this whole conception. For, as he says, it presupposes just what we want to explain. It takes the relation of signifying for granted, as something the children already grasp, or that can unproblematically occur to them ('ils parvinrent insensiblement à faire, avec réflexion, ce qu'ils n'avoient fait que par instinct' (para. 3)). Condillac, says Herder, presupposes 'das ganze Ding Sprache schon vor der ersten Seite seines Buches erfunden'. His explanation amounts to saying, 'es enstanden Worte, weil Worte da waren, ehe sie da waren'.[4]

The problem is that Condillac presupposes that his children already understand what it is for a word to stand for something, what it is therefore to talk about something with a word. But *that* is just the mysterious thing. Anyone can be taught the meaning of a word, or even guess at

---

[2] *Essay* III. ii. 8.   [3] Part II, sect. I, chap. I.
[4] *Treatise on the Origin of Language*, in J. G. Herder, *Sprachphilosophie* (Hamburg, 1960), pp. 12, 13.

it, or even invent one, once they have language. But what is this capacity which we have and animals do not to endow sounds with meaning, to grasp them as referring to, as used to talk about things?

Let us look at this. I have the word 'triangle' in my lexicon. This means that I can recognize things as triangles, identify them, pick them out as such. I can say, for example, 'This is a triangle.' But what does this capacity amount to? Let us see by comparing it with an analogous animal capacity. I might train an animal (a rat), to react differentially, say, to go through a door which had a triangle painted on it, as against one which had a circle. So my rat would be in a sense recognizing a triangle.

But there is a crucial difference: the rat in a sense recognizes the triangle, because he reacts to it. But the human language-user recognizes that this is a triangle, he recognizes that 'triangle' is the right word to use here; that this is the right description. This capacity to recognize that X is the right description is essentially invoked in our capacity to use language. Of course, we are not usually reflecting as we talk that the words we use are the appropriate ones; but the implicit claim in speaking language is that they are appropriate; and we can all understand the challenge that someone might make at any point: 'Is X the right word?', or 'Do you really mean X?' And we would all be able to give some kind of reply.

So only beings who can describe things as triangles can be said to recognize them as triangles, at least in the strong sense. They do not just react to triangles, but recognize them as such. Beings who can do this are conscious of the things they experience in a fuller way. They are more reflectively aware, we might say.

And this is Herder's point. To learn a word, to grasp that 'triangle' stands for triangles, is to be capable of this reflective awareness. That is what needs to be explained. To account for language by saying that we learn that the word 'a' stands for a's, the word 'b' for b's, is to explain nothing. How do we learn what 'standing for' involves, what it is to describe things, briefly, to acquire the reflective awareness of the language user?

Herder uses the term 'reflection' (*Besonnenheit*) for this awareness. And his point against Condillac is that this kind of reflection is inseparable from language. It cannot precede our learning our first word, which is what Condillac implicitly assumes. This is because only someone capable of using language to describe is capable of picking things out as — or recognizing things as —, in the strong sense.

But this means that language is not just a set of words which designate things; it is the vehicle of this kind of reflective awareness. This reflection is a capacity we only realize in speech. Speaking is not only the expression of this capacity, but also its realization.

But then the expressive dimension of language becomes fundamental again. In order for given words to mean something, to designate their respective objects, we have to be able to speak, that is, give expression to this reflective awareness, because it is only through this expression, through speech, that this reflective awareness comes about. A being who cannot speak cannot have it. We only have it, in contrast to animals, in that we talk about things. Expression realizes, and is therefore fundamental.

This is once again an expressive theory. But this time it is an expressive theory of language, rather than an expressive theory of the cosmos. On the traditional view, creation expresses the ideas of God; but these exist before/outside creation. The new expressive theory of human language that we find in Herder is, by contrast, constitutive; that is, reflective consciousness only comes to exist in its expression. The expressive dimension is fundamental to language, because it is only in expression that language comes to be.

The theorists of the Romantic period were, of course, very influenced by the earlier expressivism of the cosmos, as we might call it. We could say that in a sense they transposed what belongs to God on this older theory on to man. For man like God embodies his ideas and makes them manifest. But unlike God, man needs his expression in order to make his ideas manifest to himself. Which is another way of saying that his ideas do not properly exist before their expression in language or some other of the range of media men deploy. That is what is meant by saying that language, or expression in general, is constitutive of thought.

In this connection, it is no accident that the Romantic period sees a revolution in our conception of art. The traditional view understood art in terms of mimesis. Art imitates the real. It may select, imitate only the best, or what conforms to the ideas, but basically what it attempts to do is hold the mirror up to nature. The Romantics gave us a quite different conception, by which, in one formulation, the artist strives to imitate not nature, but the author of nature. Art is now seen not as imitation, but as creative expression. The work of art does not refer beyond itself to what it imitates; rather it manifests something; it is itself the locus in which the meaning becomes manifest. It should be a symbol, rather than an allegory, to recur to the distinction which the men of that generation often invoked.

As Herder put it: 'the artist is become a creator God'.[5] The artist creates in his work, as it were, a miniature universe, a whole which has its goal in itself, and does not refer beyond to anything else. Novalis makes the comparison with the divine creation in these terms: 'artistic creation is thus as much an end in itself as the divine creation of the universe, and one is as original and as grounded on itself as the other: because the two are one, and God reveals himself in the poet as he gives himself corporeal form in the visible universe'.

But to return to the theory of language. We see that language is no longer an assemblage of words, but the capacity to speak (express/realize) the reflective awareness implicit in using words to say something. Learning to use any single word presupposes this general capacity as background. But to have the general capacity is to possess a language. So that it seems that we need the whole of language as the background for the introduction of any of its parts, that is, individual words.

This may seem to pose insuperable obstacles for any account of the acquisition of language; and indeed, Herder in spite of the title of his work (*Ueber den Ursprung der Sprache*) ducks the issue altogether. But it does point to a feature of language which seems undeniable, its holism. One might say that language as a whole is presupposed in any one of its parts.

Herder again is the one who formulated this insight. It is ultimately implicit in the point above, that to use a word to describe is to identify something as —. When I say 'This is a triangle', I recognize it as a triangle. But to be able to recognize something as a triangle is to be able to recognize other things as non-triangles. For the notion 'triangle' to have a sense for me, there must be something(s) with which it contrasts; I must have some notion of other kinds of figures, that is, be able to recognize other kinds of figure for the kinds they are. 'Triangle' has to contrast in my lexicon with other figure terms. Indeed, a word only has the meaning it does in our lexicon because of what it contrasts with. What would 'red' mean if we had no other colour terms? How would our colour terms change if some of our present ones dropped out?

But in addition, to recognize something as a triangle is to focus on this property; it is to pick it out by its shape, and not by its size, colour, what it is made of, its smell, aesthetic properties, and so on. Here again some kind of contrast is necessary, a contrast of property dimensions. For to say of

---

[5] Quoted in T. Todorov, *Théories du symbole* (Paris, 1977), p. 185.

something 'This is a triangle' is to apply this word as the *right* word, the appropriate descriptive term. But someone could not be applying a word as the right word and have no sense whatever of what made it the right word, did not even grasp for instance that something was a triangle in virtue of its shape, and not its size or colour.

So it appears that a word like 'triangle' could not figure in our lexicon alone. It has to be surrounded by a skein of other terms, some which contrast with it, and some which situate it, as it were, give its property dimension, not to speak of the wider matrix of language in which the various activities are situated in which our talk of triangles figures: measurement, geometry, design-creation, and so on.

The word only makes sense in this skein, in what Humboldt (who followed and developed Herder's thoughts on language) called the web (*Gewebe*) of language. In touching one part of language (a word), the whole is present.[6]

This expressive doctrine thus presents us with a very different picture of language from the empiricist one. Language is not an assemblage of separable instruments, which lie as it were transparently to hand, and which can be used to marshal ideas, this use being something we can fully control and oversee. Rather it is something in the nature of a web, and to complicate the image, is present as a whole in any one of its parts. To speak is to touch a bit of the web, and this is to make the whole resonate. Because the words we use now only have sense through their place in the whole web, we can never in principle have a clear oversight of the implications of what we say at any moment. Our language is always more than we can encompass; it is in a sense inexhaustible. The aspiration to be in no degree at all a prisoner of language, so dear to Hobbes and Locke, is in principle unrealizable.

But at the same time, we need to connect this with another feature of language on this scheme which Humboldt also brought to the fore. What is crucial to language is what is realized in speech, the expression/realization of reflection. Language is not, once again, a set of instruments: words which have been attached to meanings; what is essential to it is the activity in which by speaking words we pick things out as — (among other

---

[6] Another very persuasive argument is the famous one in Wittgenstein's *Investigations* i.258ff, dealing with sensation E. If you try to give the name 'E' to an inner sensation, and avoid saying anything else about it, not even that it is a sensation, then you find yourself just wanting to make an inarticulate noise. For in saying nothing else, you deprive 'E' of the status of a word. You cannot know what you are saying. Cf. also his arguments against private ostensive definition; *Investigations* i.29.

things, as we shall see). The capacity which language represents is realized in speech.

As Humboldt puts it, we have to think of language as speech, and this as activity, not realized work; as *energeia*, not *ergon*.

But if the language capacity comes to be in speech, then it is open to being continuously recreated in speech, continually extended, altered, reshaped. And this is what is constantly happening. Men are constantly shaping language, straining the limits of expression, minting new terms, displacing old ones, giving language a changed gamut of meanings.

But this activity has to be seen against the background of the earlier point about language as a whole. The new coinages are never quite autonomous, quite uncontrolled by the rest of language. They can only be introduced and make sense because they already have a place within the web, which must at any moment be taken as given over by far the greater part of its extent. Human speakers resemble the sailors in Neurath's image of the philosopher, who have to remake their ship in the open sea, and cannot build it from the base in a dry-dock.

What then does language come to be on this view? A pattern of activity, by which we express/realize a certain way of being in the world, that of reflective awareness, but a pattern which can only be deployed against a background which we can never fully dominate; and yet a background that we are never fully dominated by, because we are constantly reshaping it. Reshaping it without dominating it, or being able to oversee it, means that we never fully know what we are doing to it; we develop language without knowing fully what we are making it into.

From another angle: the background web is only there in that we speak. But because we cannot oversee it, let alone shape it all, our activity in speaking is never entirely under our conscious control. Conscious speech is like the tip of an iceberg. Much of what is going on in shaping our activity is not in our purview. Our deployment of language reposes on much that is preconscious and unconcious.

So the expressive view yields us a much broader and deeper conception of language. It is an utterly different phenomenon than the assemblage of designative terms which empiricism gave us. But the implicit extensions go further. The designative theory sees language as a set of designators, words we use to talk about things. There is an implicit restriction of the activities of language. Language primarily serves to describe the world (although designative terms can also be given extended uses for questioning and giving commands).

The expressive theory opens a new dimension. If language serves to express/realize a new kind of awareness; then it may not only make possible a new awareness of things, an ability to describe them; but also new ways of feeling, of responding to things. If in expressing our thoughts about things, we can come to have new thoughts; then in expressing our feelings, we can come to have transformed feelings.

This quite transforms the eighteenth-century view of the expressive function of language. Condillac and others conjectured that at the origin of language was the expressive cry, the expression of anger, fear, or some emotion; this later could acquire designative meaning and serve as a word. But the notion here was that expression was of already existing feelings, which were unaltered in being expressed.

The revolutionary idea of expressivism was that the development of new modes of expression enables us to have new feelings, more powerful or more refined, and certainly more self-aware. In being able to express our feelings, we give them a reflective dimension which transforms them. The language user can feel not only anger but indignation, not only love but admiration.

Seen from this angle, language cannot be confined to the activity of talking about things. We transform our emotions into human ones not primarily in talking about them, but in expressing them. Language also serves to express/realize ways of feeling without talking about them. We often give expression to our feelings in talking about something else. (For example, indignation is expressed in condemnation of the unjust actions, admiration in praise of the remarkable traits.)

From this perspective, we cannot draw a boundary around the language of prose in the narrow sense, and divide it off from those other symbolic-expressive creations of man: poetry, music, art, dance, etc. If we think of language as essentially used to say something *about* something, then prose is indeed in a category of its own. But once one takes language as being expressive in this way, that is, where the expression constitutes what it expresses, then talking *about* is just one of the provinces constituted by language; the constitution of human emotion is another, and in this some uses of prose are akin to some uses of poetry, music and art.

In the Romantic period, there was a tendency to see this constituting of the human emotions as the most important function of language in a broad sense. Language realizes man's humanity. Man completes himself in expression. It was natural in such a context to exalt art above other forms of expression, above the development of merely descriptive language; or at least to give it equal weight and dignity. It was then that art began to replace religion for many as the centrally important dimension of human life – which it remains for many today.

But the expressive view not only transformed and extended the conception of the uses of language. It also transformed the conception of the subject of language. If language must be primarily seen as an activity – it is what is constantly created and recreated in speech – then it becomes relevant to note that the primary locus of speech is in conversation. Men speak together, to each other. Language is fashioned and grows not principally in monologue, but in dialogue, or better, in the life of the speech community.

Hence Herder's notion that the primary locus of a language was the *Volk* which carried it. Humboldt takes up the same insight. Language is shaped by speech, and so can only grow up in a speech community. The language I speak, the web which I can never fully dominate and oversee, can never be just *my* language, it is always largely *our* language.

This opens up another field of the constitutive functions of language. Speech also serves to express/constitute different relations in which we may stand to each other: intimate, formal, official, casual, joking, serious, and so on. From this point of view, we can see that it is not just the speech community which shapes and creates language, but language which constitutes and sustains the speech community.

IV

If we attempt to gather all this together, we can see that the expressive conception gives a view of language as a range of activities in which we express/realize a certain way of being in the world. And this way of being has many facets. It is not just the reflective awareness by which we recognize things as —, and describe our surroundings; but also that by which we come to have the properly human emotions, and constitute our human relations, including those of the language community within which language grows. The range of activity is not confined to language in the narrow sense, but rather encompasses the whole gamut of symbolic expressive capacities in which language, narrowly construed, is seen to take its place. This activity, even as regards the production of normal prose about the world, is one which we can never bring under conscious control or oversight in its entirety; even less can we aspire to such oversight of the whole range.

If we now look back over the route we have been travelling, we see how language has become central to our understanding of man. For if we hold on to the intuition that man is the rational animal, the animal possessing logos or discourse-thought, at least in that we concur that this has something to do with what distinguishes us from other animals, then the effect of the expressive doctrine is to make us see the locus of our humanity in the power of expression by which we constitute language in the broadest sense, that is, the range of symbolic forms. For it is these which make thought possible. It is this range of expressions which constitute what we know as logos.

The whole development, through the seventeenth-century designative theory and the Romantic expressive view, has brought language more and more to centre stage in our understanding of man; first as an instrument of the typically human capacity of thinking, and then as the indispensable medium without which our typically human capacities, emotions, relations would not be.

If we follow the expressive view, then we have to come to understand this medium, and the extraordinary range of activities which constitute it, if we are ever to hope to understand ourselves. What I want to suggest is that we have all in fact become followers of the expressive view; not that we accept the detail of the various Romantic theories, but in that we have all been profoundly marked by this way of understanding thought and language, which has had a major impact on our civilization. I would venture to claim that even those who would want to reject expressive theories as metaphysical rubbish and obfuscatory mystification are nevertheless deeply affected by this outlook.

I want to make at least a feeble attempt briefly to defend this outrageous claim. My point now is that the profound influence of the expressive view in modern culture is what underlies our fascination for language, our making it such a central question of twentieth-century thought and study.

This would also explain why language is more enigmatic to us than to previous ages – admittedly another highly controversial claim. For on the expressive view, language is no longer merely the external clothing of thought, nor a simple instrument which ought in principle to be fully in our control and oversight. It is more like a medium in which we are plunged, and which we cannot fully plumb. The difficulty is compounded in that it is not just the medium in virtue of which we can describe the world, but also that in virtue of which we are capable of the human emotions and of standing in specifically human relations to each other. And flowing from this the capacity we want to understand is not just that by which we produce prose about the things which surround us, but also those by which we make poetry, music, art, dance, and so on, even in the end those by which we have such a thing as personal style.

This means that the phenomenon of language becomes much broader as well as deeper when we move from a designative to an expressive perspective. We are tempted to ask what this range of capacities have in common. And even if we have been taught by Wittgenstein to resist this temptation, the question cannot but arise of how they hold together as a 'package'. For this they seem to do. It is not an accident that the only speaking animal is also the one who dances, makes music, paints, and so on. Finding the centre of gravity of this range is a much more difficult and baffling question than tracing how words designate, that is, until we come to see that the latter question leads us back to the former.

But this is what the expressive understanding of language puts on our agenda; that we find this centre of gravity, or, in other terms, come to some insight about this extraordinary capacity we have for expression.

Or we can get to the heart of the same issues in another way, if we ask what is the characteristic excellence of expression. On the designative view, this was clear. Language was an instrument. It was at its best when it best served its purpose, when the terms designated clearly distinct ideas, and we maintained their definitions clearly before us in our reasoning. On this understanding language was an all-purpose tool of thought. But for the expressivist, it is an activity which constitutes a specific way of being in the world, which Herder referred to as 'reflection', but which it is hard to find a word for just because we are so baffled to define what I called its centre of gravity.

Another way of asking what this centre of gravity is is to ask when this way of being is at its best, its fullest, in other words, what constitutes its excellence. When are our expressive powers most fully realized? We can no longer assume that just attaining maximum clarity about the things we describe and explain constitutes perfection.

But to know what it is to realize our expressive powers to the fullest must be to know something about the characteristic perfection of man, on the premises of the expressive understanding; and so this question must come on our agenda.

Again, the question of what expression is can arise in another way, We try to understand how expression can *arise*, how a new medium of thought or understanding can come to be through expression. And since we cannot study the genesis of language in human life, our question takes the form of asking when we come close now to forging new modes of expression; what happens when we extend our capacity for expression? How does this come about?

For a variety of reasons, many contemporaries have thought it plausible that it is in artistic creation that we come closest to understanding this, to understand the mystery of original expression; and this is one of the reasons why art is so central to our self-understanding.

But the baffling nature of language extends to more than the nature of expression. It also touches the question, who expresses? We saw above that language for the Romantics could not be seen as the creation of the individual. And indeed, it is hard to fault them on this. We are all inducted into language by an existing language community. We learn to talk not only in that the words are given to us by our parents and others, but also in that they talk to us, and hence give us the status of interlocutors. This is what is involved in the centrally important fact that we are given a name. In being given a name we are made into beings that one addresses, and we are inducted into the community whose speaking continually remakes the language. As interlocutors, we learn to say 'I' of ourselves, one of the key stages in our becoming language users.

Language originally comes to us from others, from a community. But how much does it remain an activity essentially bound to a community? Once I learn language can I just continue to use it, even extend it, quite monologically, talking and writing only for myself? Once again, the designative view tends to make us see this as perfectly possible. My lexicon is under *my* control. And common sense tends to side here at first sight with the designative view. Surely, I very often do talk to myself, I can even invent private names for people, and why not also private terms for objects which surround me?

Of course, I can invent private terms. But the question is whether my speech does not always remain that of an interlocutor in a speech community in an essential way. We might ask whether my conception of what it makes sense to say, of how things may be perspicuously described, of how things can be illuminatingly classified, of how my feelings can be adequately expressed, whether all these are not profoundly shaped by a potential terrain of intersubjective agreement and full communication. I may break away now from my interlocutors, and adopt quite another mode of expression, but is it not always in view of a fuller, more profound and authentic communication, which provides the criterion for what I now recognize as an adequate expression?

So the question remains open as to whether the subject of speech is not always in some sense, and on some level, a speech community.

Another related question concerns the place of the subject in expression. It is in a sense the question, What is expressed? or, What comes to expression? Of course, our developing language, in so far as it is descriptive language, responds to the shape of things around us. But we have seen that there is another dimension to language, that by which its development shapes our emotions and relations. Expression shapes our human lives. The question is, what is it that, in coming to expression, so shapes our lives as human?

For the expressivists of the late eighteenth century and the Romantic period, the answer was quite unproblematical. Expression was self-expression. What comes to full expression are my desires, my aspirations, my moral sentiments. What comes to light in the full development of expressive power is precisely that what was striving for expression all along was the self. This may not have been so in the earlier ages of human history, when men were prone to see themselves simply as immersed in a larger cosmos and not also as centres of autonomous will and desire. But as it comes to greater self-clarity expression comes to be recognized as self-expression.

But the basic expressivist insights might also suggest another account. What comes about through the development of language in the broadest sense is the coming to be of expressive power, the power to make things manifest. It is not unambiguously clear that this ought to be considered as a self-expression/realization. What is made manifest is not exclusively, not even mainly, the self, but a world. Why think here primarily in terms of self-expression?

Now the expressivists of the Romantic period did not really need to pose this question, because in a sense they could accept both answers at once. They could do so, because of the notion, common in the Romantic period, of God as a kind of cosmic subject, of which we finite subjects are in a sense emanations. This view, which hovers on the brink of pantheism, allows us to see what we make manifest in our language both as our own and as God's, since God lives in us. We express both ourselves, and a larger reality of which we are a part.

With the receding of this too indulgent pantheism (as it must appear to us), we are left with the choice. Is the expression which makes us human essentially a self-expression, in that we are mainly responding to our way of feeling/experiencing the world, and bringing this to expression? Or are we responding to the reality in which we are set, in which we are included of course, but which is not reducible to our experience of it?

The common sense of our society takes perhaps too easily the position

of the Romantics, without even the excuse of their pantheistic justification. It assumes that in our paradigm-expressive activities, for instance, in
artistic creation, we are expressing ourselves, our feelings and reactions.
But this answer is also challenged. Some contemporaries would argue that
our most expressive creations, hence those where we are closest to deploying our expressive power at the fullest, are not self-expressions; that
they rather have the power to move us because they manifest our expressive power itself and its relation to our world. In this kind of expression,
we are responding to the way things are, rather than just exteriorizing our
feelings.

Heidegger springs to mind in this connection. Something like this view
may lie behind this passage, quoted from *Dichterisch wohnet der Mensch*:

> Man behaves as if he were the creator and master of language, whereas on the
> contrary, it is language which is and remains his sovereign ... For in the proper
> sense of these terms, it is language which speaks. Man speaks insofar as he replies
> to language by listening to what it says to him. Language makes us a sign and it is
> language which first and last conducts us in this way towards the being of a thing.[7]

On this view what we strive to bring to expression is not primarily the
self. Expressivism here becomes radically anti-subjectivist. And of course,
this issue raises from another angle the one mentioned above, about the
characteristic excellence of expression, and hence of man.

These questions are all difficult and deep. I mean by that latter term not
only that they touch fundamental questions about ourselves, but that
they are baffling and very difficult to formulate, let alone find a clear
strategy to investigate. But they are among the questions which the
expressive view puts on our agenda. My hypothesis is that we are fascinated and baffled by language in part because we are heirs of this outlook.

But I must face the objection which must have been urging itself
forward all this time: surely I cannot be claiming that we all accept the
main doctrines of the expressive view of language, that there are no more
designativists, or even more implausibly, that there are no more proponents of objectifying science? Of course, I agree, that would be absurd.
The stock of objectifying science is as high as ever. The virtually inarticulate belief that only an objective account is a truly satisfactory one
has invaded the sciences of man, has shaped the procedures of widely
practised academic disciplines, like psychology, sociology, political
science, much of linguistics. Moreover one of the underlying motives of

---

[7] *Dichterisch wohnet der Mensch*, in Martin Heidegger, *Vorträge und Aufsätze*, part II
(Pfullingen, n.d.), p. 64.

an objective account that we saw with the seventeenth-century designative theory, that it seems to promise control over the domain under study, is as forcefully operative today as then; indeed, more so.

But in spite of this, I want to maintain my claim that the expressivist reasons for bafflement are to some extent shared by all of us. I should like to offer two grounds for this.

The first is that much of the Romantic view of language has come to be generally accepted by both metaphysical camps, objectivists and their opponents. We now see language capacity as residing in the possession of an interconnected lexicon, only one part of which is used at any time. We see that the individual term is defined in relation to the others. Ferdinand de Saussure made this point at the beginning of the century, and it is now common property.

At the same time we recognize the central importance of speech activity for language. Language as a code (Saussure's *langue*) can be seen as a kind of precipitate of speech (Saussure's *parole*). Speech activity itself is complex: the declarative sentence is not just the result of concatenating words with their attached meanings. It involves doing different things, picking out an object of reference, and saying something about this object. These different functions and their combination in the declarative utterance determine to a significant degree the kind of language we have. But on top of this we also recognize that speech activity goes well beyond the declarative utterance, and includes questions, orders, prayers, etc.

We are also ready to recognize that this activity involves mechanisms of which we are not fully aware and which we do not fully control. We do not find strange a thesis like Chomsky's, that our grasp of grammaticality involves the application of transformations of which we are not consciously aware, relating a depth structure to a surface structure. We accept without too much demur that there may well be a 'depth structure' to our language activity.

And we are perhaps even ready to agree that the language which is evolved through this speech activity is the language of a community and not just of an individual, in other words, that the crucial speech activities are those of the community. We may not be entirely sure what this means, but we have a sense that in some meaning it contains an important truth.

Of course, this does not mean that everyone has become an expressivist. We are not in any sense forced to abandon the metaphysical stance in favour of objective accounts. But what we now have to do is apply them in a new way. We see language as a whole, as an activity with – potentially at least – a depth structure. The task is now to give an objective account of this depth structure and its operation, which underlies the activity of language we observe. This is now the agenda.

In this the science of language is simply one example of a global shift in the objectivistic sciences of man since the eighteenth century. The shift is away from a set of theories in terms of 'surface' or observable realities, principally the contents of the mind available to introspection, in favour of theories in terms of 'deep' or unobservable mechanisms or structures. The shift is one aspect of the virtually total disappearance of the seventeenth- and eighteenth-century 'way of ideas', the attempt to understand the mind in terms of its introspectable contents, the science that came to be called 'ideology' at the moment when it had passed its peak.

This was grounded in the view, common to Descartes and his empiricist critics, that the contents of the mind were in principle open to transparent inspection by the subject himself. Thinking was, as we saw, 'mental discourse', which ought to be entirely self-possessed and self-transparent. This view seems very implausible today, where the importance of unconscious structures and processes in thought seems very plausible, indeed, close to undeniable.

But the scientific goals and norms of the seventeenth and eighteenth centuries easily survived the demise of the 'way of ideas'. In place of the 'surface' psychologies of the past, we now have explanation by-passing consciousness; in some cases by ignoring the psychological altogether, and explaining behaviour in terms of stimulus and response; or else in terms of a depth theory which is physiological; in others by what remains a 'psychological' theory but one drawing heavily on mechanisms unavailable to consciousness, such as Freudian psychoanalysis, or computer-modelled theories of our intelligent performances. In place of 'surface' sociologies, based on the adjustment of conscious interests, or the existence or absence of individual habits of mind, we have theories of social structure, in which individuals are caught up in a dynamic which they do not and perhaps cannot understand; where the explanation is at the level of the social whole, and of properties of this whole which are not evident to the participants. These follow the laws or obey the constraints of historical materialism or structural-functionalism.

Now in many of these cases, for example, Freud, Marx, structural-functionalism, the depth structures elaborated obviously owe a lot to earlier Romantic theorizing. But the fact remains that the intent of these theories is to give an objectivistic explanation.

And in this, of course, they are following a lead set by the 'hard' sciences of nature, which also have had recourse more and more to unobservable depth structures, even including some which violate our ordinary macroscopic understanding of things.

If we were to try to explain this shift which has gradually taken place over the last two centuries, away from the way of ideas, then undoubtedly the example of the hard sciences, always the paradigms of objectivistic science, is an important factor. But it cannot be the only one. Something would have to be said about the change in our condition. Perhaps it is that in modern mass societies we feel less of a sense that the factors which are decisive for our behaviour are under our purview – that what society claims of us is something we give knowingly even if not willingly – than did the educated classes of the earlier epoch. I think something like this is true, but even so, a great deal remains to be explained. Why do we understand ourselves so readily in depth-psychological terms? Something very important about the whole development of modern society is waiting here to be uncovered.

But in any case, the science of language has followed this pattern. We are no longer satisfied with surface accounts of the application of words to ideas. We want an account in terms of depth structure. But many want the same scientific goals to be paramount.

But although the metaphysical goals survive unscathed into the new sciences of depth structure, the fact that so much has been taken on board from the Romantic conception makes it inevitable that something like the same questions arise as those expressivism puts on the agenda. For instance, there is a continuing issue about how to understand the notion of depth structure, as the philosophical debates around Chomsky's work attest. Is depth structure to be understood as the operation of an unconscious capacity, for instance, do we know how to make transformations, even though we are unaware of doing so? This seems to many unbearably paradoxical. Or should we see depth structures in terms of underlying operations, analogous to those in machines? But then what is their relation to the intelligent and conscious uses of language? From either direction, some mystery surrounds the status of the language capacity as a whole which plainly underlies our ability to say specific things on specific occasions. The baffling questions the expressive view gives rise to will not disappear just because we stick to our objectivist metaphysic. Some seem to arise inescapably with the intuition that language involves some global underlying capacity, and not just a set of particulate dispositions to utter certain words in certain circumstances.

This threatens to create something of a dilemma for objectivistic thought, and leads to the characteristic gamut of modern would-be scientific theories. At one extreme are those who are highly sensitive to the metaphysical dangers of allowing depth explanations. They would like ideally to develop a behaviourist theory, in which the utterance of certain words is made a function of environmental stimulation. Skinner is the most spectacular protagonist of this view.

But the weakness of this strategy is that the explanatory power of such a theory is very poor, and it even comes close to absurdity at times. And so we gain greatly in plausibility by moving along the spectrum, to what we might call 'neo-designative' theories of meaning, like that, for example, of Donald Davidson. This theory can be called 'neo-designative' because it attempts to give an account of meaning in terms of the truth conditions of sentences. These truth conditions are observable states of affairs in the world; hence once again we have the basic *démarche* of a theory which tries to explain the meaning of language in terms of the relation of linguistic elements to extra-linguistic reality. Only here, the modern theory has profited from our understanding of language as a structured reality; so that the elements so related are not words, but declarative sentences.

These theories – another example might be explanations of the functioning of language on the model of information-processing mechanisms – are more plausible than behaviourism, but they still give no recognition to the expressive dimension. But it is possible to move further along the spectrum, to give some recognition to this, while trying to explain it in objectivistic terms.

Two examples spring to mind, which however are not concerned with theories of language in the narrow sense, but with – in different ways – symbolic expression. These are the views of Marx and Freud.

Freud recognizes symbolic expression, in our symptoms as well as in what he calls symbols. But these are explained in terms of desires, which are not themselves desires for symbolic expression, nor do they involve such expression in their proper fulfilment. On the contrary, the symbolic proliferation results from their blocking or inhibition. The symptom gives my object of desire in symbolic form, because I cannot (will not allow myself to) go after it in reality. Moreover these desires should ultimately be explicable physiologically; hence Freud's electrical and hydraulic languages.

With Marx, we also have a recognition of symbolic expression in ideological consciousness: religion, for instance, gives us a distorted expression of the human social condition of its age. With the liberation of classless society, and the victory of scientific over ideological consciousness, such symbolic forms of awareness are swept aside. And from the standpoint of scientific consciousness, the ideological symbolism is fully explicable, again in terms which have nothing to do with a motivation directed to symbolic expression. This rather is seen as a distortion of the reality, and hence of the underlying motives, which come to clear self-recognition in scientific consciousness.

This account may be somewhat unfair to Marxism, as it may also be to Freud, in giving an unduly reductive cast to their explanations. But whether we have here portrayed true or vulgar Marxism and Freudianism, the theories obviously have their weaknesses, in that they have trouble dealing with the place of expression, of symbolism in normal, undistorted or non-pathological life. When they try to say something in the domain of aesthetics, for instance, Marxism and Freudianism must develop more refined interpretations on pain of sounding philistine and implausibly reductive.

We have examples of such developed – and semiologically sensitive – Marxism and Freudianism in contemporary French structuralism (e.g., in different ways, Lacan, Barthes, Althusser). But this structuralism has taken a step further along the spectrum. It allows expression a central place in human life. It understands that man is the language animal, in that language is more than a tool for man, but somehow constitutes a way of being which is specifically human. We have to understand the growth of language as bound up with the development of a form of life which it makes possible. So that the question can arise of the characteristic excellence of language, of when expression is at its best.

As a matter of fact, modern structuralism owes quite a bit to the reflections of expressivist philosophers. For instance, Lévi-Strauss read Merleau-Ponty with interest. Lacan has been very influenced by Hegel and Heidegger (his Hegel being mediated through Kojève, who picked Heideggerian themes out of Hegel).

But the intent remains 'scientific', that is objectivist. In Lévi-Strauss' case, for instance, drawing from the work of Marcel Mauss, the basic idea – at least of his early theory – seems to be that language arises in a drive to classify, which in turn must be understood as ultimately aimed at social/moral order. We order our lives through classifications, of things forbidden and allowed, enjoined or neutral. The classificatory scheme, of our totems, of segments of the universe, is ordered to a classification of partners and actions, which alone makes possible social integration.

This theory sees the expressive function as central; sees it as necessary indeed to the very existence of human society. But it lays claim too to objectivity, presumably in that its account of language is functional and reductive. For the function which explains language is not the manifestation of anything, but the maintenance of a social order. (In this it shows the Durkheimian roots of so much French social thought.) Once more language is to be explained in terms of something else.

But as we come to this end of the spectrum, the questions which the expressive view brings forward become harder and harder to avoid. With contemporary structuralism, great mysteries surround the status of the underlying structures, for example their relation to the uses of language in everyday life, and their relation to the individual subject. These are comparable to the questions that arise from the expressive view; indeed, in some cases the questions are the same.

I ran through this gamut in order to illustrate the dilemma of modern objectivist theories of language. They can avoid the intrusion of the baffling questions concerning the nature of expression only by espousing narrower and more primitive theories which are either implausible, or which fail to explain an important range of the phenomena of language, or both. Or they can win plausibility and explanatory range, but at the cost of opening themselves to these questions.

This is the first ground I would put forward for my claim that we are all affected to some degree by the expressivist reasons for bafflement about language. It concerns the predicament of scientific theorizing about language. My second ground can be put much more tersely. Regardless of scientific considerations, modern students of language remain children of our age, and immersed in its culture. And this has been so massively affected by the Romantic-expressivist rebellion, that no one can remain untouched by it. This effect is particularly visible in our understanding of art, its nature and its place in human life. One of the most obtrusive effects is the concern of much contemporary art with the process of its own creation, with the properties of its own medium, with the experimental creation of new media. Expression itself becomes its theme; how it is possible, just what it consists in, and what point it can give to human life. The artist becomes his own subject, and/or the process of creation his theme.

It is very difficult to live in this civilization and not have the problem of expression obtrude on us, with all its enigmatic force. And that is the reason, I want to maintain, why we are all so concerned and fascinated with language, so that even the most tough-minded and empiricist philosophies, like logical empiricism, are 'linguistic' in cast.

V

I hope that this historical odyssey has cast light on our contemporary fascination with language. I hope that it has also shown why we find it baffling, and has done something to explain the paradox that, with all the advance of science, this central human function seems more mysterious to us than to our eighteenth-century predecessors.

In fact, seen from this historical perspective, the development towards our present understanding of language as both central and enigmatic seems irreversible. We cannot recapture the earlier perspectives from which language could appear more marginal or less problematic. The view of the universe as an order of signs is lost for ever, at least in its original form, after the coming of modern science and the modern notion of freedom; and the view of language as a set of designative signs, fully in our control and purview, is lost forever with the seventeenth-century view of the punctual subject, perfectly transparent to himself, whose soul contained nothing that he could not observe. From where we stand, we are constantly forced to the conception of man as a language animal, one who is constituted by language.

But I do not hope for agreement on this. Because in our bafflement, we naturally split into two camps. This reflects the pull on us of the contradictory metaphysical demands: for the clarity and control offered by an objective account of ourselves and our world, on one hand, and towards a recognition of the intrinsic, irreducible nature of expression, on the other. There are very few of us who do not feel the force of both these demands. And perhaps just for this reason we divide with polemical fervour into opposing parties, expressors and designators.

The battle between expressors and designators is one front in the global war between the heirs of the Enlightenment and the Romantics; such as we see in the struggle between technocracy and the sense of history or community, instrumental reason versus the intrinsic value of certain forms of life, the domination of nature versus the need for the reconciliation with nature. This general war rages over the battlefronts of language as well. Heidegger is one of the prophets of the stance of 'letting things be', one of the great critics of modern technological consciousness; the neo-designators defend a notion of reason as instrumental reason. All this is no accident. It shows only how much rides on this issue.

The issue concerns the nature of man, or what it is to be human. And since so much of this turns on what it is to think, to reason, to create; and since all of these point us towards language, we can expect that the study of language will become even more a central concern of our intellectual life. It is in a sense the crucial locus of the theoretical battle we are having with ourselves.

As a civilization, we live with a compromise. In our scientific understanding, we tend to be men of the Enlightenment, and we accept the predominance of Enlightenment – one might say, utilitarian – values in setting the parameters of public policy. Growth, productivity, welfare are of fundamental importance. But it is recognized that, without prejudice to the perhaps ultimately available scientific explanation which will be reductive, people experience things in expressive terms: something is 'more me'; or I feel fulfilled by this, not by that; or that prospect really 'speaks to me'. Along with this tolerance of experience goes a parallel in the public domain. The main limits of public policy are set by the requirements of production within the constraints of distribution, and these are meant to be established by scientific means, and in a utilitarian spirit. But private experience must be given its expressive fulfilment. There is a 'Romantik' of private life, which is meant to fit into a smoothly running consumer society.

However effective this compromise may be politically, it is a rotten one intellectually; it combines the crassest scientism (objectivism) with the most subjectivist forms of expressivism. But I suppose I say it is rotten mainly because I think that both of these are wrong; and that they leave out the really fruitful line of enquiry, a contemporary expressivism which tries to go beyond subjectivism in discovering and articulating what is expressed.

But even leaving aside my commitments, it is certain that in the absence of a strong expressivist critique, scientism remains smugly satisfied with its half-baked explanations, and the subjectivist conception of experience veers towards formless sentimentalism. The issue of language goes by default; which means the issue of what it is to be human goes too.

CHAPTER TEN

THEORIES OF MEANING

I

How are we to approach the phenomenon of language, that people say things and others understand them? The fact that words and other signs have meaning can seem incredibly deep, enigmatic, difficult to understand. The sense of depth comes both from the realization that language is somehow essential to human life, that is, to whatever we unreflectingly want to identify as essential to being human; and also from the very pervasiveness of meaning in our lives, the difficulty of getting the phenomena in focus. We are in a sense surrounded by meaning; in the words we exchange, in all the signs we deploy, in the art, music, literature we create and enjoy, in the very shape of the man-made environment most of us live in; and not least, in the internal speech we rarely cease addressing to ourselves silently, or to absent others.

The sense of depth can easily turn into a sense of mystery. But here something in us, or our modern culture, may resist. We can call it our commitment to reason, or to scientific thought. Language must be a phenomenon of nature just like all others. Perhaps it is a characteristic of only one species (and even this is supposedly challenged by work on chimps), but this does not make it any less a natural phenomenon. It should therefore be understandable in the same way. It should be open to investigation, and ultimately understood/explained by some theory. The problem is just to find the right one.

This stance towards language goes back quite a few centuries. We find it clearly in evidence in eighteenth-century attempts to give a naturalistic account of the origin of language (Condillac's was one of the best known). But these theories in turn were based on the polemical, no-nonsense nominalism of the seventeenth century which we find, for example, in Hobbes and Locke.

This nominalism had complex motivations, and finding a scientific understanding of language was not the primary one. But finding an adequate language of science was. One of the principal concerns of both Hobbes and Locke was to ground our picture of the empirical world in the firm foundations provided by clear unequivocal definitions of basic terms. But doing this meant demystifying language, showing it up to be a pliant instrument of thought, very important, but still an instrument. It was perverse to seek in language a domain of authority for our beliefs. 'Words are wise men's counters ..., but they are the money of fools', says Hobbes.[1]

Of course, the temptation to do something which empiricists could identify as misplacing one's trust in language itself sprang from a conception of the universe as in some sense a meaningful order, that is an order of being which could be explained in terms of the ideas it embodied, or the correspondences it exhibited between different domains, or some other such ultimately semiological categories. The new nominalism was a centrepiece of what has been called the disenchantment of the world. It was close, that is, to the spirit of the nascent modern science.

It castigated these semiological cosmologies as projections, 'sciences as we would', as Bacon called them. The whole attempt to find the ideas or forms basic to reality involves us in the delusive game of placing there what we supposedly discover. What we must seek is not to identify ideas or meanings, but to build an adequate representation of things. The notion of a representation can be seen as playing an important role implicitly and explicitly in this period, as Foucault has argued.[2]

When we hold that knowing X is having a (correct) representation of X, one of the things we establish is the neat separation of ideas, thoughts, descriptions and the like, on one hand, and what those ideas, etc., are about on the other.

A representation (in the sense of the term of art I am using here) is of an independent reality. This is not the only possible model for knowledge; nor is it the only possible model that springs to philosophically uninstructed common sense. These are all kinds of knowing, from knowings how, to knowing people intimately, which do not have to be construed representationally. We have temptation to do so when we reflect, because we are heritors of this modern movement in philosophy which made representation basic. I am suggesting that one of the stronger motives for making it so basic was the desire to overcome projection, and what we later call 'anthropomorphism', that promiscuous mixing of our own intuitions of meaning, relevance, importance with objective reality.

---

[1] *Leviathan*, ch. 4.   [2] *Les Mots et les choses* (Paris, 1966), ch. 3.

Rational thought seeking knowledge of the world tries to build representations. Words are indispensable instruments for such buildings, for they allow us to deal with whole classes of ideas at a time, and avoid our having to construct our picture of the world particular by particular, as it were. But if they are to be useful such instruments, it has to be clear what elements of the world (represented reality) they attach to; or alternatively, if we take seriously the 'way of ideas', we must be clear what ideas, that is part representations, they designate. On either construal, their role is to connect with things either mediately or immediately; and the connection must be fully in our control, if we are to use them to understand.

What naturally emerges from this is a highly designative view of meaning. Words have meaning because they stand for things (or perhaps ideas, and thus only mediately for things). They 'signify' things, to use the old language. So you capture the phenomena of meaning if you see how words attach to their designata in this way. And this ultimately is explicable by the fact that minds use them as marks or notes for things (or ideas).

And so we get the notion which our contemporary theories had to overcome: the meaning of a word is what it designates. Meaning is designation. This theory was partly motivated by (what were seen as) epistemological considerations, the need to have an adequate language for valid knowledge.

But there was another way in which the modern conception of science could help generate an approach to meaning, and this can come into play when we try to consider man as an object of science. Suppose we try to apply to man the same naturalistic strictures: no projection. Then we can conceive the idea of understanding a phenomenon like language as we would any other in extra-human nature, that is without invoking any underlying ideas or thoughts. For this extreme naturalism the basic phenomena of language are the sounds we emit, the marks we make; understanding them is seeing how they are evoked by what surrounds us, and in turn trigger off behaviour.

Extreme naturalism, of course, abstracts from ideas and thoughts, and everything 'inner', as it does also from intentions. But with this important distinction, it is very much on the same wave-length as the modern designative theory. Both consider the question of meaning in terms of correlations between words and things, words and behaviours. So extreme naturalism could grow quite easily, one might say naturally, out of the designative tradition. One can see it, in a sense, as the empiricist view with its scientific scrupulousness pushed a stage further, to the denial (or the ignoring) of the mental altogether. But it retains the idea of the word functioning as a designator. The line of descendance between, say, Helvétius and Skinner is very evident. And indeed, the extreme mechanism of this radical naturalism was prepared for in the classical tradition by the recourse to such mechanistic explanations as the association of ideas (ancestor of S–R).

Now the tradition of naturalist explanation, the interdict on anthropomorphic projection, is what can give us pause before our sense of mystery. But not necessarily in the form of radical naturalism. This tends to be discredited. Of course, it has its contemporary defenders, most spectacularly B. F. Skinner who shows its application to language in his *Verbal Behaviour*.[3] But Chomsky and others have destroyed this in our eyes, and rendered this approach wildly implausible. Our emitting the different words we do is just obviously too loosely related to the supposedly correlated environmental stimuli. We cannot seem to get away with an understanding of language which does not have recourse to thoughts, intentions and the like.

But the undermining of radical naturalism in this domain has also been abetted by the decline of pure designativism. The major breaches in this view for this philosophical culture were those made by Frege. And we can see how closely they are involved with the considerations weighing against extreme naturalism.

We could put it this way: what Frege shows to be wrong with a pure designative theory of meaning is that it ignores the activity underlying meaningful uses of language. Only in the context of a sentence does a word have meaning, because it takes a sentence to do what we do with words, that is, in highly general terms, say something. The designativist, one who tries to explicate meaning in terms of the things designated by the terms, has to take account of this activity, because it affects how words relate to things. In the assertion, we must distinguish two important roles, referring and saying something of a referent, and the way words relate to what we might think of as their designata is different in these different roles.

Or to come at what is ultimately the same point from another direction: sentences are not just lists of words. If the meaning of a sentence can be grasped from our knowledge of the meaning of the constituent words, this cannot just be by concatenating the designata. Understanding a series

---

[3] London, 1957.

of designata is not understanding what is said. For this, we have to know what is being done with the words, and grasping this activity requires that we understand something of the roles different words play in the sentence.

Even more clearly than with his concept/object distinction, Frege shatters the designative view with his sense/reference distinction. He forces the designativist to recognize that we cannot give an account of meaning just in terms of words and what they designate. We have to distinguish this latter, the reference, from the sense. Specifying the sense is specifying the speaker/hearer's route into the reference. But this Fregean image of a route invokes the underlying activity. Words are not just attached to referents like correlations we meet in nature; they are used to grasp these referents; that is they figure in an activity. And thus they differ in the way or manner or route by which they effect their ends.

So the designative view is undermined for the same kind of reason as radical naturalism, viz., that neither can take account of the matrix of activity within which the connections between words and their referents arise and are sustained. Their models are either natural correlation, or arbitrary labelling, but neither even approaches adequacy to our linguistic activity. The discrediting of the designative theory of meaning has played an important part in the decline of behaviourism.

But what emerges in the Anglo-Saxon world is a range of theories which are still in line of descent from the original epistemological and naturalist insights. They are still founded on the notion of a representation. While based on the understanding that meaning is not simple designation, they identify the crucial activity relevant for linguistic meaning as the framing of linguistic representations. By this I do not mean of course that they espouse the picture theory of meaning attributed to the early Wittgenstein; rather I mean that the dimension of speech activity which is the focus of a theory of meaning is seen as that whereby it offers depictions, potential or actual, of an independent reality, wherein it codes information, one might say, potential or actual, about reality.

This is evident in truth-conditional theories of meaning, for instance. It has been argued that there must be one key concept which applies in deriving the meaning of all sentences; and that this concept must be truth. But to say that the key concept of our theory of meaning will be truth – *the* key concept – is to say that what we must primarily focus on is the way that words form depictions, or clusters of potential information, that is candidates for truth or falsity.

And even those writers who feel chary of asserting from the beginning that truth is the key concept, and that the theorems of a theory of meaning can take the form: 's is true if p', wish to argue for it in a way which clearly makes representation central. The theory of meaning is seen as one component of a global account of people saying what they do (or emitting the noises they emit). It is a component which maps what is said on to what is the case in such a way that along with plausible hypotheses about people's desires and intentions it issues in plausible ascriptions of propositional attitudes to the speakers.[4]

Of course it is no part of the intentions of these theorists to claim that making potential depictions is all we do in language; as though our only interest were in describing things, and making assertions. On the contrary, they recognize that we also ask questions, give commands, make requests, and so on. But the claim is that the kernel which is similar in all these speech acts, and which is relevant for the theory of meaning, is the representative or depictive. A request, order, question, also depict: they give a linguistic representation of a state of things, viz., that we are asking to be brought about, or ordering to be brought about, or about which we are enquiring whether it holds or not.

Thus in developing our truth-conditional theory of meaning from the facts of language use, one important phase, according to McDowell, followed by Platts, will be the sifting out of the various speech-acts a certain basic component, similar in form in all. This, which Platts calls the 'monistic transformational component',[5] is in fact what has been described in other terminology as the 'propositional content' of the different acts. It is the depiction they are all held to contain of some possible state of affairs. And extricating this in each case is clearly necessary if we wish to account for meaning in terms of truth, to account for the meanings of words in terms of the contributions they can make to depictions or representations of things.

Thus truth-conditional theories, and others in the Anglo-Saxon world which share this basic orientation, remain faithful to the modern conception of language at least in this, that they take the primary linguistic phenomenon, the principal object of a theory of meaning, to be representation. What is it we have to understand in order to understand meaning? Primarily this, that with words we manage to frame representations. These representations are used for a host of purposes: we not only encode information by them, and transmit it; we also make known our desires,

[4] Cf. J. McDowell in Evans and McDowell (eds.), *Truth and Meaning* (Oxford, 1976), pp. 42–66; and M. Platts, *Ways of Meaning* (London, 1978), pp. 58–63.
[5] In M. Platts (ed.), *Reference, Truth and Reality* (London, 1980), p. 3.

get people to do things, ask for information through these representations, and so on. Not to mention all the playful and ironic and imaginative uses. Some of these purposes might be effected without language. We
might silently bend some stranger to our will through pointing and
threatening gestures. But when we effect them in language, then the question of meaning arises. And this phenomenon, that words have meaning,
which can appear so deep and enigmatic, this is to be understood ultimately as residing in the fact that words serve us in our framing of
representations. Once we have understood this, we have understood
meaning. So give us a theory of how we combine words to make such
descriptions, and we have a theory of meaning.

The stress on a theory showing how we combine is obviously well-
motivated. Because the striking fact about language is its potentially
endless inventiveness. There is a non-definite number of discriminable
such depictions that the competent speaker can devise, or understand. His
ability to devise/understand new ones seems mediated by his familiarity
with the words that they are composed of. Indeed, we find it easy to
assume that the vocabulary of any given speaker, although perhaps very
large, is finite. And so it appears that his ability to produce/understand an
indefinite number of sentences is a case of achieving infinite ends through
finite means, to quote Humboldt.[6]

Thus a theory showing how this combination comes about, how depictions are generated in language, would be a theory of meaning.

So, the contemporary theories of meaning, although they have broken
with the crass designativism which was born out of seventeenth-century
nominalism, remain faithful to it at least in this, that they see meaning in
terms of representations. Understanding language is understanding how
we represent things in language. In this way they remain faithful to the
concerns of modern epistemology: we have to show how language can be
a vehicle of knowledge as modern epistemology conceives it.

But these theories also remain in the line of modern naturalism. They
are meant to be theories derived through naturalistic observation. As in
the accounts of McDowell and Platts above, or in Davidson's 'Radical
interpretation' paper,[7] we see these theories as potentially derivable from,
and verifiable in, the behaviour, linguistic and other, of some foreign
tribe. We could imagine coming to learn their language this way, through

---

[6] *Ueber die Verschiedenheit des menschlichen Sprachbaues,* in *Gesammelte Schriften*
(Berlin, 1907), vol. 6.
[7] *Dialectica,* 27 (1973), pp. 313–28.

observing the noises they make, the situations in which they make them, what they seem to be desiring and intending, what knowledge of things it is plausible to attribute to them, and so on.

In other words, like all naturalistic theories, these theories are framed as theories elaborated by an observer about an object observed but not participated in. This is not to say that there is a bar on participation in the object studied; or even that there might not be crucial advantages in participating, that this might make evidence available that was otherwise unobtainable. But the form of the theory is such that it is meant to be comprehensible to the pure observer. It is not cast in language, nor does it invoke connections, which could only be comprehensible to one who in some sense participated in the reality studied.

This is the importance, I think, of the Quinean fable, taken up by many other writers in the field, of the foreign observer, ignorant of the local language, who develops a theory by observing the natives, and noting what noises they make in what circumstances. So powerful is the underlying theoretical *a priori* that many philosophers convince themselves you actually could learn a language this way. Which is what I want to challenge.

We can sum up by saying that there seem to be two crucial features of currently dominant theories of meaning in the Anglo-Saxon world: their stress on representations, and their assumption of the observer's stance. These are both linked, of course. They have the same roots in the seventeenth-century concern with epistemological reconstruction, and the ensuing stress on naturalistic explanation. And indeed, they are inwardly connected. Seeing theory as observer's theory is another way of allowing the primacy of representation: for a theory also, on this view, should be representation of an independent reality. A theory of meaning is a representation of a process which is itself the generation of representations. It all hangs together.

Both these features undoubtedly will seem obviously inescapable to many. What other key semantic notion can there be beside truth? And what else can a theory do than represent an independent reality? But both can be challenged, and are by another conception of meaning, to which I now want to turn.

II

This alternative conception of meaning that I now want to look at is the one that comes to us through Herder and Humboldt, in different ways also through Hamann; and it has been taken up in our day by Heidegger and others. I could call it the 'Romantic' theory, or family of theories; I could call it 'expressive', which is a term I have used elsewhere. But maybe the best policy is to avoid any descriptive mode of reference, and call it simply the triple-H theory.

This view also protests against the classical designative view, that it neglects the activity of speech. Humboldt argues that language seen as a lexicon, a system of terms linked to designata, or a quantum of resources now available for the description of things, in any of these ways is secondary; what is primary is the activity of speaking, within which this system is constantly being made and modified. What is important is to understand language as *energeia*, not just *ergon*.[8] This is a criticism which seems parallel to the one I claim can be seen as underlying the Fregean contribution.

But there are very important differences. The most important concern the HHH conception of what is going on in language. Perhaps most of us would agree today on some version of the Humboldtian thesis of the primacy of activity. But the important question remains of what the activity or activities is/are within which our lexicon, or linguistic resources, develop and change. Is the primary such activity that of framing representation? In Saussurian terminology, we know that the *langue* is formed by the many acts of *parole*. But what is the nature of this speaking activity?

I want to abstract from the various theories of the HHH type three important aspects of language activity. I do not claim that these are found together in this form in any writer. But I think that together they are both highly plausible, and force us to look at the theory of meaning in a different light. These are three (mutually compatible) answers to the question: what are we bringing about in language and essentially through language, i.e. such that it can only be brought about through language?

The list of things that one could bring forward as plausible answers to this question is probably indefinite. Some would be relatively peripheral, some extremely important to our understanding of language and our linguistic capacity. The three I want to mention now are supposedly of great importance in this respect.

I

The first aspect I want to mention is this: in language we formulate things. Through language we can bring to explicit awareness what we formerly

---

[8] Humboldt, *Ueber die Verschiedenheit des menschlichen Sprachbaues.*

had only an implicit sense of. Through formulating some matter, we bring it to fuller and clearer consciousness. This is the function that Herder focuses on in his critique of Condillac in the essay *On the Origin of Language*.[9]

Let us look more closely at this activity. What happens, for example, when we have something we want to say and cannot, and then find the words for? What does formulation bring off? What is it to be able to say something, to make it explicit? Let us say I am trying to formulate how I feel, or how something looks, or how she behaved. I struggle to find an adequate expression, and then I get it. What have I achieved?

To start with, I can now focus properly on the matter in question. When I still do not know how to describe how I feel, or how it looks, and so on, the objects concerned lack definite contours; I do not quite know what to focus on in focussing on them. Finding an adequate articulation for what I want to say about these matters brings them in focus. To find a description in this case is to identify a feature of the matter at hand and thereby to grasp its contour, to get a proper view of it.

In the above paragraph, I find myself using visual metaphors, which are the ones that seem to come naturally to us, at least in our civilization, when describing what is involved in articulation. The point of these metaphors is that coming to articulate our sense of some matter is inseparable from coming to identify its features. It is these that our descriptions pick out; and having an articulated view of something is grasping how the different features or aspects are related. We use 'articulate' both as an adjective and a verb, but the first is derivative from the second. We speak of someone who can express himself as 'articulate', because he can articulate and lay out the contours of what he has a sense of.

We can see this by contrast with another kind of case where I am looking for a word: for instance, where I seek the word in a foreign language, already having it in English; or where I seek the technical term for a feature of some engine or plant, or the terrain, which I can quite well identify with some adequate description: 'the long metal part sticking out on the left', or 'the elongated blue tube between the petals'. These are very different from the cases where I am seeking a language to identify how I feel, or to make clear just how it looks, or to define just what it was that was peculiar about her behaviour. Finding language in these latter cases is a matter of articulating what I sense, and therefore of getting a more

[9] *Ueber den Ursprung der Sprache* (Berlin, 1959), pp. 28ff.

articulated view of the matter. It is success in this effort, not in finding the right German word, or the correct technical term, that I want to call formulation. In the translation or technical term case, it is not true to say that I do not know what I am looking for until I find it. I can circumscribe what I want to know exactly enough to look it up in a dictionary or hand-book. But in cases of genuine formulation, we only know afterwards what we are trying to identify.

So the first thing that formulating does for me is that I can now get an articulated view of the matter, and thus focus on it properly. The second change is related to this: now that I have delimited what I am concerned with, I can draw in however rough a fashion its boundaries. These clearly go together, in that an articulated view of some matter is obviously one in which certain distinctions are drawn. The terms I apply have meaning only in contrast with others; in applying certain descriptions I make certain features salient, features which my description has now identified, hence delimited. The drawing of boundaries is essential to language; and con-versely, it is only in language that we can draw this kind of boundary, through language that we can delimit what we are attending to in the matter at hand. We can say of an animal on behavioural grounds that he is attending to this feature of an array and not that, because that is what he is responding to. For example, we can say: he is responding to the shape, not the colour. But the animal cannot make the distinction between attending to the shape and attending to the colour, as we must be able to follow the instruction 'don't mind the shape, look at the colour' in order to focus on one rather than the other.

Making the distinction here, where you grasp each by defining it contras-tively with the other, is something only a linguistic creature can do. And it is one of the main offices of language to delimit, make boundaries, so that some features can be picked out, not just in the sense that we respond to them oblivious of the others, but that we pick them out from the field of others.

The terms of language are inherently contractive, as Spinoza and Hegel argued. Which is why language is a capacity to apply a web of terms, and never the ability just to use a single term. A one-word lexicon is an imposs-ibility, as Herder and Wittgenstein have both argued. It is language which enables us to draw boundaries, to pick some things out in contrast to others.

Thus through language we formulate things, and thus come to have an articulated view of the world. We become conscious of things, in one very common sense of this term, that is we come to have explicit awareness of things.

2

Second, language serves to place some matter out in the open between interlocutors. One might say that language enables us to put things in public space. That something emerges into what I want to call public space means that it is no longer just a matter for me, or for you, or for both of us severally, but is now something for us, that is for us together.

Let us say that you and I are strangers travelling together through some southern country. It is terribly hot, the atmosphere is stifling. I turn to you and say: 'Whew, it's hot.' This does not tell you anything you did not know; neither that it is hot, nor that I suffer from the heat. Both these facts were plain to you before. Nor were they beyond your power to formulate; you probably already had formulated them.

What the expression has done here is to create a rapport between us, the kind of thing which comes about when we do what we call striking up a conversation. Previously I knew that you were hot, and you knew that I was hot, and I knew that you must know that I knew that, etc.: up to about any level that you care to chase it. But now it is out there as a fact between *us* that it is stifling in here. Language creates what one might call a public space, or a common vantage point from which we survey the world together.

To talk about this kind of conversation in terms of communication can be to miss the point. For what transpires here is not the communication of certain information. This is a mistaken view; but not because the recipient already has the information. Nothing stops A making a communication to B of information already in B's possesssion. It may be pointless, or misguided, or based on a mistake; but it is perfectly feasible. What is really wrong with the account in terms of communication is that it generally fails to recognize public space. It deems all states of knowledge and belief to be states of individual knowers and believers. Communication is then the transmittal, or attempted transmittal, of such states.[10]

But the crucial and highly obtrusive fact about language, and human symbolic communication in general, is that it serves to found public space, that is, to place certain matters before *us*. This blindness to the public is of course (in part anyway) another consequence of the epistemological tradition, which privileges a reconstruction of knowledge as a property of the critical individual. It makes us take the monological observer's standpoint not just as a norm, but somehow as the way things really are with the subject. And this is catastrophically wrong.

[10] The Gricean account too ultimately makes this same mistake. Cf. my review of Jonathan Bennett's *Linguistic Behaviour*, *Dialogue*, 19:2 (June 1980), pp. 290–301.

This is therefore another crucial feature about formulation in language. It creates the peculiarly human kind of rapport, of being together, that we are in conversation together. To express something, to formulate it, can be not only to get it in articulate focus, but also to place it in public space, and thus to bring us together *qua* participants in a common act of focussing.

Of course, given this human capacity to found public space, we can and do ring all sorts of changes on it. There is a whole variety of conversations, from the deepest and most intimate to the most stand-offish and formalized. Think of a heart-to-heart talk with a lover or old friend, versus casual chatter at a cocktail-party. But even in the latter case, what is set up is a certain coming together in a common act of focus. The matter talked about is no longer just for me or for you, but for *us*. This does not prevent us from putting severe limits on how much will be in the common realm. In the cocktail-party context, by tacit but common consent, what will be focussed on are only rather external matters, not what touches us most deeply. The togetherness is superficial.

In another dimension, we can distinguish various kinds of public space, all the way from small conversations (here including both the heart-to-heart and the cocktail-party chat) on one hand, to the formal public space established in institutions on the other: discussions in Parliament, or on the media, or in convocation. These various kinds of institutional or pan-societal public spaces are, of course, a very important part of the dispensation of human life. You cannot understand how human society works at all, I should like to maintain, unless you have some notion of public space.[11]

3

Language thus serves to articulate, and to found public space. But thirdly, it also provides the medium through which some of our most important concerns, the characteristically human concerns, can impinge on us at all.

Some of the things I can formulate are such that I could attribute some pre-articulate sense of them to animals. And the same goes for some of the matters I can place in public space. Its being hot in here is an example for

---

[11] The usual use of this term 'public space' is to refer to the institutional, societal manifestations. I am extending it to conversations, and everything in between, because I want to stress that the same human power of bringing us together in a common focus through speech is at work in these other contexts. And the public space of our political discussions, what we refer to for instance when we say that such and such a fact is 'in the public domain', constitutes a special case – albeit a crucial one – of this general capacity.

both of these. But there are other thoughts which it would not make sense to attribute to an animal even pre-articulately.

Among these, of course, are thoughts of a high degree of complexity, or those involving theoretical understanding, for example thoughts about the molecular constitution of some objects. Also thoughts on a meta-linguistic level, in a very broad sense of this term, that is thoughts about the properties of those symbolic systems in which we think, are out of bounds. Animals cannot be said to entertain propositions of number theory, even the simplest.

But I am thinking of certain concerns which could not conceivably be concerns of a non-linguistic animal. We can take the well-known example, the contrast between anger and indignation. Anger we can attribute to (some) animals, at least in some sense. But indignation we can not – at least if we leave aside our anthropomorphic indulgence for our pets.

The difference is that we can only ascribe indignation to a being with something like the thought: this person has done an injustic. One is only indignant at a wrong-doer (or believed wrong-doer). One can be angry at anyone who is provoking, even innocently, even though he is in the right, and you are in the wrong (especially so).

But what are the conditions for some agent's having a thought like that? It must be that he can make discriminations of the form right/wrong, as against just advantageous/disadvantageous, or hurting me/helping me. But this requires that the agent have some notion of standards that hold of a given domain; here it is a matter of moral standards, which hold of human actions. And by this I mean that he must be aware of these standards, and recognize that there are standards.

For many living things can be said to 'apply standards' in some loose sense: the cat turns up its nose at sub-standard fish, and only goes for the best. There are some standards, in the sense of criteria of acceptability, which will help explain its behaviour. There are standards here *an sich*, but not *für sich*. The cat does not recognize that it is applying standards, has not focussed on or articulated the standards *qua* standards.

But that is what an agent must be doing to be considered a moral subject. There is no such thing as morality completely *an sich*. Imagine a non-linguistic animal which always behaved according to what we identify as morality, for example it was unimaginably benevolent. We still would not call it a moral subject if it had no sense that this action was meeting some standard, or was something that it ought to do, or had in some way a higher significance and was not simply on all fours with anything else it was inclined to do, or might be inclined to do. This is, of course, the insight that Kant elaborates from his distinction between duty and inclination. But one does not need to take it where Kant does, into a sharp dichotomy. Nothing rules out the spontaneously good person, one who is benevolent out of love of human beings. Only for him as a moral agent there must be some sense that acts of charity have an additional, a higher significance than other things he may be inclined to do, for example eat ice cream, or feel the breeze in his hair. And indeed, this is part of our portrait of the spontaneously benevolent person, the natural philanthrope: the love for human beings that moves him incorporates a sense of their special importance, of their dignity and value. We would not think of him as a naturally *good* person if the quality of his feeling for human beings, and the joy he took in *beneficence* towards them, were not quite different from his inclination to other desired ends and the pleasure he found in them. For a start, we would even be reluctant to call anyone really *beneficent* who had no sense of the dignity of his human *beneficiaries*.

But to be open to this kind of significance, to recognize for instance that some acts have a special status because they meet some standard, we have to have language. For we are not talking any more about a discrimination which is shown in, because it shapes, our behaviour. The cat exhibited that. But no mere pattern of behaviour would suffice to induce us to call a given subject a moral subject. What we require is his recognition of the standards, recognition which does not reduce to our behaviour being controlled by them.

But to recognize in this sense, to mark the discrimination between, for instance, mere inclination and the right, or between what we love and what also calls on our benevolence and respect, we need to have articulated the domain of actions and ends or at least to have marked the relevant discrimination through expressive behaviour, for example through ritual, gesture, or the style of comportment. A creature incapable even of expressive behaviour could never be said to distinguish right and wrong. By this, I do not just mean that we as observers would lack the evidence we need to say this of him. Rather I want to claim that the very notion of an agent recognizing standards which are neither articulated nor acknowledged anywhere in expressive activity makes no sense. In what could this recognition consist? What would make it, even for the creature himself, a recogition of *right* and *wrong*?

Thus, taking 'language' in a broad sense to include expressive activity, we can say that only language animals can be sensitive to standards *qua* standards. And hence only linguistic animals can have this kind of concern, for moral right and wrong. But something similar can be said for the whole range of concerns that we consider characteristically human. For instance a being can only feel shame who is aware of some demands which are laid on him in virtue of his being an agent among others. The same goes for someone who is capable of a sense of dignity, or a sense of pride, of an aspiration to fulfilment, to integrity, and so on.

We are by no means talking only of admirable concerns. Some that we may consider petty or even despicable partake of this essentially linguistic nature. Animals could not aspire to machismo, any more than they could to sanctity or wisdom. For contained in the notion of the macho is that a man have a sense of the confidence, power, swaggering self-assertion that is proper to masculinity. There are standards here too; and that is why contempt awaits the weakling, the one who is 'like a woman'.

Thus man is a language animal, not just because he can formulate things and make representations, and thus think of matters and calculate, which animals cannot; but also because what we consider the essential human concerns are disclosed only in language, and can only be the concerns of a language animal.

III

Thus there are three things that get done in language: making articulations, and hence bringing about explicit awareness; putting things in public space, thereby constituting public space; and making the discriminations which are foundational to human concerns, and hence opening us to these concerns. These are functions for which language seems indispensable.

If we examine these functions, three points seem to emerge which are relevant to a theory of meaning, and I would like to discuss two of them at some length here.

I

The first concerns the role of what one could call expression. Language not only articulates, it also expresses. And this plays an essential part in the second and third functions above (and an indirect role even in the first). Concerning the latter two functions, we could put it this way: language does not have to be used to describe or characterize things in order to fulfil them. I strike up a rapport with someone. I can do this by opening a conversation. My opening gambit may be: 'Nice weather we've been having lately'; which is an assertion about recent meteorological conditions. But the content of my assertion may be secondary to the enterprise. And frequently we may strike up a rapport without an assertion, or a question, or a command, or any use of the characterizing, representing function at all.

Think again of the case where I turn to my neighbour in the hot train carriage; and instead of saying, 'Whew, it's hot in here', I just smile, look towards him, and say 'Whew!', wiping my brow. This can establish a rapport, which phase will indeed normally be followed by usual conversation; but might not be – let us say we have no language in common.

But even in this case, where we cannot have any conversation in the normal sense, we have created a rapport which is typically that of language animals. That is, we are now experiencing this heat/discomfort together; this matter of the stifling heat is not just one for you and for me severally, it is now for *us*. Or to use my above jargon, this matter of the heat/discomfort is now in a public space between us, which I have set up by my expression and gesture.

Here we have an expressive use of signs, which is unconnected with a characterizing or representative use. There is no depiction in my whole utterance, which combines speech and gesture. Even my mopping my brow is not a depiction. I really need to wipe the perspiration. What I do is lay it on thick, I mop ostentatiously. That is in the nature of this kind of expressive sign. But I really mop.

This ostentation is what makes my brow-wiping part of a sign, an expression. And it is this expression which puts the matter of the heat/discomfort into public space between us. Expression discloses here; not in the sense that it makes known to you my discomfort; you were well aware of that from the beginning. Rather it discloses in the sense of putting this in a public space, that of our rapport. That is, the discomfort is now an object for us together, that we attend to jointly. We enjoy now a complicity. This is an experience that we now share. Thanks to this expression, there is now something *entre nous*.

Thus expression reveals, not in the ordinary way of making something visible, as you could do by removing some obstacles to vision. We have a sense that to express something is to put it 'out there', to have it out before us, to be 'up front' about it. All these images point to the notion that expressing something is revealing it, is making it visible, something out there before us. But on reflection, we can see that this space before us is the public space of what is *entre nous*. The space of things which are objects for us together.

We completely miss this point if we remain with the monological model of the subject, and think of all states of awareness, knowledge, belief, attending to, as ultimately explicable as states of individuals. So that our being aware of X is always analysable without remainder into my being aware of X and your being aware of X. The first person plural is seen here as an abbreviated invocation of a truth-functional connective.

What I am arguing here is that this analysis is terribly mistaken; that it misses the crucial distinction between what is *entre nous* and what is not. It makes us think of cases of being 'up front', of avowal, as being of this sort: I impart information to you about myself; or I give you further warrant to believe some information (you may already have suspected) by asserting it before you. But the case I have been discussing shows how much is left out here. In the train, you cannot lack the information that I am hot, and you need no further warrant for it. Yet some kind of revelation is brought about by my expression. It is the revelation into public space, and it is this which has no place in the monological model.

So there is an expressive dimension of the signs we deploy, which is so far from being reducible to the representative dimension that it can sometimes exist without it; and this expressive dimension plays an important role in establishing the kind of rapport which is peculiar to us linguistic animals, and which I have referred to with the terms 'public space' and *entre nous*.

But although the expressive can exist without the representative, it seems that the reverse is not the case. Certainly not in normal conversation. Even when I open up with 'Nice weather we've been having' or 'Read any good books lately?', the nature of the rapport established – friendly, intimate, casual, easy; or on the contrary rather formal, cold, distant, or barely polite, or slighting, or ironical, or subtly contemptuous – is determined by the expressive dimension of my speech: the way I stand, look at you (or away), smile (or not), my tone of voice, manner of speaking; as also by my choice of words. I may choose between words which must be considered synonyms as far as their depictive function is concerned, but the expressive effect of each may be very different. That is, my choice of words may display a certain stance towards the subject matter, for example one of detached disinterest, or one of passionate involvement, or one of ironic affection, or one of cynical *schadenfreude*. And at the same time it may display a stance towards you as an interlocutor; brusque and businesslike, rather formal and distant, or eager and open, and so on.

I say 'display' here, because this is a matter of expression. My stance towards the subject, to you, are things that I reveal in the way expression reveals. I am making them evident in public space, and in so doing, I am shaping the kind of public space there is *entre nous*. One could say that the type of revelation here has to be expressive, because what I am revealing concerns public space. I am showing how I stand to this public space, the nature and style of my participation, and hence the kind of space it is between us. But public space is constituted by expression, and so any revelations concerning it have to be expressive.

And second, my display is a matter of expression, because I am not in any way depicting my stance in either my choice of words, or my tone, or my manner of speaking, smiling, and so on. I could also say: 'This matter barely interests me', or 'Talking to you is rather a chore for me', or 'Our conversation is just a peripheral pastime for me while I'm at this party and there's no one more interesting'. What is expressed can often also be articulated in a depiction. This may indeed be one way in which I alter how I feel or how I stand, as we shall see below.

But to articulate my stance so does not do away with the expressive dimension. It just displaces it. These things too I should say in a certain tone, with a certain choice of words. Perhaps I have an ironic twist to my voice and words which conveys that I am already taking some distance from the absurd social world in which people hold such dead conversations, and I am half inviting you to stand together with me at this vantage where we can survey the folly of men together. In which case, paradoxically, such seemingly cutting remarks could create an unaccustomed intimacy.

Can one ever do away with the expressive dimension? It would appear perhaps that this is the aim of those austere forms of language that we have developed for science, philosophy, and learned matters generally. At least the aim has been to step out of the conversational context where what presides over the choice of words is so much one's display of one's stance, or one's sense of the nature of the relationship. And philosophy itself has found that it is intermittently at war with one special class of such expressive displays, those we subsume under the heading 'rhetoric'. Rhetoric is the science of how to talk persuasively in the larger-scale, more official public spaces, those of political deliberation, or judicial argument, for instance. The rhetorician may not lie, in the sense of knowingly offering depictions at variance with the truth. But he is still suspect to the philosopher, because it is known that the crucial thing for him is what is displayed through his words. But what is depicted is an object of more explicit awareness than what is merely displayed. The rhetorician is under suspicion, because it would appear that he does not care all that much how accurately things are depicted, or even if very much gets depicted clearly, as long as the display succeeds, that is he presents himself or the matter he deals with in the right light in public space. As I argue in the *ekklesia*, I want you all to see me as the inspired, dedicated leader, willing to sacrifice myself; or as the long-patient, aggrieved party, and so on.

But this very concern with display can appear the cardinal sin for philosophy, for which what matters above all is the degree of correct explicit awareness of things. And so we develop the ideal of a non-rhetorical speech. This can be further refined to the notion of a mode of speech which is pure depiction, utterly undetermined by its place in a potential conversation, for example that it was said by X, to Y, on occasion Z, their relations being ABC, and so on. This would be a language where the only determinant of the expressions chosen would be the requirements of encoding the information to be depicted. The expressions chosen would be exclusively determined by what is to be represented, and by considerations of the most perspicuous way of encoding it.

No normal human prose approaches this ideal. The writings of scientists and learned men do indeed attain a certain austerity. They strive to abstract from the normal type of conversational context, in which we are so much concerned with self-display. But they do this by creating a special context, that of the exchange between serious thinkers dedicated above all to the truth of their depictions. Of course, the old Adam returns; one has only to think of all the special tricks of argument in which one displays oneself as more authentically a participant in this exchange than one's adversary. But this does not mean that there was not an important gain for human knowledge and rationality in developing the notion of such a context, and of the stance of disinterested search for truth that is meant to inform its participants.

To see the ideal fully realized, of depiction without expression, we have to go to artificial languages, to mathematical representations, or machine codes. But these succeed precisely because they are artificial languages, that is, they are deliberately shorn of what they would need to be languages of conversation. Their depictions can thus exist in a kind of conversational limbo, wherein alone this purity is attainable.

We have seen that we display our stance through expression, and that the expressive dimension of language is central to the second function. But it also can carry the third function. The essentially human concerns are only open to language creatures, I argued, because to be sensitive to them we have to have in some way articulated or expressed our recognition of the appropriate standards, and of the crucial discrimination they require.

Clearly it would have been too strong to demand that we have articulated them, in the sense of finding a description for them. What is required is that we be sensitive to the standards *qua* standards. And for this it may suffice that we give expression to this sensitivity, even if we have as yet no words to describe the kind of virtue or vice, good or bad, or in general the shape of the concern we have here.

Take the example of machismo above. We could easily imagine a culture in which the words 'macho', 'machismo' had not yet been coined, but in which something analogous existed. The sensitivity to the analogous ideal of manhood would be carried in their style of acting and speaking (as indeed, it is also carried among the macho today). The swagger with which I walk, the stance of domination with which I address women, my readiness to fight when my male dignity is infringed, all these mark my sensitivity to machismo-prime, the value in this analogous, pre-articulate culture.

But this is still different from the case of an animal; we are still dealing with a linguistic creature, who is capable of recognizing the standard involved. He recognizes it, because it is not just the case that it controls his behaviour, but he also gives expression to it. (And indeed, the standard itself here requires that he give expression to it: machismo requires that I act out of the proper *sense* of my maleness.)

And in fact, it is evident that there are standards expressed in people's personal style for which they have as yet no descriptive vocabulary, of which they have frequently no explicit awareness. The clipped way I talk, the way I stand, ready at any minute to spring into action, the distance I stand from any conversation, display what I admire and want to be taken for: the man of action, whose real concern is elsewhere, where the great battles are being fought. Or the exaggerated speed, obsequiousness, over-reaction to your every wish, project me as the dedicated servant.

This appears, indeed, to be another context of expression from which we cannot escape, I mean the way we project ourselves in public space. And in this display is a standing expression of our sensitivity to what we admire, and what we want to be admired for. This sensitivity can then be transformed by our articulating our concerns in descriptions. Our manner of projecting ourselves may be disrupted by our coming to see just what it is we are expressing. We become awkward, and have to find a new poise, projecting on a higher level of sophisticated awareness of the whole human game of self-presentation. But the articulation in descriptions can never displace the display through expression altogether.

As in the second function, so in the third. Language operates by expression as well as description. And in some sense, the expressive dimension seems to be the more fundamental: in that it appears that we can never be without it, whereas it can function alone, in establishing public space, and grounding our sensitivity to the properly human concerns.

Looking at the expressive dimension, and its role in these functions, gives us another view of the phenomena of language, and their boundaries. If we focus on representation, it will appear that prose speech, and the information-bearing uses of language in general, together with other media of depiction, form a domain quite distinct from the expressive uses of language and other expression activities, like gesture, stance, not to speak of expression through other media, like art for instance. We might think that the principles of explanation are quite different in these two domains. And certainly this must be so, if language is primarily to be understood as representation. Then clearly, the account of language will differ from the account of these expressive activities. This leads to a rather narrow circumscription of the phenomena we wish to account for in terms of meaning.

But if we follow the insights of the HHH view, and see the importance of expression, and also its intrication into our depictive uses of language, this narrow circumscription will be more difficult to sustain. We then get a much broader view of the phenomena of language, the phenomena which a general theory of meaning must cast light on. Language, in the sense of prose speech, is not seen on its own, or together only with other media of depiction. It is part of a wide gamut, along with expressive gesture, and different media of art: the whole gamut of what Cassirer called the 'symbolic forms'. This wider circumscription is typical of the Romantic view, the family of theories descended from the HHH.

2

The second point which emerges is that all three functions involve in different ways disclosure, a making things plain. Articulating something makes it evident in making it an object of explicit awareness; articulating it in conversation discloses it in the sense of putting it in public space; while the articulations foundational to our human concerns disclose in the sense of making it possible for these to be our concerns at all. Hence it is easy to group them together, as Heidegger does under this one term –

my 'disclosure' translates his *Erchlossenheit* – and expressions which similarly evoke images of bringing to the light, bringing into a clearing – like his *Lichtung*.

3

But the third point, which I want to examine at a little more length, is what I want to call the constitutive dimension of language. Language does not only serve to describe or represent things. Rather there are some phenomena, central to human life, which are partly constituted by language. Thus the kind of explicit awareness which we call consciousness in the full sense is constituted by our articulations. The public space between us is founded on and shaped by our language; the fact that there is such a thing is due to our being language animals. And our typically human concerns only exist through articulation and expression.

This means that articulations are part of certain of the crucial phenomena of human life, as becomes evident when we examine them more closely. Thus the nature of some of our feelings, those which touch the essentially human concerns, is partly shaped by the way we articulate them. The descriptions we feel inclined to offer of ourselves are not simply external to the reality described, leaving it unchanged, but rather constitutive of it.

Thus when we come to articulate a feeling in a new way, it frequently is true to say that the feeling also changes. Let us say that I am confused over my feelings for X; then I come to a clarification where I see that while I disapprove of some things I admire some quality in him; or after being confused about my feelings for Y, I come to see it as a kind of fascination, and not the sort of love on which companionship can be built. In both these cases, the change in descriptions is inseparable from an alteration in the feeling. We want to say that the feelings themselves are clearer, less fluctuating, have steadier boundaries. And these epistemic predicates have application here because the self-understanding is constitutive of the feeling. And this should not surprise us, because these are feelings which touch on those concerns which are essentially articulated.

All this, of course, says nothing about the causal order underlying the change. It may not be, for instance, that we simply come to a better understanding and therefore our feelings change. It is just that one change is essentially linked to the other, because self-understanding is constitutive of feeling. Nor does it follow that our feelings can be shaped at will by the descriptions we offer. Feelings are rather shaped by the descriptions that seem to us adequate. The formulations we offer of our concerns are put forward in an attempt to get it right, and it is implicit in our practice that we recognize a category of 'more or less accurate' here. That is, we recognize that self-descriptions can be more or less clairvoyant, or deluded, or blind, or deep, or shallow, and so on. To say that self-description is constitutive of feeling is to say that these epistemic descriptions can be aptly transferred to the feelings themselves. Our feelings can be shallow, or self-delusive, for instance.

Or again, let us say that I feel very guilty about a practice, and then I later come to hold that there is nothing wrong with it. The quality of the feeling of guilt changes. It may disappear altogether. But it remains, it is very different from the very fact that now I understand it as a kind of residual reflex from my upbringing. I no longer accord it the same status, that of reflecting an unfortunate moral truth about me.

It follows from all this, of course, that people with very different cultural vocabularies have quite different kinds of feelings, aspirations, sensibilities, experience different moral and other demands, and so on.

But it is not only our feelings which are partly constituted by our self-descriptions. So also are our relations, the kinds of footings we can be on with each other. These too notoriously vary from culture to culture. There are forms of hierarchy and distance which are important in some societies and absent in others; there are modes of equality which are essential to others, which are unknown elsewhere. There are modes of friendship peculiar to some societies. And each society has its gamut of possible interpersonal relations, different nuances of familiarity, intimacy, or distance, which form a gamut of possibilities which may be unrepeated elsewhere.

Now these footings are constituted in and by language. This is not to say that they are not shaped by relations of power, property, and so on. On the contrary; the point is that relations of power and property themselves are not possible without language; they are essentially realized in language. Language is essential because these different footings represent in fact different shapes of the public spaces established between people; and these spaces are maintained by language.

In the case of some of the more face-to-face spaces, the shape may be set with a minimum of explicit articulation. Its articulation may lie in modes of address, for instance, or in the style of speech used. In very differentiated societies, like traditional Japan, one addressed different qualities of people in different dialects. But even here, and *a fortiori* in the larger-scale and more official public spaces, the essential discrimination will be carried by explicit taxonomies: through the naming of different classes and ranks, titles, as well as rules setting out the rights of different classes, and so on.

The point could be made again in this form: the maintenance of these different footings, of hierarchy and subordination, or equality, of intimacy, familiarity, distance, requires some degree of common understanding by the potential participants. But among human beings, common understanding is brought about and maintained in language as a general rule. This is not to say that there is not tacit, unspoken common understanding between people. But it is necessarily interstitial. It exists within a framework of what is expressed. Without language at all, we could not have what we describe as common understanding. And indeed, much of what we call tacit common understanding is directly dependent on language. We call it tacit because the content of the understanding is not overtly formulated, but it may be expressed in such things as mode of address, choice of words, degree of volubility and so on, by which we display the common recognition of the footing we are on with each other.

And as with feelings, so here; the degree and manner of the articulation is an essential determinant of the nature of the relation. If some aspects of the footing people are on become explicitly formulated for the participants, the nature of the relationship will be altered. By the same token some kinds of social relations would be impossible without a certain degree of explicit articulation.

Take an example, which has been very important to us politically, the type of regime which has come down to us from the Greek polis, and to some extent also the Roman republic, where there is a fundamental equality between the citizens *qua* citizens, equality which is essential to their conception of self-rule and a free people. This type of regime is impossible without there being some formulation of the demand of equality, without this becoming a term of assessment, held to apply to certain societies, or in certain contexts, and not others. We could imagine certain kinds of primitive societies where what we could call equality could exist unformulated, but not for example a Greek polis, where equality was bound up with the norms for who should rule and how, and where it thus had to be recognized in some form as norm.

Thus the Spartans describing themselves as the Equals, the norm of *isêgoria* in democracies, the battle around *isonomia*, and the like, are not accessory features which we could imagine having been quite absent while those societies remained essentially what they were. The self-description as equals is an essential part of this regime, that is of this relation of equality, and this because the regime requires a degree of explicit common understanding which is impossible without the self-description.

The above are examples of what I want to call the constitutive dimension of language. We see ways in which the language we use enters into, is an essential part of, our feelings, our goals, our social relations and practices. The aspect of language which is so essential may be purely an expressive aspect in some cases, such as when modes of address are what carry the burden of marking the different kinds of footing. But it may also be that what is essential to a given feeling or relation is certain descriptions. This we see with the case of the polis. Self-description as equals is essential to the regime. And this not in virtue of some merely casual condition, as one might say that relative isolation, or an infra-structure of slave labour were essential to these regimes. Rather the point is that this kind of practice of equality essentially requires the explicit recognition of equality. It would not be classifiable as this practice without that recognition, just as the benevolent creature above could not be classified as a moral agent without the recognition of the standards his action followed.

And so, to sum up my three points, the HHH view shows us language as the locus of different kinds of disclosure. It makes us aware of the expressive dimension and its importance. And it allows us to identify a constitutive dimension, a way in which language does not only represent, but enters into some of the realities it is 'about'. What does all this bode for theories of meaning?

IV

Are these insights bad news for theories of meaning which focus on representation as the basic phenomenon to be explained? It might appear so at first blush, because the striking thing in the above exploration of the HHH is that it turns up two important aspects or dimensions of meaning which are irreducible to representation: the expressive and the constitutive.

But on further reflection, it might be thought to pose no problem to something like a truth-functional theory of meaning. The very image of a 'dimension' which I have been using seems to show the way out. A truth-functional theory might be thought to be coping with one dimension of meaning, giving an account of how meaningful utterances are generated which represent the world and the situation of the speakers. It would leave the other dimensions of language to be dealt with by other theories.

Thus I say in conversation 'That was a rather effective reply'. I mean this without irony, but it is an understatement. A truth-conditional theory of sense will work out its truth-conditions, and the corresponding theorem of the theory will offer a plausible account of what I meant, because it will make sense of my behaviour in a plausible way. Presumably, together with other facts about my situation, my relation to my interlocutor, the nature of the object described, and so on, it is quite likely that I should want to make an assertion in this understated mode.

There would be other theories, for example a theory of expression, which might help to explain how I project myself, how I display with understatement the reserve that is part of my manner of being in general, or that I feel in this relationship, or relative to this matter, or that I am projecting in order to keep a certain distance from my interlocutor. This would be a theory of expressive sense, as it were; parallel to the theory of (depictive) sense.

Then our theory of human emotions, and social relations, would cope with the constitutive dimension, by taking account of the fact that feelings, goals, footings, and so on, are partly constituted by our expressions and descriptions.

Thus we might imagine a neat division of labour; and the insights of the HHH would not threaten the truth-conditional theory in any way. It would simply point to other phenomena to be dealt with by other theories. Different philosophical schools would have pioneered theories in the different domains, but neither need be threatened by the other. And, it might be added, neither would be compelled to read the other's literature; and a long, audible sigh of relief rises on both sides of the Channel.

But unfortunately, this separation will not work. The t-c theorist maps the words uttered on to their putative truth-conditions in such a way as to preserve plausibility of propositional attitude ascriptions. The theory of sense characterizes linguistic utterances in terms of the truth-conditions of what are identified as the incorporated representations, so that along with the forces ascribed to the utterance, people's saying something like this makes sense in the light of their situations, desires, relations to others, what they know/believe, and so on.

But this requires that we identify the putative truth-conditions independently of the target language. That is, we must have a way of formulating our own adequate grasp of the truth-conditions independent of the formulations of the target language. For our coming to understand these formulations, on this view, just consists in our being able to match them systematically with the descriptions of truth conditions. Hence it is acknowledged that the language in which we formulate the right-hand side of our T-formulae must be one we already understand.

Even in the homophonic case, it cannot be strictly exactly the same as the target language. The meta-language must go beyond the target language at least in this, that it reformulates a number of the formulae of the latter when giving disquoted on the right their truth-conditions (or satisfaction-conditions). If in principle, nothing can be reformulated, then we have no kind of T-theory, but just an instruction: for any sentence, quote it, add 'is true iff', then repeat it disquoted.

And the difference is, of course, quite clear in the heterophonic case. In the Quinean fable of the radical interpreter, he identifies the truth-conditions in his own language, and must be able to formulate them in it, prior to understanding the target language.

Now this may work for the domain of middle-size dry goods, the ordinary material objects that surround us, and are likely to be salient both to observer and native, in virtue of their similarity as human beings. Perhaps depictions of these can be understood by offering truth-conditions formulae in our language.

But when we come to our emotions, aspirations, goals, our social relations and practices, this cannot be. The reason is that these are already partly constituted by language, and you have to understand this language to understand them. One can, perhaps, reformulate a description of them in some other, more theoretical language; this is the hope of all social science (and what Winch seems to be negating; if he is, wrongly). But one can only do this effectively after one has understood them in their own terms, that is, understood the language in which they are formulated for the agents concerned.

In the case of the Quine–Davidson fable, the difficulty would arise in the well-known way, that for any tribe with a way of life sufficiently different from ours, a host of words for their virtues, vices, emotions, concerns, social ranks, relations and practices would have no adequate translation into English. In competent works of anthropology, these terms are often left untranslated for that reason; the writer hopes to give us an idea of their meaning by showing the role they play in the life of the tribe.

But the general form of the difficulty for the t-c theory is that we cannot adequately grasp what some of the truth-conditions are without some grasp of the language. Observers from some totally despotic culture, dropped into classical Athens, we keep hearing this word 'equal', and its companion 'like' (*isos, homoios*). We know how to apply these words to sticks, stones, perhaps also houses and ships; for there is a tolerably exact translation in our home language (Persian). And we also know *a* way of applying them to human beings, for instance physical likeness or equality of height. But there is a peculiar way these Hellenes have of using the words which baffles us. Indeed, they have a pugnacious and perverse way of applying them to human beings who seem to us not at all like, some tall and some short, some of noble birth, some of base, and so on.

Now our problem is not just that we have to grasp that this is a metaphorical use. Presumably this kind of thing is not unfamiliar to us. What we have to grasp is how this word gets a metaphorical grip in politics. Maybe it is not hard for us to see that these short, base men are refusing to be subordinate to the taller nobility. That much will be evident from all the aggressive gestures, and perhaps actual fighting which goes on.

But what we have not yet got is the positive value of this mode of life. We do not grasp the ideal of a people of free agents, that is, in which no one just takes orders from someone, which therefore must rule themselves, and yet which has the courage, initiative and patriotism to get it together when they have to fight for their freedom. These agents exercise their right to deliberate together about what they will do, but the right to talk does not make them any less effective as agents and warriors when the time comes to act.[12] We do not see, in other words, the nobility of this kind of life, or what its practitioners identify as noble, their conception of the dignity of a man residing in his being this kind of agent, having this kind of freedom.

A similar point could be made in connection with the word 'freedom'. Let us take another observer, now hostile to the polis, and pleading the case of a despotic culture. This notion of freedom, as a status within a certain kind of social practice of self-rule, seems utterly devoid of sense. Freedom can only mean the absence of physical obstacles, or perhaps stretching a point, the absence of legal prohibitions.[13]

What our Persian observer could not see, and what Hobbes would not see, is the way in which 'equal', 'like', 'free', and such terms as 'citizen', help define a horizon of value (if I can use these Nietzschean expressions without espousing his theory). They articulate the citizen's sensitivity to the standards intrinsic to this ideal and this way of life. These articulations are constitutive of the way of life, as we saw, and therefore we cannot understand it unless we understand these terms.

---

[12] Cf. Pericles' funeral oration in Thucydides, *Peloponnesian War*, Book II, pp. 34–6.
[13] T. Hobbes, *Leviathan*, ch. 21.

But reciprocally, we cannot understand these terms unless we grasp what kind of sensitivity they are articulating. They cannot be understood simply on the representative model, as potential descriptions of an independent reality; predicates which can be 'satisfied' or not by certain kinds of independently existing objects. They function, true, to describe certain social conditions and relations. But these conditions and relations only exist because the agents involved recognize certain concerns, defined in a certain way; they could not sustain just these relations and states if they did not. But the terms are themselves essential to these concerns, under this definition, being recognized. It is through them that the horizon of concern of the agents in question is articulated in the way it has to be for just these practices, conditions, relations to exist.

Hence to understand what these terms represent, to grasp them in their representative function, we have to understand them in their articulating-constitutive function. We have to see how they can bring a horizon of concern to a certain articulation.

Thus I argued earlier that a term like 'equals' had to be articulated in the polis, because it carried this sense of mutually non-subordinated agents who are nevertheless part of the same society, who owe allegiance to the same laws and must defend them together. Equals, likes (*isoi, homoioi*), we are bound together, and yet also not hierarchically. Equals is the right term; and it had to be *articulated* in the society, because this kind of society, based on pride in this kind of ideal, could only exist if it was seen as an achievement, the avoidance of an alternative to which lesser peoples fell prey – the Persians in one context; in Pericles' exaltation of Athens, the comparison is with the Spartans. That is why there is no such society without some term like 'equals'.

But this is also the reason why there is no understanding 'equals' without seeing how it functions to articulate just this horizon of concern. This is *not* the same as seeing how it describes an independent reality, because there is no independent reality. Rather it is a matter of seeing how within a certain context of other concerns, and the practices in which they are pursued, the term in question could serve to articulate our concerns in just this shape and definition.

But then the whole range of terms of which this is true, and the sentences and expressions deploying them, do not seem to be fit candidates for a t-c theory of meaning. They cannot be related to truth- or satisfaction-conditions specifiable in another language, not unless, that is, we already understand them and have found or coined translations. Rather to grasp their truth- or satisfaction-conditions we already have to understand them. But the kind of understanding we need for this purpose is not of them in their representative function, but rather in their articulating-constitutive function. And once we have understood them in this way, there is no further search necessary to establish their truth-conditions. We have understood them fully.

In short, it is just a mistake to think that understanding these terms could consist in developing a theory which gave the truth-conditions of sentences using them. It is to misconceive their role in language; to see them on the model of an exclusively representative conception of meaning. If this kind of model were right, then t-c theories would make sense.

Imagine a human language made up of an artificial language, whose only function is to code information about an independent reality. It operates free from any conversational context; this if it exists at all must remain utterly unreflected in it. It has no expressive or constitutive dimensions. Now we can relax the picture, and imagine that human beings are using this language, but they keep their expressive function quite separate, and any constitutive uses as well. These are carried by certain noises they emit, like our purely expressive sounds: 'whew'; or by gesture, the way they walk, and so on. All description is thus insulated from the expressive and constitutive. Of course, the people concerned would have to be utterly inarticulate about themselves, for they could not talk about those aspects of their lives which were partly constituted by expressions.

In any case, in this weird world, the descriptive language, the descriptive core, we might say, of their language, similar to our artificial language, would be susceptible to understanding in a theory of meaning of a t-c kind. But this is very far from our world. For linguistic beings who even begin to understand themselves such a thing is inconceivable.

Nor will it do to object here that we should not insist on the objective of understanding, that the notion of a t-c theory offering us a picture of what those who understand the target language understand is in the end too psychologistic, that the aim is not at all to generate understanding of sentences the same way as human speakers do, or at least that we are not concerned to give an account of the way in which they come to recognize that the truth-conditions hold. This is too 'psychologistic' an objective.

For this kind of declaration of modesty does not lift the above difficulty. It does no good to say that we are looking for a t-c theory which abandons the goal of matching speaker's understanding, or bringing it to light. Our problem is that we cannot identify certain crucial truth-conditions until we have gained a great deal of insight into speaker's understanding. The difficulty cannot be solved by retreat, by scaling down our objectives, but only by advance, by becoming more ambitious. A t-c theory of meaning by itself is not viable, not because it might be seen as too ambitious, but because it manifestly is not ambitious enough.[14]

The impossibility of a t-c theory can also be seen in another way. As explained by Platts,[15] for instance, it involves ascribing truth-conditions to utterances which, along with some conception of the speech acts being performed, end up ascribing plausible propositional attitudes to the speakers, given their desires, situations, and so. But how are we to come to an adequate understanding of their speech acts? To do this we have to have an understanding of their social practices: the way they pray, invoke gods, and spirits, curse, bless, exorcise, establish rapport, put themselves on and off the different footings which are possible for them in this society, and so on. In short, to get an understanding of their speech acts is to get quite a far-reaching grasp of their social conditions and practices and relations. But to do this, as we saw, we have to get quite an understanding of a big part of their vocabulary, as well as coming to understand their expressive activity; which includes the way they may in talk about anything – sticks, stones, rivers, games, etc. – express their goals, values, or relations.

It seems then that the insights of the HHH do offer reasons to lose confidence in t-c theories. And it is *qua* theories which see meaning entirely in terms of representation that they are so undermined. But these insights also serve to undermine the other major feature of theories in the contemporary Anglo-Saxon world: their assumption of the observer's stance.

For the type of understanding needed when we have to grasp the articulating-constitutive uses of words is not available from the stance of a fully

---

[14] It may seem that I am intervening here in the McDowell–Dummett debate. But I think the point I am making stands somewhat outside it. Because I am not concerned with the question of how the speaker exercises his capacity for recognizing that the sentence is true or assertable. And therefore the whole question of assertability conditions, and the debate between realism and anti-realism, are not relevant to my problem. But I think in another way that there is a connection. Because I think that Dummett's intuition is right, and strikes a chord in everyone, when he argues that a truth condition theory leaves something crucial out, that it does not seem to give an adequate picture of language as something people understand; that there is something more to understanding than just successfully matching representations to objects. And this intuition turns out be entirely founded. There is something vital missing in t-c theory. Cf. J. McDowell 'On the sense and reference of a proper name', *Mind*, 86 (1977), pp. 159–85, and M. Dummett, 'What is a theory of meaning?', in S. Gutenplan (ed.), *Mind and Language* (Oxford, 1975), pp. 97–138.

[15] *Ways of Meaning*, pp. 58–63.

disengaged observer. This is because, to understand the articulating use, we have to see the term within the context. This context is made up both of the horizon of concerns which is further articulated by the term in question, and also by the practices connected with them. The practices are an inseparable part of the horizon, not only because the concerns will have to do with certain practices – as in the above example, 'the equals' was bound up with the practices of ruling and being ruled, of obeying and making laws, of deciding and exercising power, and so on; but also because some concerns are most fully expressed in social practices and institutions, those precisely which lack some explicit articulation of the values involved. When this is so, the horizon of concern may be defined in the practice itself, and the pattern of right and wrong, violation and compliance which it defines. Implicit in our social practices are conceptions of the subject, and such values as freedom, individual inviolability, and so on. We in our society are less attentive to this fact, because we also have theoretical articulations of these values.[16]

But this kind of context cannot be fully understood from a detached observer's standpoint. By this I do not mean that you have to be a participant in a society to understand it. But rather, two things are true: (a) to understand this kind of context, and the kind of difference the term in question could make in it, you have to understand what it would be like to be a participant.

Thus you understand the key terms to the extent that you have some grasp of what would be the appropriate thing for a participant to do in certain situations. This is an essential condition of anything we would count as grasping some social practice; and the same point can be made about the horizon of concern. You have no grasp on the conception of honour of a foreign society, if you have no idea of what is suitable and what unsuitable, what is a bigger derogation than what, what must be done to expiate, and so on. Some degree of participant's know-how, some ability to 'call' the right responses, even if for a host of other reasons, including insufficient command of the language, you could not actually wade in there and participate, is an essential part of understanding.

(b) In addition, we only arrive at this understanding by some exchange of mutual clarification between ourselves, or some other member of our culture, and members of the target culture. An anthropologist has visited the tribe, and we are now reading his account. He is interpreting it for us in terms of our culture. But the anthropologist's understanding is arrived

---

[16] I discuss this in volume 2 chapter 1.

at not simply in his language, nor simply in the language of the target people, but in a kind of language negotiated between the anthropologist and his informants. There has to take place a kind of 'fusion of horizons' if understanding is to take place.

I believe with Gadamer that something analogous goes on in cases where there can be no living exchange with the target people, when we study past societies, for instance. In trying to understand them, we have to elaborate a language which is not simply our language of self-understanding, and certainly not theirs; but one in which the differences between us can be perspicuously stated without distortion of either one. To the extent that we fail in this, we end up judging them anachronistically, as inferior attempts at what we have attained, or equally wrongly, as inhabitants of some golden age which we have lost. Avoiding anachronism always involves being challenged enough by them to put in question our own terms of self-understanding, whether these are self-congratulatory, or self-depreciative.

Now this is incompatible with adopting what I called the detached observer's standpoint, the kind we naturally adopt towards the natural world. For this involves neither the kind of understanding mentioned above, that of a potential participant, nor does it in any way present the challenge to our self-understanding. To treat some reality as a detached observer is to treat it as the kind of thing participation in which, self-clarifying exchange with which, is either impossible or irrelevant.

But it is plainly impossible to learn a language as a detached observer. To understand a language you need to understand the social life and outlook of those who speak it. Wittgenstein put it very well: 'To imagine a language means to imagine a form of life.'[17] And you cannot understand a form of life as a pure detached observer. That is what is bizarre in the Quine–Davidson fable of the observer in a foreign tribe, learning the language by matching truth-conditions to utterances. It is the companion mistake to believing that you can understand a language with a truth-conditions theory. Maybe if you could – as you can the artificial language – then maybe you would not need to be in any sense a participant, or even a potential one. Maybe you could do it purely by external observation, trying to find the formulae matching utterances, situation, motivation, and so on. But the need to understand the way their language articulates their horizon and practices makes the pure observer an absurdity.

The absurdity is seen at its purest in Quine's notion that any understanding of one person's language by another is the application of a theory. As

---

[17] *Philosophical Investigations*, i. 19.

though we could ever understand each other, if we stood to each other in the stance of observers.

This can only seem plausible because of the hold of the epistemological tradition, as I have argued above. The ideal of knowledge it proposes is that of a monological observer. By a fateful shift, this norm of knowledge is transposed into a conception of the nature of the subject of knowledge. At base we have to understand ourselves as monological observers, who have acquired the capacity to exchange information. This conception leaves no place for public space, and thus entirely blocks out one of the most significant features of human language.

If this picture were true, and each of us operated as a monological observer, then indeed we would all need theories of each other. My receiving information from you would ideally be subjected to tests for reliability. I should need a theory to assess your trustworthiness as an informant. But also, since what I receive is simply the raw data of your making noises or signs, I would need a theory to interpret these as information.

But once we understand that language is about the creation of public space, and that public space has participants – indeed, it is just what exists between participants, making them such in the act of communication – then we can see that there cannot be a totally non-participatory learning of language. The whole idea is at base inconsistent.

V

The insights of the HHH thus seem to put in question the basic premises of many contemporary theories of meaning: that meaning can be treated in terms of representation, and that we can come to an understanding of language as monological observers.

But does this mean that a t-c theory, for instance, is without value? Even if we grant that learning the meaning of many words has to consist in understanding their articulating-constitutive function; and that once we have understood them in this way, we know all we can about their satisfaction conditions: even so, is there not room for a T-theory?

After all, one of the major aims of a T-theory was to show how we can derive an infinite number of sentences, which we can produce or understand as grammatical/meaningful, from a finite stock of understood terms or expressions. One of the important phenomena of language is that we are able to go on and ring an indefinite number of changes on the sentences we have already produced or heard. From the sentences 'X is black' and 'Y is white', we can go on to produce the sentence 'X is black and Y is white'. Having mastered 'He said that p', we can go on to 'She said that he said that p'.

Now the aim of T-theory could be to explain the boundless creativity of sentence-production on the basis of what we normally believe to be a finite vocabulary. And this would be matched in the theory by the ability to derive an indefinite number of theorems of the form 's is true iff p' from a finite list of axioms.

But we might object that we could not hope to account for our creativity in this way, or only in small part. What is most striking about linguistic inventiveness, is the coinage of new terms, of new turns of phrase, of new styles of expressing oneself, the inauguration of new extensions of old terms, the metaphorical leaps, and so on. The very assumption of the finiteness of vocabulary is questionable, since it would appear that our existing terms are full of potential extensions. To take just one example (I owe this one to Steve Holtzmann): we speak of feeding an animal; then we go on to speak of feeding a parking meter; then we speak of feeding someone's ego. There is quite a rich image here of the ego as a voracious devourer of praise and assurances.

The reply of the T-theorist would be that indeed, metaphorical extensions are another matter, but that they presuppose some grasp of the literal meaning. What a t-c theory of meaning is in business to map is the literal meanings of the terms in the language, and the sentences built from them. And mapping this is basic, since to understand the figured sense of any term you already have to have a grasp of its proper sense. Hence a theory of this kind, while not explaining all of linguistic creativity, would account for the essential basis of whatever it left unexplained.

And it is clear that a T-theory needs something like the notion of the 'strict and literal meaning' of the terms it explains.[18] For owing to the different stances we take in speech, irony, sarcasm, rhetorical exaggeration, understatement, and so on, it is plain that the conditions obtaining in all correct and appropriate uses of a given expression will vary wildly. If we take an assertion like 'That was a clever remark', it is clear that it can be appropriate and quite correct in one tone of voice following a clever remark, and in quite another tone of voice following a very stupid remark. If the T-theorist is going to learn to map such sentences on to their truth-conditions, he has to be able to control for these rhetorical shifts, for irony, sarcasm, and so on, and this seems to

[18] Platts, *Ways of Meaning*, pp. 52–3.

require on one hand that he isolate a literal meaning of the expressions studied, and on the other that he identify the various rhetorical changes that can be rung on it.

T-theorists thus seem to have a great deal invested in the following propositions: (a) that each expression that can be used to characterize things has a literal meaning (or in the case of polysemy, meanings) along with any metaphorical or figured meanings it might have; (b) that grasping the figured meanings presupposes a grasp of the literal meaning; and (c) that observing the conditions in which speakers make their utterances, along with what we can surmise about their motivational states, beliefs, and so on, should permit us to isolate this literal meaning.

The point seems to be this: the way that an expression can relate to the appropriate conditions of its utterance can be varied through all the rhetorical stances available, and also by the variety of speech acts available in the culture. Thus, as we saw above, sarcasm can even reverse the appropriate conditions for applying an expression like 'clever remark'. But there must be one way of relating to conditions which is basic, which anchors the others. If we think of language as primarily for depiction, then this basic way will be depictive. The primary way that an expression relates to its truth or satisfaction conditions is as an adequate representation of these. And indeed, if there were not such a basic way, it is hard to see how the different rhetorical stances could exist, that is could have the particular point they have. The whole point of my saying sarcastically 'That was a clever remark' would be lost if 'clever' did not have the literal meaning that it does of showing intelligence and acumen. It seems that the rhetorical flourish can only exist as a flourish thanks to this primary way of relating. Let this straight relation of depiction to truth/satisfaction-conditions be called the literal meaning of an expression. Then all descriptive terms must have literal meanings.

And so we get a doctrine of the primacy of the literal, which can perhaps be summed up in this way: 1. Each expression which can be used to characterize, make assertions, questions, commands, called for short a 'descriptive' expression, has at least one literal meaning. 2. The literal meaning of an expression is determined by its role in a straight, accurate, unadorned depiction of what it applies to. 3. The literal meaning is primary, i.e. (i) grasping any figurative or non-literal sense presupposes we grasp the literal sense; (ii) the other uses are defined, get their characteristic point, only in relation to the literal use.

This sounds plausible to us as a general proposition about language, and thus something you can count on in learning any language in any culture. But in fact it is parochial, culture-centric. In our civilization, which has made the accurate, dispassionate representation of things one of its central goals, a culture in which science is so important (and this we have been in different ways arguably ever since the Greeks), it comes as no surprise that there is always a proper sense, that this is to be understood in terms of description, and so on. But in interpreting other cultures – and also some more or less suppressed aspects of ours which are similar to these cultures – this may lead to nonsense and distortion. I would claim that it does. It is the kind of thing that leads us to postulate absurdities like the 'pre-logical mentality'.

Let us look at alternative possible primacies. There is another very important use of language, besides describing, and that is to invoke. This is of particular importance in what we call a religious context. For instance in a ceremony the presence of a god might be invoked by a suitable form of words.

Names play an important role in invocative uses of speech. But they function here not to fix reference, but to call, to call up, to invoke. If you know the name of someone you can call him. (Wittgenstein too was trying to shake us out of our obsession with the centrality of description when he said: 'think ... [of] the use of a person's name to call him'.)[19] You have some kind of power over him. That is why in certain cultures a man's real name is hidden, and known only to certain people. That is why knowing the names of the gods gives one power. And that is why the name of the God of Israel was forbidden to men to pronounce.

But descriptions can also figure invocatively. The Greeks called the Pontic the Euxine Sea. They wanted to *make* it kindly. When the Portuguese explorers returned after turning the southern tip of Africa and reported the 'Cape of Storms', Henry the Navigator ordered it renamed 'Cape of Good Hope'.

But surely, we want to say, this invocative use is secondary. It was only because the Greeks knew how to apply the expression 'kindly sea' as a description that they could use it as an invocative name. It is rather like an order to the sea: 'be kindly'. Like all orders we can understand it as a propositional content joined with a command. But to understand the propositional content is to understand how language can represent. So the representative turns out to be basic after all.

Or so we tend to think. But let us work out a case of a culture where invocation is more than marginal. Let us say that we invoke the God

---

[19] *Philosophical Investigations*, i. 27.

through reciting his high deeds. Certain myths about him, as we would call them, expressed in canonical style, are central to his ritual.

All right, but then are these myths, as accounts of what he did, not examples of speech in its representative function? In a sense, yes. But the question is whether the representative here is primary. What makes the story correct, more precisely the formulation in the recitation? That it depicts correctly certain events? Or that the words have power? It may be impossible to answer this question. In particular, the people concerned may not be able to understand the alternative. There may be nothing like a Cardinal Bellarmine or a Vienna Circle in this culture which would enable some experienced hand among shamans to say something like: 'I don't know about the truth status of these utterances, but they sure bring the crops up.'

A more correct account (which they may not have worked out; this is *our* question) might go further like this: the words are true/right because they have power, they invoke the deity, they really connect with what he is. This must mean that what they assert of him is in some sense right and appropriate. But this relation we do not really understand, and cannot hope to understand. It is quite possible that the myths give accounts which look incompatible to someone from a culture where the representative is primary. But that is not a problem for us. As invocations, these recitations truly connect with deity, they function in tandem so to connect us; and so they are both right. They both reveal something about him.

Or there is another possibility. Certain words may be privileged because they are words of power, now not of us invoking God, but of God himself. The Qur'an (meaning 'recitation') is an example of this. The words here are special not because they fit an independent reality, but because they are the words of the creator, who made everything. But this is not to say that we have simply reversed the direction of fit, and that they offer depictions of the world in the form of commands (like the 'Let there be light' of Genesis). This would allow the primacy of the representative. The relationship of these words to reality is not clear to us; all we know is that these words of power underlie everything which is.

But now it looks as though we have in this domain something like a primacy of the invocative. The ultimate context in which an expression is anchored is the invocative one. Its basic, correct use is determined, that is, out of the invocative context. Its representative correctness follows from this, is derived from this. For this domain we can reverse the doctrine of the primacy of the literal – which is simply the primacy of the representative. For the key expressions here, there is a sense they have in the invocative context, not perhaps a finitely denumerable meaning, but nevertheless a meaning (this corresponds to 1 and 2 above). 3. This meaning is primary, for (i) it is presupposed in any other uses; i.e. a merely representative use, what you can say correctly about the God outside the invocative context, can only be validated by what you rightly say within it; and (ii) even what we mean by describing God correctly is unclear, and has to be determined from our knowing how to invoke him, and connect with him. For instance, it is this which determines what is contradiction, what says something profound, and so on.

This seems to be valid for the sentences pronounced in the invocative context. But it is also clearly true for the key terms which are intrinsic to this domain: e.g. 'God', 'spirit', 'mana', 'baraka', and so on.

But, we want to object, how about all those terms for ordinary 'profane' things that get taken up into this discourse? We say that the God lives in the heavens, or under the seas, that he took the form of a bull, and mated with the daughter of X, that he slew his enemies, ate them, and then vomited them up, and so on. Surely some form of the literal primacy thesis is true for all these; that is, we have to be familiar with skies, seas, bulls, mating, daughters, slaying, eating, vomiting, to make sense of all this. These are like metaphorical extensions of our ordinary uses. We have to have these words in our ordinary descriptive vocabulary in order to be able to use them in the mythic recitation. In Lévi-Strauss' famous phrase, a myth is the result of *bricolage*, but the elements which are lying around to be put together surely come from the mundane world. So there must be some acquaintance with these terms in their ordinary, descriptive meaning for the myth to be comprehensible. Hence at least 3(i) is true of them.

But this confuses two things. When we come at these people with naturalistic explanation in mind (and we rarely seem to get it out of mind), we want to say something like: clearly their acquaintance with profane skies, seas, bulls, and so on was an essential part of the causal story of their developing this mythical world-outlook. That may be true, in some sense, is bound to be true. But that is quite different from the thesis that for them what we characterize as the literal sense is primary.

This would mean that they have a practice of describing bulls, and so on, independently of the mythical context, possibly even prior to it, but certainly autonomously relative to it. This would mean that they identify criteria for bulls, different classifications within the class bulls, different properties of bulls, which in no way find their rationale in the mythical stories about bulls. These profanely identified bulls are then taken up and used in the mythopoeic process.

But this may be just wrong. It may be that there is nothing significant about religiously important animals that surround them, no criteria of identification, no important discriminations of types, which does not have its basis in myth. For instance, the salient features of the animal may be the object of an aetiological myth (why do pigs have curly tails, why do moose have huge antlers? etc.). The manner in which the people concerned observe, classify, perceive these animals may be very thoroughly connected with the way the animals figure in myth; so that no important feature is without its mythical significance and aetiology.

When we take up our naturalistico-Marxist perspective we feel like saying things like: 'Of course, the reason for the central role of the cow in their culture is not its closeness to the God, but the fact that it was the principal economic resource; the myth is rationalization, or ideology ...' But that is quite a different matter from understanding their language/culture. For them the invocative context is primary, not just for those special terms which figure almost exclusively in it, but also for a whole host of others, which can indeed be used to refer to (what we identify as) profane objects, but where these objects are seen, identified, classified in ways that dovetail with and are shaped by the mythical-invocative context.

A tribe's classification of animals for totemic purposes, or for cosmological purposes, or to define certain tabus, which serves to connect them to spirits, or cosmos, or whatever, cannot be without link to the way they see and identify members of these species that they meet. The two dovetail closely and may reciprocally mould each other in the tribe's universe of discourse, whatever the order of our naturalistic explanation.

Put in terms of the discussion of the previous section, we can say that, for instance, a totemic classification of animals will have an articulating-constitutive use for the tribal society – as 'equals' did for the polis – as well as a representative use applied to the surrounding fauna. To believe in the primacy of the literal is to hold that the latter use is primary, and that the former is derived and 'metaphorical'. In the 'literal' use, the animals are presumably identified and discriminated purely by their objective properties; the concerns, norms, relations that they help articulate *qua* totemic beings play no role. These only become relevant when the animal terms are taken up in the derived 'metaphorical' sense where they serve, for example to identify clans.

Now my point here is that this analysis in terms of literal/metaphorical meanings may be quite wide of the mark, indeed seems thoroughly implausible. The traffic is more likely to be two-way, the articulating-constitutive use helping to shape the criteria of identification in the representative use as well as vice versa. If we wanted to put this in a thoroughly paradoxical way, we could say that the metaphorical is primary here.[20] But it would be best to say that the whole distinction 'literal sense/metaphorical sense' cannot apply to a case like this. There are not two senses of the term here, one of which deserves to be called literal. It serves no purpose to talk of a 'literal sense' here; and will not until a more rationalizing culture develops with a concern for objective description, which descriptions will in turn make a range of more 'subjective' uses stand out, as mere tropes.

It is an important step in what we see as the development of knowledge and rationality when people break free of this dependency on the invocative/constitutive, and set themselves to observe and describe for the sake of representative accuracy. This has come about over several stages of our culture. Once a culture has conceived the norm of representative accuracy, and made this primary, then there is such a thing as the literal meaning, or such can be worked out for the first time. But exactly for that reason, it is anachronistic to look for this in a culture where the mythic-invocative is still primary. We find such people saying things like 'twins are birds',[21] or 'leopards are Christians',[22] which baffle us. In our bafflement, we may grope for an account in terms of the figured sense of the words. But the contrast with a primary sense is unrecognized by the people concerned, and this analysis leads us astray.

The assumption that there is such a thing as the strict and literal meaning of an expression turns out to be an ethnocentric assumption. But it is essential to a t-c theory. That is because it sets itself to match utterances *qua* representations to the world. It is essential to the theorist to believe that there is a representative kernel to be found in all the various speech acts. This seems plausible when one looks at assertions, questions, commands, and notes that one can abstract a propositional content, a depictive core, from each. But this procedure reaches an impasse when one comes to a culture in which invocative uses are still dominant. Invocations do not have depictive cores; they are not all just like commands, like 'Let there be light', or 'Come Holy Ghost, our souls inspire'; and in many cultures they are not like commands at all.

---

[20] As Rousseau does to make an analogous point: 'le langage figuré fut le premier à naître', *Essai sur l'origine des langues*, chap. III.

[21] Evans-Pritchard, *Nuer Religion* (Oxford, 1956), pp. 128–33.

[22] Dan Sperber, *Rethinking Symbolism* (Cambridge, 1975), pp. 129ff.

More generally, it is clear that developing a T-theory will not be the way we can define the meanings in any language of those descriptive expressions which are partly shaped by their invocative or constitutive uses. For the T-theory will attempt to define expressions by identifying the satisfaction conditions of their literal uses. But these do not exist. Rather we cannot hope to understand the pattern of application of expression to world in this kind of case without an understanding of its invocative/constitutive role in the culture. If we look for its meaning to a supposedly primary, purely representative use, we will be continually baffled.

What we need to understand a language of this kind is to scrap t-c theory and cotton on to the nature of the invocative and constitutive uses in the culture under study. But to do this we have to transcend the limits of modern theory defined by the two assumptions I mentioned above: that meaning be seen in terms of representation, and that theory be from the standpoint of the monological observer. The invocative can only be understood if we draw on the insights of the HHH, and become cognizant of the expressive and constitutive dimensions of language.

And as a matter of fact, we can begin to understand it from our own practices which are analogous, and which writers of the HHH have discussed.

'Think ... how singular is the use of a person's name to call him' said Wittgenstein (I consider him an honorary member of the HHH).[23] You address someone, open a conversation. That brings about a public space between you. That public space is shaped, modified, made colder and more distant, or warmer and more intimate, and so on, by what you say, your choice of words, your tone, manner, and so on. Public space is invoked in speech. More, it can invoke qualities in us. It is a peculiar power of the saint to be able by seeing the good that we are, and naming it, to bring us closer to this good. There is a symmetrical power that some evil people have. The invocative is far from being dead in our culture. It is transposed. And above all, it is invisible to those influential self-understandings which have taken the primacy of the representative for their principle. You need the insights of the HHH to bring it to light. Once you do, then some of the seemingly bizarre beliefs of primitives, such as, for example, that knowing my name gives power over me, seem less incomprehensible.

But we suffer from a powerful temptation to interpret ourselves in

---

[23] *Philosophical Investigations*, i. 27.

terms of representative primacy. This starts as a norm: it is essential to our scientific practice, to what we understand as the correct search for knowledge, that we set ourselves the goal of making an accurate representation of things. And this has meant shaking ourselves free from earlier views in which the demands of connection, communion, or attunement with the cosmos were still intricated with those of attaining an adequate picture of the true state of affairs. This norm is obviously justified, indeed, indispensable to our scientific culture.

But the norm has ended up being forgotten as a norm. Somehow the pressure seemed irresistible to see this picture of the subject, the disengaged observer making and testing representations, as the correct theoretical account. But nothing could be more disastrous. We cannot understand the past, and distort the present. And above all we utterly fail correctly to conceive what the *task* is that the norm prescribes. We think in some confused way that we are already really there at the point it calls us to.

The theorists of meaning dominant in Anglo-Saxon philosophical culture, who share the dual premise I have mentioned, are prime victims, I would argue, of this transposition of norm into theory, which is so typical of modern culture. That is why they can believe that a theory of meaning could be elaborated which took account only of the representative dimension.

But as a matter of fact, not only is this not the only dimension, it is in a sense not even the primary one. The first thing we need to do in understanding a language is to see the place that representation has in that culture. If it is given normative primacy, well and good. Even there, as we have seen, a purely representation-based theory will by no means suffice. All our language of individual and social self-understanding would be opaque to such a theory. We will only think it will work, if we have fallen victim to the transposition from norm to theory.

But at least our theory will have some fit with our culture. It will not at all if the culture we are studying does not give primacy to representation. What the nature of the culture is, what kinds of speech acts are primary, has to be established first, as it were. The Wittgensteinian slogan turns out to be completely true: to understand a language, you have to understand a form of life.

But this just takes further what I argued was the lesson already implicit in Frege's critique of early designativism. You cannot understand how words relate to things until you have identified the nature of the activity in which they get related to things. Here the point is taken further and applied to those who have claimed Frege's mantle: you cannot understand how sentences relate to their truth-conditions, or expressions to their satisfaction-conditions, or their assertability-conditions, until you have understood the nature of the (social) activity, the form of life, in which they get so related. The way in which they relate to the world is very different in invocative cultures than it is in representative ones. Get this straight first. Proceeding as though the representative were a quite autonomous dimension is a road to disaster, even as among your spiritual forebears proceeding as though designation were the only relation turned out to be.

This is the message of the HHH.

INDEX

Printed in the United States
131029LV00004B/6/A